Where the Magic Happens

Carole Coren

Printed in the United Kingdom
First Printing, 2020

ISBN: 978-1-8380508-0-1 (Paperback)
ISBN: 978-1-8380508-1-8 (eBook)

Guided Light Publications
Littlehampton, West Sussex

DEDICATION

To my mother, son, granddaughter
and friend Maggie
for all their love and support
&
to everyone who feels strongly enough
to make their world a better place

and my thanks to Terri Windling for her excellent editing

To Cara
with Best Wishes
Carole

CONTENTS

Shomas

INTRODUCTION

I am a Channeller, Spiritual Healer and Teacher and have been in communication with the world of Spirit for over 25 years. This book has been written, using Automatic Writing, by many beings of the Spirit Realm.

Shomas is my Spirit Guide, and he, The Elohim, The White Brotherhood and The Twelve Elders of the Universe, who work with Melchizedek[4], have all contributed to the content of this book. They were its inspiration and are all wonderful souls working for the betterment of mankind on Earth.

Shomas told me: "This book is our gift to you, for you to give to mankind as a manual on how to live a life so beautiful it will make everyone glow with a spiritual vibrancy.

"We are many and we bring the love, Light and the wisdom of the Ancients to your presence to heal the planet for the future. You can help heal the world with our words.

"This book is for future generations to read and understand our world and how we are here to help and heal all mankind. We would like to bring those with little or no knowledge of the Spirit Realm, into the fold; to open their hearts to endless possibilities of Light and Love in their lives, and for them to see what working in the Light[2] really means; so they may live their life accordingly. We hope to direct souls to their true pathway for life and help them comprehend how to care for their world and what to expect from ours."

Spirit Guides[1] are non-physical beings who are assigned to us, often before we are born, to guide us through our lives. I am fortunate to have this wonderful Spirit Guide, Shomas, whose advice and wisdom has come to me over many years through Automatic Writing – a process in which I channel messages and guidance from Spirit Guides and/or Angelic beings directly through the written word.

Our Spiritual Guides have our welfare at heart, and with profound and gentle persuasion they hope to change the ways of man towards a brighter and happier future, where there are no wars, and where peace and happiness prevail. The writing in this book has a resonance which comes from their hearts, and my heart, to flow through your hearts, to slow your pace of life and to bring you into harmony with your Guides in the Spirit Realm.

The following chapters are teachings written by the Spirit Realm, in the form of a story in which a grandmother introduces her granddaughter to many aspects of the Spirit World and what they offer mankind. The two main characters' experiences show the synchronicity of Spirit messages, with facts offered to both of them to disseminate. These two characters bring life to the pages with an essence of fun and fragility. They experience life as we all know it, but within that life they have a contact with pure Spirit[1] and can share the knowledge received with everyone around the world.

Each chapter stands alone in its information, so you may pick and choose what you wish to read. Often the guidance will say 'we' rather than 'I', as the information comes from them all, and they will speak of 'man' for ease of writing, but this also means 'woman'.

Shomas and the other Guides hope you will enjoy the content of this book, that it will make you think, and at times make you smile.

They send love, Light[2] and power to us all so that we may discover the true meaning of happiness on the Earth plane before engaging in the pleasures of the Spirit world.

CHAPTER ONE

SHOMAS

Olivia knocks on the front door and opens it tentatively, thinking, "Typical Granny, unlocked as usual. She trusts everyone."

On walking through the house she can see her Grandmother Jane in the garden, her favourite place. Wisps of grey hair dance in the breeze, like the daffodils she is gently tending. Jane looks up, drops her gardening gloves and rushes towards Olivia to give her a hug.

The kettle is on and the cake is cut as they lapse into their normal friendly banter of family events and everyday news. There is such a comfortable camaraderie between these two women; it goes beyond love and respect. It is deeper and more profound. There is an innate knowing between them that defies words. Olivia has been visiting her grandmother all her life, and even now, in her twenties, she still looks forward to the warm welcome she always receives when she visits.

Jane's home is a treasure trove of artefacts from time immemorial. She is an avid collector of anything unusual, and she herself is as ageless as some of the items she has collected. Olivia loves to explore the different rooms, touching priceless items from Egypt, Peru, the Azores, and to see crystals of every shape and hue casting beautiful facets of colour across the walls of each room they occupy. Jane has been collecting since she was a child, and can bring alive stories of every item. Her house has a kind of magic, a timeless quality all of its own.

There is one room though which Olivia loves more than most: Jane's special room – the room where the magic becomes even more real. A room where you can be transported through time and space, to see and hear of the lives of the ancients and more!

Jane has always been psychic, and Olivia has followed in her footsteps: a gift handed down through generations. A gift so precious that only they, in the family, now share.

Jane does Automatic Writing, where her hand is overtaken by her Spirit Guides, who use her pen to write and portray a cinemascope of information telling of lifetimes lived from the beginning of time. Where Angels impart knowledge to guide and advise humankind of its purpose on Earth and how to share the Earth's gifts in peace and tranquillity. Jane couldn't even dream of some of the things she has been told, and her granddaughter enjoys asking her questions to see where they lead.

Olivia feels at peace here, and today, with tea drunk and family matters sorted, the two women head toward Jane's special room as today Olivia is being invited into the magic.

Stepping through the door, they are both excited, and the sensation of anticipation is electric. The light in this room is beautiful; orbs of light dance in the rays of the afternoon sun, which illuminate every corner. It is warm, but they do not want to open a window and ruin the magical feeling of this space. They sit opposite one another on the big comfy chairs and lapse into a comfortable silence as they tune into the essence of just being, which radiates around them.

After a while, Olivia enquires, "How did you know you could do Automatic Writing Granny? Tell me how it all started."

"Well Livvy, it all really started in August 1992, whilst sitting watching the television. I suddenly had this strong urge to write; so sitting down with pen and paper, I waited. I wasn't sure what I was waiting for or what to expect, as I had never experienced anything like it before. Suddenly my hand started to move of its own accord; and although, looking back on it, I could have been frightened, I wasn't. To start with, all I wrote were loops. For many days all I wrote were loops, loads of loops, which linked themselves across the page; and then one day, in the middle of all the loops there suddenly appeared '8 a.m.'!

"From then on, every morning at 8 a.m. I would sit with pen and paper and wait to see if anything happened. Initially, I would feel a strange tingling in my right hand and then the pen would move across the page. The loops eventually began to form words – not easily decipherable at first, but as they appeared on the paper I could hear these words in my head as though the writing was being explained to me. I realised all I had to do was put my own mind to one side, so I could let the writing flow freely."

"I would have been terrified," Olivia interjects.

"Strangely, I wasn't. The initial messages weren't very clear. They were mainly about signs, and someone being beside me, and me understanding (I wasn't sure what). Each time I wrote the messages they were signed, 'love you Robert'. Robert was my father, who had passed away some years before, so I found this signature comforting. Our bond had always been so strong, and I knew that if these messages were coming from him, then no harm could come to me.

"As you can image, at the start, I needed confirmation that I wasn't going mad. I was a College Lecturer so I was very grounded; I needed proof that it really was my father speaking to me. So a friend suggested I ask a question that only he could answer. I remembered he had been a rear gunner in a Lancaster bomber in World War II – and as I know absolutely nothing about aeroplanes, I asked how many crew would have been in a Lancaster. 'Four airmen and three gunners – why?' was the reply. I checked and it was correct; the crew would have been a pilot, navigator, flight engineer, bomb aimer (doubled as front gunner), wireless operator, mid-upper gunner and rear gunner. As you can imagine, this was quite mind blowing. The next statement was: 'Don't doubt us, we are here to make it easier, please trust us, don't let your doubts stop you from listening to us'."

"How wonderful to have a link with your Dad again," Olivia exclaims.

"Yes, it was. I missed him so much, so our chats were very comforting." Jane pauses for a moment and smiles, remembering her father fondly.

She then says: "The writing from my father continued for some months, then one day the style of writing changed. 'I am Shomas,' it said. 'I will be your Guide through this lifetime and all others; we are intrinsically linked for eternity. I was with you in Tibet in 805 AD; it is lovely to talk with you again. I will now be writing. I am going to give you words and messages so you can understand what is going to happen. Your father spoke to you initially, as I just wanted to establish the link and get you used to working with Spirit. It is so good to be able to talk to you; I have wanted to for so long. We can catch up on lost time.

"'Let the pen flow, just let it go, and I will write through you to tell you all you want to know. You will feel me pushing the pen and the writing will just happen. Other Spirit Guides and myself are here for you, to help you understand. We are here for many others too, but they cannot get our messages as you can. There are times when there are a few Guides here and times when there are many: we can be in more than one place at a time. Don't go rushing on ahead in your mind, let us do the writing. We will plant the words in your head as we write them; take time to listen. Don't be frightened of doing this, the pen will help you. We just want to talk to you. The time will come when you trust us fully and will use us to help you. You need reassurance that this is real. It is real, trust us; we come to help you, not to frighten or create doubts. The writing will get clearer and faster as you get used to us using you, and we need you to believe in us'."

Jane explains that Shomas is a Spiritual being of love and Light who always appears as a Tibetan Monk – which was how she would have known him in their previous lifetime together, and how Olivia will come to know him too. Jane's writing, from years of teaching, is a backward sloping scrawl, but Shomas writes with a beautiful copperplate script, so very different to her own. Olivia is excited to know more.

"As you can imagine, it's a strange concept to grasp and accept: that someone, not from this level of existence, is using your hand to write messages which will affect mankind in the future.

"Firstly, I thought: *Why me*? I doubted my ability to receive information from a higher plane[5]. I was convinced that it was my subconscious making things up; but it is impossible for me to have even considered half the things I have been told. It is incredible that I can 'talk' to someone who knew me from so many centuries before. But, I have realised, as time has gone by, that Shomas is just like me, he even has the same sense of humour. I feel this wonderful closeness – and a sense of being looked after and watched over, just as I did when my father 'spoke' with me.

"Shomas has stayed with me ever since. I cannot imagine life without him; he is always by my side, and I can call on him whenever I want. If ever I am unsure of anything, I just have to ask and he will advise me and help me to follow my path. I am so lucky."

Jane watches Olivia's eyes widen, then she resumes her recollections.

"A while ago, Shomas told me: 'You have been given a gift to help others. We want you to tell everyone about the messages. There are many souls who you will be able to help with messages and healing. You will know when the time is right and what they need from you. Listen to your heart. The information we give you is for people of like minds and hearts.'

"My Guides tell me that they are giving me statements from their world to ours to help humanity find its way – not only during these troubling times but in all the years and generations to come."

"That's incredible," says Olivia, in awe.

Jane agrees. "Over the years, the messages have become clearer and clearer. Each word, initially, was linked by a fine pen line as the pen could not lift off the paper; then these lines gradually cleared as the writing became more and more decipherable. The writing now is a beautiful copperplate script. I even get dotted i's, crossed t's and punctuation.

"Recently I have also been honoured to receive messages from the Elohim, who are Guides from such high realms I could not understand why they would want to channel through me, but apparently they do. Often first thing in the morning they tell me of events to happen that particular day, and when I watch the evening news, everything they have said is accurate! I have received all sorts of information over the years – a lot of which is about the Earth. Over time I will share with you some of the wonderful philosophies that have been given to me. Would you like to meet Shomas now, Livvy?"

Olivia nods enthusiastically. "I've waited a long time for you to share this with me."

"Hold out your hands," Jane advises as she places a large quartz crystal into her granddaughter's hands. "Now relax. I will take you into a meditation and leave you to talk to Shomas."

The room fills with rainbows as sunlight hits the crystal and cascades in a spectrum of colour around the walls. Olivia closes her eyes as Jane encourages her to go into a meditative state, where, after a while, she is transported out of the room and up, up to the realms of Light.

A crystal cave opens before her. She can see through the doorway, and as she walks into the cave, there is a seat of pure quartz crystal, where she feels encouraged to sit. As she does so, a kindly being appears before her.

"Good afternoon, Olivia," he says, "it is lovely to be able to speak with you. Your grandmother told us she was going to bring you to visit us today."

"Can you tell me who you are and all about yourself, please?" Olivia asks confidently.

His gentle manner brings no fear; he has a lovely smile and the kindest eyes. "My name is Shomas. I am your grandmother's Guide. I have come to see you, as you and your grandmother are so close, and I would like to tell you my story."

"I look forward to that," Olivia enthuses.

Shomas begins: "Your grandmother and I were training to be Buddhist Monks in a monastery high in the mountains north of Lhasa, Tibet, in 805 AD. Planet Earth was a very different place when we were young: it was a green and pleasant land, no pollution, no contamination. We were friends from eight years of age until around the age of eighteen. Ten years! It seemed a lifetime, we were so close. We joined the monastery, near our homes, at the same time, entering the temple at eight to learn the disciplines of prayer and meditation. It was such a happy and peaceful time. Our life in Tibet was austere: there were no material possessions, and food and clothing were spartan, but we were content living our lives in devotion and prayer. The world was a much more peaceful place then and we, in isolation in our Monastery, were in touch with a 'higher power' and few other men. We were totally self-sufficient and had very few visitors.

"When we were together, it was as an extremely spiritual band of souls. Because we were children when we entered the monastery, we played; we were not stopped from childish pursuits. We played much as you probably did: with kites, and often skipping and running in the fields around the monastery. The older monks were good to us young folk. There were mountains behind our monastery, but the foothills were mainly fields and pastures, which we shared with the animals who grazed there.

"As young men we travelled higher into the mountains and the views were phenomenal. We could see for miles and there was nothing to mar the view. No chimney stacks, no factories or skyscrapers, just the blending between the green and blue of land and sky. The seas and rivers teemed with fresh fish, fish you could eat safely. Birds and animals roamed the land freely, none were caged or chained. I remember the sense of freedom, of space, of light, the colours and the clarity of the water. Life was an idyll.

"We had to learn stillness and quiet to train our minds to higher thoughts for meditation, which is difficult when you are so young, but it developed as the years went by. We appreciated our role in life to serve and worship in the monasteries, and to learn monastic disciplines, mantras and prayers. We also took it in turns to shoulder the responsibility of the daily chores of the monastery. But when the bells rang we knew we had to sit and meditate and listen to the bells.

"The Tibetan bells are a very powerful sound which you *enter*; I cannot think of a better word. You vanish into the sound, and from there, you acquire stillness. We became one with the sound; it is deep, very deep, and we learnt from a very early age that when the bells ring you become still and go into that sound. Even so young, you cannot avoid going into the quietness. Your mind stills and you develop a reverence for the sound. Once we were trained, we did not speak very much in the temples; we were allowed to speak when we were at rest. Meal times were silent, and we had to learn respect for the elders within the monastery, and obviously for the Head of the Order. We had a great deal of respect for him because of his position in the monastery and within the spiritual world.

"It was a wonderful time, although many people would think it cruel to take a small child and put him through the rigours of that regime. We had so many friends, it was lovely, and the older monks treated us as their children. They joined in our play and enjoyed our company too. It was a good time, a very good time.

"Not all young males were taken for training. The Head of the Order always knew who would be the chosen few, and their parents were told that their children would be taken to the temples in the monastery at the age of eight. These children were born to the position, and obviously this role was chosen before they came to the Earth plane, but you did not know that as a small child. It was a great honour for these children to be chosen, so their parents did not mind having their children taken away from them, as it was of great esteem. We were, of course, able to visit our parents and they us. Even though we were in training, we were not separated from our families.

"Our training took a lifetime. We would go in as children and continue. You never stop learning, ever. Even the Head of the Order today, the Dalai Lama, is still learning; he is always in a process of self-discovery. He is one of the perfect Masters currently working with humanity.

"There were a great many monasteries up the mountainside. We were in the main monastery with the Head of the Order. There were other monasteries up the mountainside, I cannot remember how many. The Head of the Order had to visit them all, of course, and he took us, as trainees, to visit them too. These monasteries were high – very high in the mountains – and it was a very long trek to get there.

"Monks were trained to be able to walk many hundreds of miles, without their feet hurting. It was a kind of meditative state: you could walk with no pain; it felt as though you walked on air. It felt as though it had only taken five minutes but it could be days, or even weeks, to get from one monastery to another. We did not need much food, so there was no need to stop often, but when we did stop in the villages they would feed us, as it was an honour for them to do this.

"The people of Tibet have always had great respect for the monks, and they would always bring food. Mothers would bring loaves of bread and pies they had baked for us to eat. We ate quite well, never needing much food. One pie would probably feed us all, just a small portion each. We would not consume the amount that you Westerners do; you seem to need this for energy. We did not need much food for energy; we always had an abundance of Spiritual energy.

"It was wonderful that the people cared for us as we cared for them. Everywhere we walked, the minute we came into a village we would be welcomed into homes and fed and watered. It was with great reverence they welcomed us into their dwellings. Even though they were poor and had very little themselves, they would share what they had with us always. It was wonderful, and it is a shame that there is not more of that generosity in the world these days. The world is a very different place now to the land that we lived in, very different. It is so sad.

"As we got older, we did skin breathing, to increase our energies and if we ever did get tired we could sit, and we could levitate. This was very restful as it was not necessary to lean on any part of our body; that feeling of lightness was wonderful. We were trained in a different method of meditation, a different way of emptying our minds, for levitation. I cannot describe it, it was just different. It is difficult to remember...it was a long time ago.

"The Tibetan way of life, with its spirituality and peace, is sadly being destroyed these days by others who wish to rule our land. It was such a peaceful nation, but Tibetans these days are fleeing their own country to save themselves from the takeover. The Dalai Lama has already left his home; he is now living in a place of safety, and spreading his messages of Light and love throughout that nation and to the world.

"Our land was sacred, it was our home. Now it is being taken away from the people who have loved and nurtured it for thousands of years. We watch from here and it brings us much sorrow." Shomas's face saddens, as he continues to speak of his memories.

"One day your grandmother and I were playing in the hills around the monastery. We used to fly kites, and because of the high winds, we could take turns hanging inside the kite whilst the other held the tether. Your grandmother was hanging inside a kite which I was pulling when it crashed to the ground, and she passed away. The sadness of that loss overwhelmed me, and I have stayed by her side ever since."

He pauses, and Olivia watches him pull himself out of the past, casting off his sorrow. The look he then gives her is warm. "I have much to tell you," he says, "and we shall meet many times to share information which we would like you to use to help your planet Earth. You need to go back now. Come again another day, and we can talk further."

With that, he smiles and walks away, vanishing into a huge beam of light.

Olivia, still in her meditative state, sits for a few minutes to absorb all she has heard, and then gets up and walks out of the cave. Slowly bringing herself back to the present, she opens her eyes to find herself back in the room where her grandmother is sitting waiting and smiling. Jane asks, "Nice journey?"

"Wonderful," Olivia enthuses. "I met Shomas. What a lovely sweet soul! How amazing to have had him as your Guide all your life."

"I am so lucky to have Shomas as my Guide," Jane concurs. "I have to tell you a funny story. Apparently when I am in trance, as the channelling comes through I rock gently. I asked Shomas to explain and he told me: 'We used to rock when we prayed and meditated. I am sorry, it is a habit I cannot get out of; we all used to rock. It is relaxing for me and brings back old memories. At first I thought, *oh dear I am rocking*, but then I realised that in a way it will help Jane to know I am here, to know it is me'."

"That is so lovely. Do I have Guides of my own?" Olivia asks.

"Of course you do," Jane confirms. "Everyone has Guides, even though many people don't realise it. Our Guides and helpers are responsible for enabling us to fulfil the spiritual contract we make with ourselves, for our lives on Earth."

"I look forward to hearing more about that," Olivia enthuses. "How do I get to meet mine?"

"All in good time. We shall find out who they are another day. You will meet them and learn how they have been assigned to help you in this lifetime," Jane advises.

"Do Guides cross many lifetimes?" Olivia enquires.

"Some do, as you heard Shomas did. Our link is as strong now as it was when we first met in Tibet. He is my twin soul. We all have twin souls. If we are lucky

enough to meet them here on Earth, we can spend a very idyllic life together –
but this is rare, as many of our twin souls are still in Spirit, helping and guiding us
throughout our lives.

"I also have other Guides who often come to work with me. There is Mamoses: she
and I were hand-maidens in the Temple of Isis at the time of the Pharaohs, which
would explain my love of Egypt. I am also honoured to have been given a Carmelite
Nun, Sister Agnes, and a wonderful Atlantean Physician, both of whom have come
to help me with my Healing abilities in this lifetime.... Would you like more tea?"
Jane suddenly enquires.

"How can you switch from the Spiritual to normal so easily?" Olivia asks, bemused.

Jane smiles, "You have to live in the real world, darling, or you would be away
with the fairies half the time. Bills have to be paid, chores have to be done, but
excitement is around the next corner as you dip into their world."

Olivia is spellbound.

It is getting late by the time Jane has finished answering her granddaughter's
million questions, so Olivia elects to stay the night. She phones home, then she
and Jane make up the bed in the spare room. She often used to stay over when
she was smaller, and loved to chat until her eyes couldn't stay open any longer,
but it had been quite a while since she had wanted to stay. Life had taken over.
Work, boyfriends and parties all took up time that used to be spent with family...
but tonight, it seems right. And tomorrow? Well, who knows what tomorrow may
bring? The luxury of a lay-in, at least, and Jane fussing over her for breakfast is a
certainty. She has nothing else planned this weekend, so hopes her grandmother and
Shomas have more treasures to impart.

Life will never be quite the same again, Olivia reflects. She always knew her
grandmother was different, but now it is awe-inspiring to think she has been
receiving this kind of information for years, yet never really had anyone to share it
with in this way. No wonder Olivia's father calls his mother 'his little hippy'!

CHAPTER TWO

IN THE BEGINNING

Sunday is a bright morning. The sun shines through a chink in the drawn curtains. Olivia can hear bustling downstairs, as she lays luxuriating in the fact she does not have to get up for work and can stay snuggled in the warm for at least another hour.

She dozes for a while, then goes to the bathroom and, borrowing Jane's dressing-gown, ambles downstairs to be met by the warm smell of home baked bread. One of the luxuries of being retired, her grandmother had once told her, was that you can bake and tend the garden whenever you want, and obviously today, with company, the baking had taken the fore.

"Hello sweetheart, did you sleep well?" Jane asks as she sees a sleepy Olivia at the door.

"Bliss, thank you. I went out like a light and that bed is so comfortable. You've been busy. Is that fresh baked bread I can smell?" Olivia asks, sniffing the air.

"It is," Jane confirms, "would you like some? The honey is from my neighbour, who has his own bee hives, and couldn't be better. Do you fancy a cup of tea too?"

"Yes, please," Olivia says, smiling, "that all sounds lovely."

"I thought today, if you would like, I could explain a little about how I first became involved in all of this, and some things I have discovered over the years," Jane offers.

"I'd really like that. Just let me have a shower and get dressed," Olivia answers, starting to rise.

"Finish your breakfast first," Jane gently chastises. "Best meal of the day, they say."

Olivia sits back down and finishes off warm bread and honey and hot tea. Then, feeling very full, she wanders off to get ready for the day. About an hour later, she finds her grandmother sitting on her swing chair in the garden savouring the midday sun. The garden is so pretty, it is full of colour, and the scents on the air around the swing chair are quite heady. Scented flowers are planted to their best advantage everywhere you can sit in order to absorb their delicious aromas. Every corner of the garden is filled with colour and the grass has been mown to create rows of stripes. Olivia sits down on the swing beside her grandmother, and they rock in peaceful unison for a few minutes before either of them speaks.

Jane then starts to tell her story, beginning with the 1970s when she and Olivia's grandfather lived in the downstairs flat of a large Victorian house in a town on the Sussex Coast.

"From the first day we moved into the flat, I sensed we had company. It was a long flat: a lounge and bedroom to the left side of the hall, leading to the dining room, through which you accessed the kitchen, bathroom and utility room. On entering the dining room, there would often be a chill and a beautiful smell of lavender. I wasn't scared of the presence I sensed, as it didn't feel ominous.

"After some months there, I became pregnant, and sometimes I would relax on the sofa in the lounge – where a chill would fill the air and the scent of lavender engulf me. I still didn't see anyone, but I would say 'I'm OK, just tired'...and the smell and chill would go away. When your Dad was born, his cot was often engulfed in that beautiful scent, so I knew someone was there, watching over him.

"The couple who lived in the upstairs flat refused to believe there was anything unusual in the house, until things started to be moved around on their dressing table. One day one of their mirrors suddenly appeared on the stairs, reflecting an image of them as they came in through their front door. This scared them, so they came downstairs to ask if we had experienced anything similar!

"Some time later, a letter arrived from a woman who said she had intended to be a companion for an elderly lady, who had once lived in our house. Unfortunately, circumstances had prevented her from coming there, but she felt that the spirit of the elderly lady was still around looking for company. The couple upstairs received the letter and sadly destroyed it, so I didn't get a chance to reply and find out more – but I knew, in my heart of hearts, it must have been my 'Lavender Lady'.

"After a couple of years we left the flat and moved on. Many years went by and I started teaching at a local college. One day some students asked if I believed in ghosts, as they had moved into a student house and thought that the house next door was haunted. When I asked where they lived, it was in the house next to the flat where we had lived. I just said, 'It is'. They were flabbergasted and wanted to know more, so I told them the whole story. I realised then that the Lavender Lady was still there, so I prayed she would find peace and escape from the house.

"About fifteen years later, whilst attending a local spiritualist church, the medium came to me saying, 'I can smell lavender. There is someone here waving springs of lavender under my nose. She is asking me to tell you that she has found all her friends and family, whom she'd thought she had lost. She is very happy, and says thank you. Can you take this?' The medium had never met me before, so could not possibly have known. I was delighted, as the message was a real sign that the Lavender Lady had 'gone home' and was not tied to the old house anymore."

"What a lovely story! Weren't you frightened when you first sensed she was there?" asked Olivia, "and did you ever find out any more about her?"

"I never really thought of what happened as a problem; it was only a chill and the scent of lavender. We did have a friend who freaked out completely when she walked through the dining room, where the air went cold. She refused to come back in the house from that day on. As to finding out more, there was no way I could trace the Lavender Lady, so I was just happy that she was happy. It was all I really needed to know, and I never heard any more...although I do still think of her occasionally.

"My Spirit Guides have advised me that there is no death, just a passing to the next phase of life eternal. Once the soul leaves the body, it's not the end – it is the beginning of a new life, a life of Spirit, and for me my Lavender Lady was proof."

Jane then adds, "How sad it must be for anyone who feels that once you die that is the end, and cannot believe that their soul can go on to better things. I have been told that on leaving your body and passing into the realms of Spirit, there is a feeling of lightness and freedom. Apparently all the family who have gone before celebrate their loved one's arrival, so in a way it is their birthday in Heaven!"

Olivia smiles at that lovely thought, and gives a soft sigh as Jane continues. "I went to see a medium some years ago, as I wanted to talk to my mum and dad through someone else. To get a different perspective to anything I could receive. As you probably know from films like *Ghost*, there is a Light which everyone has to walk into on passing from this life to Spirit. But the medium told me that Dad, who had passed over about twenty-eight years before Mum, had built a bridge for her to cross over from our life to theirs, and covered it in roses, her favourite flowers."

"Oh that is beautiful. He must have loved her so very much," Olivia exclaims.

"Yes, he did; they were very close. I was very lucky, I had a great childhood. I shall tell you all about it some other time," Jane says nostalgically.

They both lapse into silence again, lost in their own thoughts about Olivia's great-grandparents and their love.

CHAPTER THREE
PLANET EARTH

Life goes on as usual for Olivia, although her everyday work seems tame to her now. There is no way she can tell her colleagues of her adventures at her grandmother's. They would think her mad. Roll on Friday!

Olivia has always known that Jane is not like other grandmothers. Her father, although he teased Jane about it, had great respect for her spiritual work, and Olivia was brought up to feel the same. Now that Olivia is ready to become part of her grandmother's amazing life, she wants to know everything.

At last Friday arrives and Olivia can't wait for her day to end so she can go and see what other adventures are in store. As soon as she arrives she receives her normal warm welcome. Jane always gives the best hugs; and after tea and a chat, they both climb the stairs to the room where the magic happens.

Olivia is excited and wonders what is on the agenda today. She sits in the comfortable chair and waits in anticipation. This time, Jane places a tiny globe made of crystals in her hands and tells her that Shomas wants to talk to her today about Planet Earth.

"In what way?" enquires Olivia.

Jane smiles. "Just wait and see. Close your eyes and relax. I want you to clear your mind, let the cares of the world drop away, and allow the life force energy[11] to heal you and bring you back to a state of balance. You may find it difficult to cut out the world, all the noise and hum-drum of daily life, but try to block out thoughts of what yesterday has brought and tomorrow may bring. I know it's hard but try. Sit very quietly and listen to your own breathing. Feel a sense of freedom, a relaxation of your muscles and mind. As you relax, your breathing will become deeper and deeper...and then you will see Shomas, and he will take you on another journey."

Olivia does as she is asked, and suddenly Shomas appears. "Good evening, Olivia," he says, "it is lovely to speak with you again. Today I want to talk to you about Planet Earth."

Olivia smiles in greeting and bows her head reverently as Shomas starts.

"In the beginning there was a beautiful planet, a glorious land of light and love. The trees and plants blossomed in profusion and the colours were so bright they would dazzle. The planet Earth is a unique and wonderful object; it was created as a jewel in the crown, the life blood of a galaxy. It is the most beautiful and most physical planet, and the most sought after on which to incarnate. It is one small dot in the Universe: a small dot that is very important to the wellbeing of every other small dot within your solar system, and that system is essential to the continuation of your galaxy and of the entire Universe as you know it now."

As Shomas speaks Olivia can 'see' in her mind's eye the beauty of the planet as it had been. The colours are amazingly bright and more vibrant than she has ever imagined.

"In the early days of the planet," Shomas continues, "beyond man's recognition now, there lived a people so diaphanous in their beauty. They lived and breathed with the planet, working in harmony with the land, and holding all the plants and animals in high esteem. They took nothing from the Earth if they could not return it sevenfold. They lived with the flora and fauna, in unity and peace. Plants flourished under their care and developed into the beauty you see around you: the vibrant colours, the floral scents. Insects and animals came into being, and bird song filled the air with sweet melodies. Earth was a molten rock turned solid, a barren land turned verdant and the waters cleared, creating the wondrous blue and green planet seen from space today.

"Back in the aeons of the past, there was an entity which hovered over your planet and filtered the water to bring a purity and cleanliness to all rivers, streams and lakes. Sadly, as time has passed this entity can no longer do this job whilst mankind pollutes and scars the land, breaking the leylines and disrupting the water table. Now, the rivers, streams and lakes are filled with silt and blocked by rubbish and decay, which contaminates the water. Man has a lot to answer for; he has tainted and destroyed a lot that is good. He needs to become aware of these issues and take more care of his home. He looks for water on other planets, but forgets to take care of his own lands and seas."

As the beautiful colours turn to decay, Olivia can see the harm mankind has caused the planet. It is so distressing.

"Earth, as you know, should be a beautiful blue and green planet, scattered with white fluffy clouds," Shomas tells her, "not polluted and choked by its own atmosphere. The orange skies are not sunsets, they are pollution at its worst, and this has to stop before it kills the planet and affects all the people on it. Sadly, today a closer look at your beautiful planet shows dirt and grime, plague and pestilence, darkness and destruction. Earth is not the land it was. It is being destroyed, and everything on it is being used and abused.

"That beauty has to be restored. Earth has to be returned to being the jewel of the Universe. The planet needs a helping hand to bring it back to its former glory – where life will be sweet once more, where birds will fly free, and animals will stroll the Earth unfettered. Men and women will find their souls anew and the planet will again be pure. Your world is filled with toxins but these shall be cleared and it will return to the beautiful world it once was. From a satellite, the Earth looks pure and wonderful; it looks as it looked before. It is only when you come close that you see the harm done, and you realise that this radiant blue world is being destroyed.

"There will come a time when man won't need the fuels he uses, as he develops a greater understanding of other means of fuelling his machines and transporting himself from place to place. In time, all will be made clear," Shomas assures Olivia, "and there will be enough knowledge to be able to save the Earth.

"Do not be afraid. There is a need to bring the Earth back into balance, to return her to her former beauty and give all upon her a chance to see how she should really be, a place of peace, tranquillity and love. A perfect island in the ocean of the Universe. Man is always looking to heaven for paradise, when he has it right there in his hands. I know sensitive souls now feel these things far more. I wish everyone was a sensitive soul, the world would be a better place. Everyone needs to help to raise the vibrations[9]. To take a stand and make all of mankind take notice, so the world will be a better and safer place. The future is all your tomorrows, and the tomorrows of your descendents. Let them live a life as full, if not better, than yours."

With that, Shomas says good-bye and leaves as quickly as he arrived. Olivia comes slowly back from the meditation. She knows, from what her grandmother has told her, that she must not rush back to ordinary consciousness – but as soon as she feels herself in the room again, she opens her eyes and looks straight at Jane. "That was mind-blowing!" she exclaims, "so much to take in!" Then she proceeds to relate to her grandmother all she has just been told, and the magic of all she has seen.

Jane ensures Olivia stays seated, allowing her time to return to 'normal'. Then she says, "Let me ground you before you leave the house. I forgot to do it for myself once. My head was in the clouds and I fell over in the road – very embarrassing and very painful! Just sit for five minutes and let me close all your chakras, then you will be okay. I shall explain why and how you can do this for yourself another day. I am so glad you understand what I do, and that it doesn't frighten you. You are so precious to me and I wouldn't want to unnerve you."

After Olivia's chakras have been closed, Jane advises, "now I think you had better go home or I shall be in trouble for keeping you so long. See you next week?"

"Yes, please. I love you," Olivia enthuses as she heads for the door.

"I love you too, Livvy, take care," Jane responds, watching with affection as her beautiful granddaughter walks down the path on her way home.

CHAPTER FOUR
LEYLINES

Olivia's week seems interminable. She can't wait to see her grandmother the following weekend. She has started reading about leylines, and wants to know what they really are and what their purpose is. She knows her grandmother will have the answer, so blurts it out as soon as she arrives.

"Whoa, whoa, whoa," exclaims Jane, "let's get you in the door first. What has prompted all of this?"

"You promised to take me to see some crop circles in the summer," Olivia explains, "so I started reading about them – and the website I was reading also had an article on leylines. Then I remembered you mentioning them before, and as I know absolutely nothing about them, I thought I would ask you. I became so excited on the way over, I forgot the usual niceties!" She gives Jane a big hug.

"No problem," says Jane. "We shall have a cup of tea and then I shall explain to you, as much as I know."

A little later, warmed from their hot drink, they stroll upstairs and Jane regales Olivia with all she understands about leylines.

"Well," Jane starts, "*Ley* is the Saxon term for a clear glade or track of open ground. In 1921 Alfred Watkins, an amateur archaeologist, explained how he had dowsed these lines of energy to trace their origins and geometrical structure all over the planet, recognising that they seemed to align places of geographical and historical interest. He wrote that during ancient times these alignments were created to make trekking easy by line of sight. He professed that they are integral to the well-being of the planet herself, and as such, to the people who live upon the Earth.

"I have been told, by my Guides, that the leylines found by Alfred Watkins overlay very ancient leylines, which were the paths trodden by pilgrims for millions of years, and by generations of nomads who traversed the planet. The St. Michael's leyline apparently starts at Land's End, and passes through several Megalithic sites and Castle mounts before it gets to Glastonbury Tor, and then on to Avebury and beyond on its three hundred and fifty mile long path. As leylines criss-cross the globe they, for the most part, link structures which are integral to the populace – such as churches, castles, pyramids and standing stones – which all lie where leylines cross and the energy is doubled in that area.

"There is a clear link between megaliths, leylines and astronomy," Jane continues. "Most stone circles, long barrows and tumuli are aligned with leylines. As I said before, they mainly trace the ancient pathways used by our forefathers and hold the energy of all the thousands of feet that trod those paths. Amazingly, Glastonbury, Stonehenge and Avebury all align to create a perfect right-angled triangle. And I am led to believe that at Stonehenge fourteen leylines converge, making it an energy portal[21] or place of power."

"That's incredible," interjects Olivia.

Jane agrees, and begins to read some writing Shomas had shared with her some years before: "'The Earth is a living being in her own right; she supports not only mankind but the plant life, the trees, the flowers and the vegetables, which would not grow without the life-giving force of the planet; and as a living thing, planet Earth needs the energy supplied by the leylines.

"'Leylines are embedded in the Earth's crust and create octahedrons, dodecahedrons, icosahedrons across the planet – and where these cross, vortices are created, from which the energy traverses beyond the parameters of the globe, to other planets within the vastness of space. They stretch out to planets within the Universe and beyond, from where they give and receive power. As the leylines traverse the ever-expanding cosmos they hold each planet in its specific place in space and time. If they cease to exist, the planets will change their courses and the Universe will not be as it is today. There are multitudinous levels of energy and development which hang in balance on this grid.

"'Earth is so very important; it is the central hub, holding together thousands of planets. There are not many planets with this capability, very few. There are others, which are of a similar level, but not for many millions of light years. They are scattered far and wide throughout the Universe but they all are integral to this grid.

"'Earth is the pivotal point of the Universe with Britain as the pivotal point on which creation depends. It holds the planetary matrix in place; and Britain is home to the Spiritual Guardians of the pathways of Light of the Ancients.

"'These days, leylines are not recognised as they were, but they still hold together the energy grid of the planet. There are places in the world where, as they cross, the veils between heaven and earth are thinnest, and it is at these points that man can connect more directly to Spirit."

Jane pauses to give Olivia time to absorb this, and then continues to read more of Shomas's writing about Leylines.

"'When Earth is alive and kicking, the whole Universe is full of vitality. The planets are vibrant with her energy. The leylines extend to the farthest reaches of the

Universe and affect all. If anything were to happen to Planet Earth then obviously those energy lines would be destroyed, creating a hole in the mesh – and this is why Mother Earth, or Gaia[18] as she is sometimes called, must maintain her position within the Universe.

"'Many leylines have been broken, dug up and desecrated through the carelessness and thoughtlessness of men. They are being blocked and scarred and the power isn't getting through, so the planet cannot recharge. There are huge scars in the Earth's crust, created by the development of roads and quarries. Something has to be done to ensure all these broken lines are re-aligned and re-connected around the planet.

"'All the minerals taken out of the planet cannot be replenished, and because of this Gaia could give up, throw up her hands in despair, and the Spirit of the planet could leave – just as the Spirit leaves your bodies when you pass on. But she is a loving, caring being, and she knows that if she leaves and the planet dies, all upon her will go too, so she is 'hanging-on-in-there'. She is determined that life shall go on, but she is shaking her body, to re-align the energy lines, so that she again receives the power she needs.

"'Man must learn to respect the planet and the laws of nature. To hold dear the strength of the leylines and crystals and acknowledge their abilities. Nature is a powerful force, respect it!

"'These days folklore is a thing of the past; it is not revered and respected as it was in ancient times, but it should be. It speaks of the lines, it speaks of the trees and the importance they play in the future of the planet – each different tree bringing a different energy and usefulness to daily life. The beech, the ash, the oak – all used for building materials, the yew as a guardian of sacred spaces, the chestnut for shelter and warmth. Each tree has a life-span of hundreds of years to grow and expand and be of use.

"'We regret to say that these days few trees are respected, they are chopped down and discarded in the name of progress. Trees are the lungs of the planet, without which man could not breathe. The tree roots hold together the soil and stop landslides. You all need to explain to the young that they must respect and revere the trees and the leylines, to keep them safe and protect the world. Teach everyone the true benefit of leylines, trees and plants, so they will respect rather than destroy them.'"

Jane looks up from the notebook she is reading and says thoughtfully, "I remember reading somewhere that roughly eight thousand years ago all trees and plant life were removed from the Sahara area to be used in building and farming. This caused the soil to erode, and is why the Sahara is now just barren desert."

She continues with Shomas's story. "'All the planets with crystals in their centre are interdependent. So if one of these planets should die, and vanish from the grid, then the whole structure and energy system of the Universe would be affected. The energy levels of the planets which connect to that one planet would be depleted, which would cause havoc. The whole interconnected network of leylines would have to realign and re-configure. It would take some time to replace this very important element, and for the energy levels to rise again on each of these planets. Some planets are very small, some very large, some with life forms, some without. The depletion of the energy levels would affect any life forms upon these planets whilst the network rebuilds and repairs itself.

"'It is very important that planets like the Earth remain as they are. Man has to do something about his planet to clear the poisons and the toxins, as Mother Earth is throwing up her arms in despair, and we cannot possibly allow this. It is vital that the planet survives; it is vital that it stay exactly where it is in the solar system, this galaxy and the Universe itself.'"

Olivia sits stunned. "I never realised leylines would be so important or were so complex. It is not something we are taught in school."

"Maybe it should be," Jane admits. "It may make younger people realise just how important leylines, and the land itself, are to the life they live. They could become involved in a tree planting project, or help the county rangers to coppice and clear scrubland, or clear the waterways of weed and rubbish – anything which would help the planet to breathe again."

Jane and Olivia discuss this a while longer, and then Jane suddenly says, "today I thought we would have some retail therapy. Our spiritual work is enormously important – but sometimes you need a change of pace, so today's the day."

So they pick up their bags and head for the door, still deep in conversation.

CHAPTER FIVE
CROP CIRCLES

Summer arrives with the heady scent of roses filling the air. The garden stretches out like a cat enjoying the full caress of the morning sun. Olivia has been busy and unable to visit Jane for a number of weeks, her visit today is filled with anticipation. They are going to visit some crop circles which have appeared in fields in the local area.

Olivia decides to drive so that Jane can navigate and tell her what she knows of this strange phenomenon. Years ago, after visiting a circle with a friend, Jane had joined a local research group. So she starts to explain everything she has learnt about crop circles over the years.

"A friend of mine was a member of the Centre for Crop Circle Studies (CCCS) and he took me along to one of their meetings which was extremely interesting and informative. There were many different factions of people who believed these circles to be created by different sources. I learnt that crop circles have been appearing in fields across the world since around the 17th century, but have only gained recognition in the past twenty to thirty years. The shapes are mainly mathematically perfect, and stunning in their execution. They tend to mainly be a northern hemisphere phenomenon – with their centre predominantly in Britain within what is known as the golden triangle: Avebury, Stonehenge and Marlborough – but they have also appeared elsewhere in the world. They are mainly found in our wheat fields, but they have also been found in oilseed rape, barley, maize, linseed and grass. They have even been found in the USA, Australia and Chinese paddy fields.

"There is a lot of information about Crop Circles in *An Introduction to Crop Circles* by Andy Thomas, who is a fascinating speaker on the subject. And in *Quest for Contact* by Andy Thomas with Paul Bura, a fantastic channel, author and poet (who sadly passed away a few years ago).

"Strangely, many instruments, when put into crop circles shortly after the circles are created, can be affected by what appears to be electromagnetic energy. This energy can often make compasses spin and watches stop. It is not advisable to go into a circle for a day or two after it has been first laid down, as the energy is so intense."

Olivia listens intently as Jane reads a section written by Shomas on the subject.

"'The circles are created with such power and speed, they are bound to affect the crystals, batteries and bulbs tested within them. The energy force is natural and comes from the planet itself; it is an indescribable power, just as the power in crystals is indescribable.

"'The patterns are an ancient language based on bygone truths that western man has largely forgotten, and tell of the trauma man is causing the planet. These amazing designs are trying to draw man's attention to this fact. It will take a lot of research before mankind will be able to trace the source of this ancient language, but he will understand who is creating these circles one day and be given clues as to their representation. Spirits from other planets may influence the way the circles are drawn, as they watch over the Earth, because she is the central link in the Universe.

"'The crop circles are a visible manifestation of the Earth's plea for help, and these symbols have been appearing in your fields for some time now. They have been produced to help man to understand about the needs of the Earth Spirit. Man has taken too much from the Earth over the centuries: he has raped the Earth of her goodness, oil, fossil fuels and there's not much left, so that is why the circle makers are giving the signs to warn you.'"

Jane stops reading and adds, "Some similar symbols have been found in ancient caves around the world. No-one is really sure what they mean, or why they were carved, but it is interesting that symbols like these are now appearing in our fields. When the circles first appeared, photographs of them were taken to a tribe who had hardly any contact with Western civilisation. Upon seeing the shapes which had been created, they cried and said, 'It is Mother crying. Brother is hurting Mother'. Mother being Mother Earth, and brother being mankind. The Hopi Indians have also always believed in Mother Earth and how she is the 'life' of the planet, and how mankind is making her unhappy with the damage he is doing."

"Oh, how sad," sighs Olivia.

Jane and Olivia eventually arrive at the circle they have elected to visit. They have had to get permission from the farm owner to walk through his crops. Farmers lose thousands of pounds in revenue because of the damage caused by a crop circle appearing in their field and will often charge visitors in order to recoup their losses.

In the field, the air is still. There is not a sound except their feet on the flattened corn and the sweet melody of a skylark in the distance. The circle is enormous; it isn't actually one circle but a series of circles making a very complex pattern. There is no way of seeing its complexity from the ground, as it has taken up most of the field. It can only really be appreciated from the air.

"When we get home, we can go on the Crop Circle website and see if they have any aerial photos of this one yet. Then you can see how beautiful it really is," says Jane.

"Brilliant," exclaims Olivia, "I have never seen one before, let alone been inside one. This is amazing."

"Did I tell you that I was once asked to ask Shomas where a crop circle would be appearing?" Jane adds.

"No, tell me more," Olivia responds, curious.

"Paul Bura (a channeller), Diana (a medium) and I all worked on a map to find an area where we thought a crop circle would be created. We all independently came up with corresponding information, which led to a place near Devil's Dyke in East Sussex. About eight or ten of us went to this specific place on the designated evening: mid-summer's night, and sat above the field where this phenomenon was supposed to appear.

"We sat for hours watching and waiting, and despite the date the night began to get very cold. The sky was clear and, as we were out of town, we really had a great view of all the stars that night. At about 2 a.m, someone asked if we would all like a cup of tea. We turned away from the field just long enough to have our cups filled, and on turning back could see tiny blue lights dancing on the field exactly where we had expected a circle to be.

"Sadly, no actual circle appeared in the field we were watching, but an existing formation at Lancing, a few miles away to the west, morphed itself from a thin cross into a full circular configuration that very night, and many other circles appeared within the vicinity over the next year."

"What a shame. Have you any idea what the blue lights were?" Olivia asks.

"I'm not sure," Jane says pensively, "but Shomas told me, 'The energy force is natural, the circles are being created by the Guardians of the Earth Spirit. The Devas[12], or spirits of the plants and trees, are Guardians of the Earth and have much to tell about the Earth Spirit's cries for help. Time will come when all mankind will understand. Many may poo-poo the idea to start with.'

"Now, I had never heard of Deva's[12] at that time, and when told that they are spirits of the trees and plants I was very sceptical, as I couldn't grasp the concept at all. It sounded way-out to me – but if you think about it, it is logical. The trees and plants are living things too, and these Devas are the spirits relating to them. If we have a spirit, then so should all other living things, and the planet must be a living being in order to support life on her surface."

"So many people say the crop circles are man made," Olivia quips.

"When the hoaxers put down a circle, they use planks of wood and flatten the cereal crop to the ground." Jane informs her. "In a 'real' crop circle the corn bends a little above the ground and then swirls for the most part clockwise from the centre. As I said to you before, they don't only appear in wheat and barley but in paddy fields and even in oilseed rape, which snaps if you try to bend it. I am sure Doug and Dave, or whatever their names are, can't be doing those!" Jane is so emphatic, Olivia has to believe. "And it would take them days to create anything as complex as this," Jane emphasises, spinning around with her arms outstretched. "And a genuine crop circle is usually formed in a very short space of time considering their complexity."

They both stand in reverie, thinking about the crop circles and their creators.

CHAPTER SIX

MINDFULNESS & MEDITATION

The morning dawns bright and clear. There is a smattering of daisies across the lawn, Jane hasn't the heart to mow today as their cheery flowers bring enchantment to an otherwise plain lawn. All across the garden everything is in full bloom. The garden looks radiant and the heady scents from the climbing plants is intoxicating.

Jane has been thinking about running Mindfulness and Meditation classes from home. As Olivia has stayed she enlists her help to plan how this should be delivered.

"Mindfulness is the new 'in' word for calming the mind," she explains to her granddaughter over breakfast. "It is a psychological process of bringing your focus solely to the experience of sounds, sensations, thoughts, feelings or actions happening in the present moment, which helps to clear the mind and allay distraction. For example, you might examine the intricacies of a petal, or listen to the soft buzz of a bee as it flits from flower to flower, or draw patterns in the sand, or feel a breath of wind caress your face. You might even slowly walk a labyrinth in order to free your mind of the turmoil of the day. It is not an attempt to exclude the world; it is just a way to be aware of the moment, and to temporarily release all the other thoughts and worries which abound in our day-to-day lives.

"Mindfulness is believed to relieve depression and anxiety, as well as to encourage healthy aging, enhance weight management and improve athletic performance. It is also known to help children with special needs to focus and calm their minds.

"It is closely linked to meditation," she adds, "and is a significant element of the Buddhist tradition, where it is used to develop self-knowledge and wisdom which will gradually lead to enlightenment[17]. It may take the form of a simple meditation, or a state of complete focus created by producing 'mandalas' which are patterns created on paper or in sand."

"Oh, I've done that," says Olivia, "I sometimes sit and draw pen-and-ink patterns and it is always surprisingly relaxing."

"Exactly the idea," Jane confirms. "Tibetan monks take several weeks to create their sand mandalas, working together as a team. There is a huge amount of labour involved, working from the centre outwards to create these really intricately detailed patterns. Once complete, the mandalas are ritualistically dismantled and brushed away, which symbolises their belief in the transitory nature of material life."

"How incredible!" Olivia exclaims, although she is devastated by the thought of destroying something so beautiful.

Jane adds, "You don't have to follow the Tibetan practice and destroy your drawings! But it is good to remember to be present and mindful in everything you do."

"There are several exercises designed to develop mindfulness, which are helped by guided meditations. Meditation itself is a great way to cut out the world, with all the noise and humdrum of daily life – to block out thoughts of what yesterday has brought and what tomorrow might bring. It encourages you to be at one with yourself, and helps you to have the right attitude to appreciate the world around you even more than you already do."

Olivia likes any chance to learn to meditate, so Jane explains more of how to do it:

"Sit very quietly in a closed room and bring your attention to your breathing. You will feel your abdomen move as you breathe, in and out. It takes time to slow your thoughts and still your mind, but meditation can be at the heart of your day to help your 'monkey mind'[16] be at peace. But," she warns, "those new to meditation (and sometimes even experienced meditators) can find it difficult to shut off random thoughts, jumping in and out of consciousness and disrupting the peace and emptiness they wish to experience. You may find it hard to go 'off' on a meditative journey at first, but gradually you will find the peace and relaxation you seek, to enjoy and absorb the meditative journey.

"There are a couple of basic solutions which may help. One is to count backwards from three hundred, and by the time you get halfway through, you are 'away'. Or, as random thoughts come into your head, visualise an open window and pop these thoughts outside. Later, you can ask Spirit to bring them back as and when you need them and amazingly, they will return to you in full flight.

"Eventually you will find the method most suitable for you. Try to practice every day for five to ten minutes, preferably away from any electronic equipment and somewhere where you will be undisturbed. Before you begin, make sure you turn off the phone!

"Sit with your feet on the floor, hands cupped in your lap," Jane says, demonstrating, "your left hand nestling in your right hand. Your spine should be straight and your head erect, as though the crown is held by a piece of string tied to the sky. Shrug your shoulders, two or three times, to help release tension. Take some deep breaths: in through your nose and out through your mouth. Take your breathing a little deeper than usual. Sit for a while, just listening to your breath. Once you can quieten your mind and enter the stillness and peace of meditation, you may just enjoy the tranquillity, a total emptiness of thought, or you could be taken on a journey to talk to your Spirit Guides.

"Some people prefer a guided meditation, where someone talks you along a visualised path, either in person or recorded. They will leave you at a certain point in the meditation to give you the freedom to explore on your own. Normally Spirit will take over then and continue on your journey with you, showing you amazing sights which you can remember and relate (if you want to) later.

"Once you are confident, you can go into the stillness and peace without aids, where immediately, Spirit will take you and lead you on a journey of your own. This is similar to what you already do when you visit with Shomas, so I don't think you will find it hard. As you grow more accustomed to meditation, it is always fascinating what images you see, often helping with questions you may be asking at the time. These experiences are magical!

"For Healers, this is an excellent time to concentrate on sending absent Healing to anyone you know who needs this help – or, alternatively, any nation or cause you feel would benefit from Healing. In meditation, you will normally 'see' a problem that you wish resolved, and with Spirit's help you can concentrate on easing the issue.

"Shomas is saying, 'Spend a few minutes a day clearing your mind. Let the cares of the world drop away, and allow the life force energy to heal you and bring you back to a state of balance'." Then Jane falls silent, her eyes closed, concentrating.

While Jane has been demonstrating meditation techniques, Shomas has popped in to add his thoughts to the mix. Olivia, realising what has happened, sits quietly and waits. She knows Jane will share it with her later.

"I should like to give you a few words on meditation," Shomas tells Jane. "Sit very quietly and comfortably in a closed room, relax every part of your body and listen to your breathing. Feel a sense of freedom, a relaxation of the muscles and mind. Breathe in deeply through your nose and out through your mouth, expelling all negativity and stress from your body. Listen to your breathing, let that be the only thing which registers in your mind.

"Let your imagination initially take you for a walk in beautiful woods or gardens: do not let anything disturb the peace. Relax your mind and body, open yourself to the Light, and follow your breathing. The cares of the day will fade away as we take you on a magical journey of discovery.

"Meditate, send Healing light not just to people and animals but to the nations and countries in which they live, to the land beneath your feet, to the sky above and to the trees and plants which sustain your life. Send love and Light to all. Breathe life and love into the Earth and you will add your part to raising the consciousness of the planet and helping mankind to rebuild it for the future.

"We ask that you all sit and meditate. To take time to look to your inner meaning, to listen to the small still voice within that tells you right from wrong. So many people never hear that voice as they catapult themselves forward through their life.

"So few people look into themselves for the real source of their God and the all-knowing eye of their soul. But it is there, if you look deep within: you will see all you need to see, hear all you need to hear, to propel yourself forward on your true path for the rest of your lifetime.

"Many Buddhists have mastered the art of looking for their God within and gained peace and tranquillity. They no longer need possessions, material wealth or the trappings of your world. They know all they need are the clothes they wear and the food they eat to have a life of peace and harmony."

Jane thanks Shomas as he takes his leave. Then she tells Olivia what Shomas had to say, and enlists her help to finalise the structure for her classes.

Jane plans to take all participants on a guided meditation for the first session.

"Why don't practice on me?" says Olivia, and Jane agrees it is a good idea.

The pair sit together in Jane's upstairs room, and as the light plays gently on the walls, Olivia sits in anticipation of the journey she is about to encounter.

They both relax and Jane begins: "Make sure you are sitting comfortably, both feet firmly on the floor, hands relaxed in your lap. Now close your eyes.

"Correct your posture, feel your neck extend as you lift your head to link to the sky, and relax your shoulders. Relax every part of your body. Quieten your mind. Throw any stray thoughts away as you become more conscious of your breathing. Breathe in through your nose and out through your mouth, inhaling positivity and exhaling tension and negative emotions.

"Feel your feet connecting to the floor and visualise roots extending from the bottom of your feet into the ground beneath. See them travel down and wrap themselves around a huge crystal in the centre of the Earth."

As Olivia follows Jane's instructions, she drifts into a deep meditative state.

"Now focus your attention on the rhythm of your footsteps as you wander slowly down a quiet, dusty, country lane, banked by hedgerow and wild flowers. As you meander down the lane, a butterfly comes to rest on the top of the hedge and you watch the jewel-like colours in its wings as it flits from leaf to leaf. Smell the honeysuckle as its long tendrils brush your face, allowing you to inhale its intoxicating scent."

Jane pauses to allow Olivia time to experience this.

"You will come to a rustic farm gate. Open it carefully and go inside. There, in front of you, is a beautiful field of corn, and a gentle breeze encourages the whole field to wave like a flag. Listen to it rustle.

"Become aware of the serenade of a skylark's song as it flies low across the field."

Jane pauses again, while Olivia listens to the skylark.

"Along a well-trodden path at the edge of the field, poppies raise their cheery faces to the sun and cornflowers dance in the breeze. Blow a dandelion head and watch the seeds spiral to the earth in a cascade of frothy white parachutes.

"Walk along this path, feeling the baked earth beneath your feet and the warmth of the sun on your back. Let this warmth envelop you like the protective embrace of the wings of an Angel, keeping you safe as you drift further along the trail.

"In a corner of the field, there is a large oak tree, it's gnarled branches overhanging a stream. You will find the dappled shade quite cooling. Sit on a rock and watch the sun glinting on the ripples of water tumbling over pebbles in the stream. Listen to the water softly calling to you, helping you to relax and be calm. Dip your feet in the stream and let the water wash away the cares of the day, leaving you refreshed and renewed.

"Rise gently from your seat and walk across the field. Half-way across, you reach a flattened circle, perfect and complete, laying amidst the corn. Lower yourself gently to the ground, lay back and relax as the breeze rustles the corn tassels and gently caresses your hair. Relish the time to just lay there, still and at peace. Clear your mind as white light enfolds you and encompasses your very being. Melt into the arms of serenity and love, allowing your Guides to take you on a journey of their own."

Jane stops speaking for much longer this time, to allow Olivia to meet her own Spirit Guide and learn at his feet.

Later, when she feels the time is right, she quietly speaks again.

"Remember all you have been told as you rise and walk back across the field...back through the gate...and out into the lane where you, again, pass the honeysuckle. Pick a small sprig and hold this in your hand; the intoxicating scent will bring back memories of this day as you stroll back down the lane...back to this house...back to your seat.

"Now, slowly come back, feeling the solidity of the chair beneath you. Wriggle your hands and toes to establish your return, and then, very gently, open your eyes to refocus on the room."

Jane waits until she sees Olivia wriggling her toes and stretching her hands, eventually opening her eyes and refocusing on her grandmother. Then she encourages Olivia to share her experiences.

Olivia is full of enthusiasm. "That was just so relaxing, Granny! Thank you so much." She then tells Jane about everything she saw and heard on her journey.

"I could feel the corn under my bare feet. I could hear the trickling of the water over the pebbles in the distance as I lay in the field looking at the bluest sky. I lay there for a while getting my bearings and my own Guide came and spoke with me. He has a gentleness just like Shomas. Meeting him was wonderful.

"When he left, I rose and walked slowly back across the field. I passed the corn – which was stilled now, as the breeze had dropped – and carried on back to the gate, where I re-entered the lane. Walking slowly up the lane, I could smell the honeysuckle again, then I heard your voice gently calling me back, telling me to open my eyes and return to the room. It was brilliant! Can we do another one on another day, please?"

"Of course," Jane assures her. "When I asked you to breathe in through your nose and out through your mouth, it is something I remember from meditations I used to go to with Paul Bura, whose main Guide was an Indian Chief. We were always told breathing in through your nose inhaled positivity, and out through your mouth exhaled negativity. I always try and practice this each time I meditate, visualising it with every breath."

Olivia smiles. She will remember that.

CHAPTER SEVEN
AURAS & HEALING

It has been raining heavily and the wind is battering the well-tended hanging baskets outside the front door. Olivia is welcomed, as always, with open arms, as soon as she arrives. She is bustled into the kitchen and given a towel to dry her hair. Grandmother and granddaughter have their usual banter about family and events over the time since they last met. Jane has been to the theatre and regales Olivia with the storyline.

Drier and topped up with the usual cup of tea, Olivia asks Jane quizzically, "Can you please tell me about all the different types of healing? What is an aura and what are chakras? You mention chakras when you 'close me down' after I have been upstairs talking to Shomas."

Jane is enthusiastic as they settle in the big comfy chairs in the Lounge so she begins: "Lets start with the aura. The aura is an egg-shaped field of subtle, luminous radiance surrounding all living things – similar to the halo in religious art, but is for the most part invisible to the human eye. The aura is waves of energy that vibrate at a certain level, which surround the whole body. It is a map of thoughts and feelings which reflect every human emotion, every intellectual and spiritual aspect – and will change as it is influenced by these factors within a person's energy system.

"Kirlain photography[23] can show your energy field, converting these waves of energy into colours, thereby creating a picture of your electromagnetic field or aura. Each different colour will be a visual measure of the state of health of your physical body on the day the photograph is taken, so you can get an understanding of your emotional, mental and spiritual state at that particular time.

"I am sure Shomas can explain auras better," Jane adds. "Go upstairs to see what he has to offer today, and I shall tell you more about Healing and chakras later."

Olivia agrees and makes her way upstairs. It is such an easy routine now for her to travel to a space where Shomas will come and impart his wisdom. After his normal polite greeting, he begins:

"Every living thing has an aura," he explains, "an invisible etheric haze which flows around its entire body. Be it a tree, an animal, a human being, they all have subtle non-physical energies which emanate around their physical form. All emotions show in a person's aura. If you are unwell your aura will be dull; if you are in tune with yourself, positive and happy, your aura will be beautiful and glow vibrantly with colour. Different colours in an aura depict different aspects of health and personality. When the body is functioning properly, the energy streams through the body like electricity through a power system and you will find you feel more positive, more enthusiastic and more in tune with life. When your aura is bright, you act as a magnet, drawing to you what is needed and desired at that time. The more it flows the healthier and happier you feel and you begin to 'glow'.

"Restrictions to this energy will make your aura dull, and can be caused by stress, anxiety, trauma, physical imbalance, improper nutrition, unhealthy environmental conditions or excesses in life-style: all of which will make you feel lack-lustre and quite low.

"A pregnant woman will get a 'bump' in her aura sometime before she even conceives, showing there will be conception. If you have an accident or an illness, dents will appear in your aura around the area of pain. Auras can survive even after living tissues with which they are associated have been destroyed. If someone loses a leg or an arm in an accident, the aura will still exist for a long time after its removal, as though that part of the body still exists – hence the patient often sensing that their leg or arm is still there.

"To keep your aura bright spend a few minutes a day clearing your mind. Let the cares of the world drop away to allow the life force energy to heal you and bring you back to a state of balance. A short meditation would be good for this."

Olivia thanks him as he moves on to the next subject, Healing.

"Healing can clear the chakras and make the aura radiant. This in-built knowledge is now coming to the fore, as is the knowledge that holistic medicine heals the 'whole person', not just part of an individual ailment.

"Mankind is re-discovering the art of Healing, by the laying on of hands and the use of sound. As the populace becomes aware that conventional medicine cannot cure all ills, more people will turn to Spiritual Healing. Anyone who believes they can be helped is open to Healing. This can be given anywhere where you feel someone needs your help. Don't be disheartened if it doesn't seem to work sometimes; the recipient may be blocking the channel, sometimes through fear or even lack of belief. You do not have to believe in Healing or have faith for it to work, but sometimes a non-believer will put up such a block in their minds, it will be impossible for the Healing to get through to help them. It is not always possible to cure everyone every time, as sometimes their illness may have been elected before birth as part of their karma[13].

"Many people across your world are losing faith in allopathic medicine, and as there are not enough doctors and nurses training to help the ever growing population of the world, Healers will become a natural port of call. Many countries worldwide do not respect or even understand Healing. Some governments even ban this from their skill sheet. Despite those regimes, good Healers will be welcomed by those who still allow the practice, to help them to understand the body and how it works.

"We want you all to know how much we appreciate the Healing work you all do across the planet. Not just Healers, but doctors, nurses, medics and ambulance staff – who all show Healing in their own way.

"Allopathic doctors are limited by the restrictive dogma of medical practice codes of conduct and are often not open to the flexibility allowed within their actual psyche. So many of them are natural Healers but cannot see the wood for the trees; they are scared to step over the line due to fear of litigation. It is sad they feel they cannot be free to offer their natural skills as well as their medical craft, as the two will readily go hand-in-hand.

"Not many allopathic medical practitioners realise how much they are aided by Spirit, to tend patients in their care. They do not realise that they are often overshadowed by carers and leaders in their field from this side of the veil[6], who help them in the medical work they perform.

"Many Healers on your planet at this time are feeling a shift in their energy as they are all being given a gift of thanks to empower them further. They will feel energised and driven and not tired after each session, as they may have been before.

"Healers give their all to help and heal hearts and minds, to bring forward this natural act to help the sick regain vigour and solace in this world of yours. Everyone has the ability to Heal, be it with hands, hearts or words. Everyone has this ability to a certain degree, and it is just a case of tapping into the source to find their gift.

"Healers must firstly have faith in themselves and their abilities. Fear is a mental block which affects your physical matrix and can obliterate the Light. We know that, as a Lightworker[3], your day to day life can take over at times and you may feel you are failing, but we shall never let you fail whilst you work in our name. You take the path of Light into your heart to help and heal others. This is the first step on the stairway to righteousness, and we hold those steps in a line for you to progress further into the Light.

"We, here in the Spirit World, use many Lightworkers[3], especially those who sleep deeply, by taking them out of their soul base at night. They are spiritually taken from their beds to help heal the war-torn areas of your world, to heal the sick, and those in transition. Also to heal the land and to stand sentinel to show the path to Light for those on their way 'home'.

"Many on your planet need Healing at this time and so, as each Lightworker passes over to our side, they are offered a gentle word of recognition, to thank them for all the work they have done in their lifetime on Earth in helping and healing others."

Shomas can see Olivia is enthralled by this topic, so continues in a slightly different vein:

"What many people do not realise is that music is also very healing: it is good for the soul and is the food of love. There is great power in music. Melodious sounds of nature, and of harp or other stringed instruments, bring peace to the heart and calm to the mind. It is relaxing and inspiring to be able to sit and listen to various types of music, each piece affecting your mood in a different way. Whatever the music, it helps you to relax, creating a feeling of tranquillity, and if you sing along it can release stress and tension, which will clear your head and heart. It is very good therapy for any lethargy in the world today.

"The music we are discussing is harmonious and tranquil music. It eases the aches of the heart, it makes one at peace with the world. A malady of the spirit can be caused by the fractious music of the youth of today. Much of this music is disharmonious and bad for the soul. Mankind needs harmonic sound. Bring everything back into harmony and the world will be a better place. Our music here is so beautiful and restful, everyone finds it calming. There is no music on Earth to match the heavenly sounds you will hear when you get to this plane⁵.

"Sound is pure energy, which can be brought into the physical matrix to be transformed into light energy, but not into Light itself. Pulsing light and sound is the way forward in Healing, it works on a molecular level. Some of your scientists are discovering 'new' ways of helping their patients, by using sound to dissolve kidney stones and other such ailments. Leeches, which are a natural but old-fashioned way of removing diseased tissue, are being used again to remove gangrenous flesh.

"On a lighter note, we are delighted that more and more of the populace are interested in the natural health movement. Clinics which do not use pharmaceuticals are cropping up in many towns and villages. Be wary, as some clinicians are untrained and may cause more harm than good, putting the treatment to ill repute. Just check before you make an appointment."

Olivia politely thanks Shomas for his insights today, and he gently glides away as she returns to the present.

After listening to her granddaughter recount Shomas's words, Jane tells Olivia some other interesting facts she has learnt over recent years.

"There are apparently inroads into curing cancer by sound," Jane says excitedly. "If this becomes possible, it will be an incredible discovery.

"Sound Healing – which uses the voice, bowls, bells, gongs and tuning forks – creates a vibrational field of Healing energy which flows over and through the body, calming both mind and spirit. Many medical therapies are becoming more holistic as people turn to alternative medicine when conventional medicine can no longer help them."

Jane pauses, then adds, "Do you know, Livvy, when I was much younger, there was a man in my home town who could just lay his hands on someone's hand if they had arthritis, and you could actually see the bones moving back into place, restoring the use of their hands. It must be amazing to be able to help people in that way – to help them recover from illnesses which cannot be cured in the conventional way.

"In the *Sunday Express* a while ago, there was an article which stated that Healing is now being recognised in hospitals for conditions which are difficult to treat allopathically. I think this is wonderful, and long awaited for all Healers.

"Healing is non-intrusive and helps virtually every known illness or malady. It is able to work in conjunction with all other medical or therapeutic techniques to relieve side effects and promote recovery. The aim is to transfer spiritual energy from the Spirit Realms through the Healer into a patient to encourage natural Healing. Everyone can do it, you know, but few realise they can. It is available to all, irrespective of religion, belief or culture.

Life gives you knocks and bruises, but like a 'weeble'[19], we wobble but don't fall down. Our Guides give us support. They catch us as we start to fall, and they dust us down and put us back on the right path. A Healer just helps to unbend the dents along the way.

"What you must remember when Healing is not to disperse or throw anything you remove from the patient into the ground. The Earth has enough problems, and doesn't need anything else thrown at it. I was at a 'Mind, Body and Spirit Show' once and walked past a Healer who was psychically removing something from the patient she was working on. She 'threw' it at the floor just as I passed by, it felt like a shot of needles or barbs into my foot! Just think how much the Earth must endure if every Healer does this each time. Always ask Spirit to take anything which has to be removed, up to the Light and disperse it, or to safely transform it into a form which will be useful for the Light."

"I wonder how many Healers know this!" Olivia exclaims.

"More now, I hope," her Grandmother says with a smile. "There are so many 'types' of Healing, Livvy. They all basically come from the same source, but vary in their implementation.

"Spiritual Healing is simple, natural and safe. The National Federation of Spiritual

Healers[30] teach Healers to hold their hands a short distance away from the patient and work over the entire body to find or feel any illness that may be there.

"Reiki is a natural 'hands-on' method of Spiritual Healing which treats the whole person: mind, body and soul. It is the art of channelling 'universal energy' through the body, and is safe and non-invasive. The name Reiki is made up of two words Rei (God's Wisdom or Higher Power) and Ki (Life Force Energy). It is a spiritually-guided source of life force energy. Reiki originated in Japan based on the concept that an unseen energy flows through our bodies. Reiki is a technique for reducing stress, promoting vitality and removing blockages in that energy. If one's life force energy is low or blocked, then we are more likely to get sick or feel stressed; once this is eased, we are more capable of being happy and healthy. Reiki encourages balance and harmony within the body, in order to restore health, wellbeing, and a sense of inner calm to the recipient. Anyone can attend courses to learn Reiki: Level One, is primarily focused on teaching how to be attuned with the energy to practice on yourself. In Level Two, you will learn to perform Reiki on others and understand 'Distance Healing', a technique where you can send Reiki to anyone beyond the limitations of time and space. At Level Three, the Master level, you learn how to teach others the practice. It is best to leave some time between each level to get used to using the energy before progressing to the next.

"Another form of Healing, similar to Reiki, is Seichem. This is an Egyptian high-vibrational energy Healing, connecting Heaven to Earth via the heart. It is also very grounding. In Seichem, they say, 'where there is love, all is possible', as it connects us to the Source or 'all that is'.

"Shamanic Healing, is performed by a person who uses an alternate state of consciousness for the purposes of Healing. This involves working between the visible and invisible realms, made up of all unseen aspects of life that affect us – including the spiritual, emotional, mental, mythical and dream worlds.

"Crystals also make excellent Healing tools. They have been used for Healing by the Hopi Indians, Hawaiian Islanders and the Chinese for centuries. Some crystals are carved into Healing wands which can be used on the body to concentrate on each specific place to be healed. Practitioners can also create a grid of crystals around someone to heal their body and aura; or crystals of each specific chakra colour can be placed on the relevant chakras to heal and align them.

"Aromatherapy is another form of Healing, where the chemicals in essential oils unlock the body's ability to heal itself. The oils remain on the body for three to four hours activating the healing process, which can continue for quite some time."

Jane pauses for a moment before continuing.

"I read an article in *Nexus magazine* that Healers' hands radiate energy and heat from their palms, similar to far-infrared radiation. This penetrates the surface of the skin, gently elevating the surface temperature of the body to help circulation and alleviate pain. Scientists are now developing lamps which create this far-infrared therapy to assist in the healing of a whole range of ailments from arthritis to ulcers, and to help in the reduction of the potential of cancer cells to grow. These lamps are currently being used in Chinese Medical Centres and German Hospitals."

Olivia again is amazed. There is so much to learn!

Jane goes on. "Another practice linked to all of this is the art of Feng Shui, in which forces determined by the routes of the sun, moon and five major planets are believed to affect our magnetic field. By changing the layout of your home, Feng Shui can improve the energy flow of your living environment, and hence improve your wellbeing.

"Do you also know that animals love Healing?" Jane asks Olivia. "They stop in their tracks whilst you perform the Healing on them, and when they feel they have had enough they just get up and walk away."

"How funny! Bless them," Olivia murmurs.

"Colour Healing is another holistic therapy dating back thousands of years," Jane continues, "when Egyptians, Chinese and other ancient cultures used it to cure the sick. It connects to the Light of the world, the aim being for coloured waves of energy to balance diagnosed conditions. Colour can be used constructively in so many ways. Colour has a profound Healing effect on humans and animals alike, especially when worn in clothing or jewellery, or used in interior decoration. Blues and greens being calming, they support balance and harmony. Pinks and purples are for love and relaxation, and tend to be used in meditation. Reds, oranges and yellows are vibrant, and can excite, helping to combat depression. Look at the decor of places you visit: most hospitals are painted green, clubs and pubs seem to have a lot of red, and therapy rooms tend to be painted pink or lilac to soothe their clients as they enter. Check these out next time you visit one.

"Now, let's have some lunch," Jane suggests. "Food is very grounding and we can discuss chakras later." The two women set to work preparing a meal, chatting all the while. When it is ready, the rain has stopped, and they sit outside to relish their repast.

CHAPTER EIGHT

CHAKRAS

Once lunch is over and the washing up is done, the two women decide to stay downstairs to continue their conversation.

"I would now like to tell you about chakras," Jane begins. "The word Chakra is Sanskrit and literally translates as 'wheel or circle of movement'. It refers to three-dimensional energy points or vortices of swirling energy and light, which regulate the flow of energy throughout our bodies. These are not physical; they are aspects of our consciousness, and are denser than auras, but not as dense as the physical body.

"Each of the main chakras is a vortex emitting from a central line in our body, running from the base of our spine to the crown of our head. These cone shaped vortices extend a short distance outside of our physical body, and are positioned to the front and to the back of our structure to create a luminous energy field.

"There are seven principle chakras located at different levels along this line. Each having its own colour, which is simply a different waveband in the spectrum of visible light. And each one has its own frequency[10] and energetic quality.

"The Base or First Chakra (colour red) is situated at the base of the spine and controls the adrenal glands, kidneys, spine and the whole of the nervous system. It links to basic life survival, courage, self-reliance and stamina, and represents our connection to the wider world. An imbalance in the energy of this chakra is linked with anger, frustration, ungroundedness and violence.

"The Sacral/Naval Chakra is the Second (colour orange), located between the naval and pubic bone. It is associated with the reproductive glands and the bladder. It promotes vitality and strength and our ability to put ideas into action. It generates kindness, tolerance, creativity, new ideas, passion, endurance and sexual energy. Imbalances include problems with boundaries and trust issues.

"The Solar Plexus Chakra is the Third (colour yellow), situated between the base of the rib cage and the navel and associated with the pancreas and spleen. It regulates our blood sugar levels and it is our centre of emotional energy, giving us our sense of identity, confidence and how 'in control' we are of our life. Imbalances are linked to irrational fears and low self-esteem.

"The Heart Chakra is the Fourth (colour green), situated in the centre of the chest, and is associated with the thymus gland and immune system. It promotes unconditional love, calm, compassion, harmony, understanding, sharing and forgiveness. Imbalances manifest as jealousy and self-hatred.

"The Throat Chakra is the Fifth (colour light blue), located in the throat area. This relates to the mouth, ears and throat. It is the link between ourselves and the world around us and is associated with communication, inner growth, peacefulness, self-expression and sound, helping our voice to be heard. It also controls our metabolic rate through the thyroid gland. Imbalances can create compulsive lying and aloofness.

"The Brow/Third Eye Chakra is the Sixth (colour indigo/dark blue), and is located just above and to the centre of the eyebrows. This controls the pituitary and hypothalamus glands and therefore controls and balances the hormones and all the other glands in the endocrine system, nose and sinuses. It promotes intuition, psychic abilities, concentration, self-knowledge, vision and insight. It is associated with wisdom, and seeing the bigger picture so one can make better decisions. A balanced individual is organised, patient, reliable and clairvoyant, but imbalances can result in dogmatism and escapism.

"The Crown or Seventh Chakra (colour violet), which is located at the top of the head, can connect to your spiritual self; it also controls the pineal gland, hair and skin. This promotes positive thought patterns, trust, inspiration and imagination. Imbalances bring depression, indecisiveness and anxiety.

"There are other chakras that our awakened consciousness can experience: The Eighth Chakra, located above the head (outside the physical body but within our personal energy field) is our connection to Spirit. The Ninth Chakra, called the Seat of the Soul is situated high above the physical body, it transcends space and time and connects us with all of life. Below the surface of the Earth, is yet another Chakra which is your Earth connection and very grounding.

"There are believed to be about one hundred and fourteen chakras around your body in all, but the seven mentioned above are the main ones. The smaller chakras are found in places such as the palms of your hands. All chakras are linked to the aura, and their energy radiates through the body and out into the surrounding aura.

"Chakras can often become unbalanced, and it is only by working directly on them that energy can be realigned and harmony restored. One of the ways to balance the whole chakra system is to place an appropriately coloured crystal on each area of the body for about fifteen minutes, to give each chakra a boost of its own vibration without altering its energies, or the overall harmony of the system. You can also place a grounding stone, such as a Haematite, between the feet to act as an anchor.

"If any of your chakras become blocked – through issues such as stress, anxiety, anger, etc. – they can manifest physical problems. Then you will need to cleanse, activate and re-align these subtle energies. Sometimes when you are feeling light-headed it is because your chakras are out of balance, so before you go anywhere, just check them. You can cleanse and clear them by moving your hand over each one, feeling its energy spin and its clockwise rotation. Pull all toxic energy from its centre, throw it up to the Light, and ask Spirit to disperse it. You can also use a dowsing crystal to align all your chakras: once the dowser spins at the same speed and distance for each chakra, they are aligned."

Jane pauses to allow Olivia time to take in the information so far. When her granddaughter is ready, she explains further:

"You can also use crystal bowls to balance your chakras. Each bowl attunes to individual chakras and the bowls are tuned to musical notes. For example, the Crown is B, Pineal is A sharp, Third Eye is A, Throat is G, Higher Heart is F sharp, Heart is F, Solar Plexus is E, Sacral is D and Base is C. Tuning Forks C & G may be used as a quick way to balance from top to bottom.

"There are also mantra sounds which relate to each chakra. The Crown is OM, Third Eye is AUM, Throat is HAM, Heart is YAM, Solar Plexus is RAM, Sacral is VAM and Base is LAM. You can use a mantra to clear any blockage by singing 'Om Gum *(insert Chakra mantra sound here)* Ganapathiyei Namaha'. You need to chant each mantra for about ten minutes. The resonance of the mantra really helps to clear any blockages and makes you feel so much more at ease.

"Shomas told me once, 'When on the Earth plane, you vibrate to the chakra notes in order to develop the skills you need to progress through that particular lifetime. Some days you will work for the good of all, some days you need to work to an end, some days you will work to help others. Each time the note will change dependent upon your mood, your awareness, the life you live from day to day, and those who share it with you. You resonate to a high note for good days, and a low note for bad days, and an intermediate one for day-to-day living. Some days you will need a base note (C) to ground you and bring you down to the Earth plane to deal with the nitty gritty of life. Some days you will play a heart string (F) as you feel profound love for your fellow man. Other days your brain will take over, and with each change of tempo your colours change in your aura. We can see this from our side and know your mood, your thoughts and your reactions to others by this. You change daily dependent upon who you work with and where you are.'

"I thought that was rather lovely," Jane adds, "and makes sense of how you can feel so differently from one day to the next."

"That's beautiful, and it relates to the different types of music you can like on different days too," Olivia reflects. "I never realised chakras were so important. Thank you for telling me all about them."

But Jane needs to explain a little more. "Whenever you are connected to Spirit or working in the Light, your chakras are open," she cautions her granddaughter. "Do remember to close them before venturing out in the world again. Generally, they open and close of their own accord, but there are times when it becomes essential for us to close them down ourselves. This protects us from outside influences, negativity, or from any adverse thoughts sent out by others.

"There are a number of ways to close the chakras, so try various methods to find which is best for you. The easiest way I have found to do this is to close each chakra front and back with a cross of light within a circle of light. Or, if you prefer, you may close a door over them, back and front. Once they are closed, it is advisable to encompass your whole body in a huge protective bubble of white Light, and imagine mirrors on the outside, so that any slings and arrows thrown at you by adversaries will rebound to keep you protected and safe.

"It is very important to do this, as it is possible for negative energies to link into you if you are not careful and are left wide open. This is why I close you down every time you come here, before you leave. If you come across anyone of an aggressive or negative nature when you are out, always close yourself down. As you get used to doing this, you will find you can do it quite quickly. Even a zip of Light from the bottom to top of your body will work if you are in a hurry."

"I wondered why you always made me 'close down'. I never asked before, as it just seemed like a natural part of all that was happening, but it is good to know. I shall make sure I always do that," says Olivia thankfully.

CHAPTER NINE
DOWSING

The weather is starting to get chilly as autumn weaves its way into winter. The trees are bare and Jane's garden has lost its lustre; glorious blooms have given way to barren twigs. A few pansies are still trying to raise their bedraggled faces to the fading sun, but not much else wants to push itself up through the mud as it has rained heavily again, and the garden is looking very sorry for itself.

Olivia arrives in a flurry of scarf, hat, gloves and boots to keep out the creeping cold. Once she has unwrapped all her layers and settled down in the big comfy armchair, Jane explains that she wants to show her how to dowse. She had once taught Olivia, as a little girl, how to use a pendulum for dowsing, but the skill has long been forgotten. Today it is time to learn again.

She hands her granddaughter a beautiful Rose Quartz pendulum. "That is yours to keep, darling," she says. "Today you will programme it for yourself. Then do not let anyone else touch it."

"Why?" Olivia enquires.

"Because once it is programmed for you it will lose that connection if anyone else touches it."

Olivia nods sagely.

"I want to give you a little bit of background information before we start," Jane begins. "Apparently the history of dowsing goes back to the times of Lemuria and Atlantis, where, it is said, the use of dowsing was commonplace.

"There are various dowsing implements which can be used. One is the V Rod, which is normally made from a forked twig, held in both hands, which will dip or rise according to what it finds. There are also L-shaped rods, which come in pairs and are held in each hand; they will normally cross over each other during use. Or there is the Wand, a single long rod which spins on a cord. Then there is the pendulum, which is probably the most commonly used dowsing instrument because of its flexibility. The pendulum is simple, compact, easily carried and is useful in so many different situations. It is mainly used to provide common yes/no answers, but it can also be used with charts to obtain all manner of information.

"What you have to realise, Livvy, is that everything in the Universe is energy, and we are allowed to tap into that energy when it is appropriate; but what you must remember is that your attitude and approach to dowsing will largely determine how successful you will be. You have to be open to receiving this information, and you must practice, practice, practice in order to develop confidence in your abilities.

"Dowsing can be used in many ways, and you can dowse for an array of items. Using charts you can you can dowse for deficiencies or intolerances in your diet, then check which vitamins or minerals to take to improve your health. If you have mislaid something you can ask your pendulum to help you find it. You can dowse for water, for emotional and spiritual information, the positions of leylines on a map, or even to help you plan a new place to live.

"All questions must be clear, precise and not ambiguous in any way. Each question can only be answered with a Yes or No, or by a given value from a chart. Also, as an Earthly being you have free will, so your Guides cannot help you to answer any questions unless you specifically ask for their help, and then they can only help if it is appropriate for you to know the answer. Always check, do I have the right to ask these questions? Are they relevant to my well-being or the well-being of others? Do I really need this information or knowledge? If the answer to any of these questions would be No, then don't dowse. If an answer to a question is unclear, either leave the question until later, re-phrase it, or, if you are not given an answer at all, then you are not meant to know it. You will have to accept that and stop trying.

"When asking questions always ask your Guides to give you an accurate answer free from personal interference; as dowsing should only be used for the highest good of all and harm of none. It is a privilege to be attuned to advice from your Spirit Guides, and as such it should not be used as a tool for materialistic or egotistical gain. Always ask for protection before using your pendulum, then close yourself down afterwards."

"Wow, that is quite a responsibility, isn't it?" Olivia exclaims.

"Yes, it is. I have to make you aware that this is not a party trick; it shouldn't be done for fun, especially not in the pub after a few drinks or just to amuse. You have to take it seriously," Jane emphasises.

"Point taken," says Olivia solemnly.

"Always remember to prepare for a dowsing session, or you may be unsuccessful and the information that you get could be faulty. As you get more used to doing this, you will find it gets much quicker and easier to do.

"When you first get your pendulum it needs to be programmed; this attunes it to your own individual vibration. Once it has been programmed, as I said earlier, it is recommended that you do not let anyone else touch it at all, ever. You can, if you wish, go into a meditation and ask to be individually linked to your pendulum. Or, as we shall do today, pick up your pendulum and ask your Guides and Angels to bless it. Then ask for it to be refreshed and cleared of any negative programming which is not of the Light, to ensure it is returned it to a pure state before it is used.

"To do this is, bring your pendulum up to your heart, then up to your third eye or brow, to your right shoulder, then your left shoulder and back to your heart. (This represents drawing the sign of the cross.) Then ask your crystal to recognise you as its partner, so that it works only with you and your Guides. Once this is done you must always ask your Higher Self and 'all that is' to let you be a pure channel of Light when using your pendulum.

"It is important to ask that your conscious mind may not interfere with the clarity of any answers and that protection is put in place on all levels of your being, so that any other energies may not interfere with the pendulum when you are using it. You can then place yourself inside a bubble of love and Light, or create a pyramid of crystal energy by placing a crystal on your brow, then your heart and at your feet to encompass you in Protection, Light and Healing and ensure a safe place for you and your pendulum to work within. Ideally, do this each time you wish to use your pendulum. I have been led to believe that Calling all Angels, an Alaskan Flower Remedy spray, or Defend and Protect, a Living Tree Orchid Essence spray, are also good for protection if you prefer to use a few drops of these.

"Now we are going to learn the orientation of your pendulum. Firstly, ask it something that only you know to have a definite Yes answer, and see which way the pendulum moves. For example, 'Is my name Olivia?'"

"It's spinning clockwise!" Olivia exclaims.

"Great! Well, now you know the Yes answer, ask your pendulum a question with a definite No answer, such as, 'Is my name Jane?', and see which way it moves."

Olivia tries this and gets a definite swing anti-clockwise in the pendulum.

"There will be times when the pendulum cannot give you an answer," Jane continues, "either because there is no answer to the question or because you are not meant to receive an answer, so you have to define what the move is for that. For me, my pendulum swings clockwise for yes, anti-clockwise for no and sways back and forth for 'I don't know' or 'I can't tell you'. These directions may differ from person to person; always check consistency of movement before you start."

They spend time working out the orientation of Olivia's pendulum until she understands the difference between all the moves.

"Now practice asking all sorts of questions to see what answers you get. But don't forget: only for the highest good of all," Jane adds. Olivia tries this.

Then Jane gets out a set of charts which she has produced to gauge a range of topics. She shows Olivia how to use these too. The pendulum sways gently in a direction to indicate the option it has determined.

"Once you have learned how to use your pendulum to read charts, you can also use it to count. If it advises you to do something in particular, you can then ask how often you should do this. Be very careful to be accurate. You can either use a chart to count, or just let the pendulum swing towards an extended finger and see how often it bangs against it.

"The pendulum is only as clear as you are, so if you feel you are not on top form, don't dowse as your connection may not be clear and this may affect the quality of the dowsing. Also take care where there are powerful electronic fields as this will also affect what you receive. You may use a chart to check your accuracy.

"If you do feel there is something affecting your energy, check your body's polarities; the pendulum should circle clockwise on your right and anti-clockwise on your left, clockwise at the front and anti-clockwise at the back. Ask the pendulum if there are any issues. If the pendulum says Yes, ask Spirit to remove them from your personal space, from your aura, from your house, from the astral, and take them up to the Light, and not let them return until they want to do good for the world. Once the pendulum stops spinning, it will have cleared them, so don't stop until it stops!"

"At the end of your session, always remember to close yourself down. Visualise a cross of light within a circle of light on each of the seven main Chakras, back and front, and below the feet for grounding, then encompass yourself in a bubble of light and put mirrors all around the outside to protect yourself from outside influences, as I have said before. This will ensure that any 'slings and arrows' thrown at you, mentally or emotionally, will hit the mirrors and recoil back, keeping your personal space clear.

"Cleanse your pendulum regularly in the same way that you cleanse all your other crystals. There are so many different ways to do this, but here are a few I use: hold it under running water, place it on a clear quartz overnight, or place it inside a singing bowl and ring the bowl. The resonance of the sound will cleanse the crystal within. There are plenty of books on the subject which you can read to improve your craft."

"I didn't realise a pendulum could be so versatile," Olivia tells her, amazed. "Or you could do so much with it. It will be invaluable. Thank you so much for showing me all of this."

They both close themselves down and go off to prepare a well deserved meal, Olivia merrily checking everything they cook with her pendulum to ensure she gets a Yes for all the ingredients!

CHAPTER TEN

CRYSTALS

Next morning, Olivia is woken by the sound of heavy rain on the window. She shivers and huddles down under the covers for another hour before getting up to greet the day.

Highly inquisitive as always, after breakfast she enquires of her grandmother, "Can I ask, why do you use so many crystals? I remember when I was younger I used to come to visit and you taught me all their names. I had a jar full of tiny tumble stones; they were so beautiful and I could name most of them, but I never really knew what they were all for."

Jane smiles and replies, "Well, Livvy, what most people do not realise is that all the different stones have secret powers which can help in our lives. They respond to our feelings, they sparkle when we are happy and lose lustre when we are ill. They amplify thought, impart information, focus and transmit energy and generate love.

"Crystals are intelligent and powerful stones. For example, quartz crystal has the ability to heal and give energy to the bearer. If you carefully look at blue lace agate, you can see where it got its name: the threads of lacy white ripple through the palest of blues, this crystal is very good for calming emotions. Each different stone is unique in the properties it possesses.

"If you hold any specific crystal in your hand and ask it to help, to give energy, to overcome obstacles, you can feel a surge of power run through your body of which there is no equal. Many crystals also amplify our connection with the Spirit world, which is why I use them so much in my work.

"Natural crystals take centuries to grow. The Earth history, impurities, bubbles, rainbows or cracks in their structure give them their character and their power.

"Man-made crystals have no imperfections, but their clarity still offers unique qualities to the bearer.

I have a few books which will tell you all about the different stones, and which ones you need at certain times in your life. You may take a few home to read if you like."

Olivia smiles with pleasure at the kind offer.

Jane continues, "As you may know, quartz crystals have been used for years to assist in the powering of radios, watches, clocks, computers, televisions, microwaves etc., by rectifying the alternating current. Quartz crystal is piezoelectric, so it vibrates at its own frequency, which creates a regular, predictable pulse per second – effectively replacing a pendulum so that a clock never needs to be wound to keep perfect time.

"Shomas told me: 'Crystals have grown within the Earth's crust since the beginning of time. They have experienced axis shifts, earth tilts, pole reversals and changing climates and still have grown and developed. They are pure minerals, naturally created, and have immense power and wisdom. Depending on their composition, they can help mankind in many ways. People are only just beginning to discover the capabilities of these beautiful stones.'

"He also told me that 'there is a crystal within the centre of planet Earth which radiates like a sun in an energy realm not perceived with your eyes. This is the powerhouse of the planet. It is an enormous crystal, and is right at the very core of the Earth, from where it emits energy. There are also other huge stones in the centre of the planet, emeralds, diamonds, elestials, opals, quartz and sapphires, all selected to help radiate energy to the world above.

'One day everyone will understand how to tap into this phenomenal piece of crystal at the centre of the world. There is so much energy, so much power which has grown right at the very core of the Earth since it was first formed. It is an energy source for the entire planet. It helps with the growth of the crops, with the gravitational field and energy levels all around the globe.

'As with crystals which have to be cleansed and re-charged to utilise and expand their power, then so must this large crystal in the centre of the Earth be cleansed. It is in dire need of re-charging due to all the harm the planet has endured. Once re-charged, the planet will be vibrant with life and will be a beautiful world once again'."

Jane picks up another book of writing she has received from Shomas over the years and starts to read it aloud. "'The Earth has for too long been ignored and now manifests symptoms of dis-ease as it screams for attention, through earthquakes, flood and famine. It is undergoing an initiation, and those on the Earth at this time are experiencing different levels of that same initiation. This is an initiation of love; and crystals, being a manifestation of love and light, are there to play a vital role. They are the integral part of the Earth's core, and once recharged and reactivated, will bring new life and energy to the planet and to the benefit of all mankind.

"'The Earth has its own resonance, and each crystalline element has its own individual power, resonating to a different level of sound, which is why different crystals have differing strengths and effects on the planet. Some have immense healing power and will be of tremendous benefit to Healers and Therapists and the people they aim to help. You will begin to realise the potential of each gem, and how they can be used in everyday life, as you work with them more. Use crystals whenever you know someone needs your help. If you feel you can ease any pain, please try to do so, and the crystals will amplify the Healing you offer.

"'Man is beginning to re-discover the power of the mineral kingdom, just as the Atlanteans did. He is becoming aware of the knowledge contained in stones used in structures around the globe which all have a power to help the planet. For example: Stonehenge and Avebury, Machu Picchu in Peru, the Mayan temples in Guatemala, the Pyramids in Egypt and Mexico, and the stone temple Angkor Wat in Cambodia. Many were built with ancient knowledge by levitating crystal energies, breaking down the molecular structure of the rocks and stones, moving them to where they were to be positioned, and putting them back together as a whole. No need for pulleys and cranes.

"'The crystals were so powerful then. They still are very powerful, but mankind is only now beginning to understand them again. He is just scraping the surface of the potential of these enormous gems, and the phenomenal energy they wield en masse.'"

"The more I learn, the more amazing it all is," says Olivia in awe. "I have read that there is a crystal which lies off Bermuda which is purported to be the cause of the problems of the so called 'Bermuda Triangle'. Can you tell me anything about that one, please?"

Jane thinks about all she has gleaned over the years on the subject. "Small crystals were apparently used in Atlantis to power vehicles," she explains to her granddaughter. "The primary crystals or power stations of the area were huge. The main crystal from Atlantis is believed to lie off Bermuda now, and the one from Lemuria lies off the west coast of South America. I have been told that both will be re-discovered in due course as the land plates move and rise. These crystals can still give off enormous power, especially when the planets are in alignment, and can throw the navigational instruments of ships and aeroplanes into disarray. Many of the small crystals from Atlantis still exist, and are scattered all over the world, they will come into their own, as energy channellers, when the time is right.

"You can obtain crystals which are said to have come directly from the ancient land of Lemuria, where the use of crystals was commonplace. Lemurian Seed Crystals are said to have been planted by these ancient peoples before the destruction of their civilisation. Each stone appears to have been carved by a human hand, as they have horizontal grooves or striations across their naturally faceted faces. Some appear to have a reddish-pink colour due to a nearly transparent coating of iron oxide, yet the inside of the stone remains clear. Each crystal is able to connect itself vibrationally with all other Lemurian Seed Crystals. They are the Record keepers of long-lost esoteric secrets, filled with compassionate love for all living creatures.

"To access the wisdom contained within each one, you must first allow a Lemurian Seed Crystal to choose you. Cleanse and charge the crystal in Sun or Full Moon Light for two to three days. Allow you and your crystal to become attuned to one another's inner vibrational frequencies. As with your pendulum, once you and your crystal have chosen and accepted one another; do not allow any one else to implant their energies into your crystal by touching it. If they do always cleanse it again.

"Meditation whilst holding your Lemurian Seed Crystal will enlighten you in ways you cannot yet perceive. These incredible gifts from a highly evolved civilisation offer, a heightened sense of awareness, expanded consciousness, and an opening to the Angelic Realm and, ultimately, to the Cosmos beyond our knowledge."

"They sound extraordinary, do you have any I can look at?"

Jane goes to find one for Olivia to see and feel the striations. Returning with a small Lemurian Seed Crystal, she places the stone in her granddaughter's hands. Olivia is awed by its history.

Jane adds, "With so many crystals to choose from, it can be difficult to know which is the right one for you. If you receive one as a gift, then it will have been chosen especially for you, but if you are choosing one yourself, browsing through the range of crystals available to find just the right one can take some time. If you want a crystal for a specific purpose, it is best to read about the properties in a good crystal book in order to select the appropriate one for your needs."

Looking straight at Olivia, Jane then asks, "Do you remember yesterday when I was teaching you how to use a dowsing crystal? Well, you can also ask your pendulum which crystals you will need for a specific job, making selection so much easier and more accurate. Just hold your pendulum over the crystals on offer and let it decide which is the one for you. Once you get a 'Yes' answer your selection will be made.

"When buying a crystal yourself, if you get a chance to see and hold it, then trust your intuition. A crystal will 'call to you'. Handle several and choose the one that makes you tingle – but do remember that big and beautiful is not always the most powerful, or the most appropriate for you. Some of the small, rough ones can be just as effective. Then you can programme your crystal to be dedicated to any purpose for which you wish to use it.

"Many crystals are fragile and friable; they can easily become scratched and damaged, or even broken, so try to keep them apart. When carrying crystals from place to place, do remember to wrap them, to protect them and stop them absorbing negative energies from their surroundings, small pouches are ideal. Tumblestones tend to be tougher as they have been turned in fine grit to get their polished surface, and will stand up to quite a lot of wear and tear; but still treat them with respect!

"Crystals need to be cleansed when you first buy them. Think of all the people who have handled them just to get them to you. Sadly, the area where they come from is often blasted as the miner digs them out of the Earth. They are then cut, shaped and maybe polished, then passed on to a shipper who sends them to a wholesaler, who sells them to a supplier, where they are placed on shelves for you to find. So many people handle them and often not in a kind or gentle way, so you need to cleanse and remove all these energies from the crystals before you can use them yourself.

"Always cleanse crystal jewellery, too, before you wear it, as it may hold the vibrations of the person who carved and set it. They may have a negative effect on it, or not, but best to be on the safe side. If you wear a crystal regularly, do ensure that you cleanse it periodically to remove any negativity it may have captured and kept from you. Also when using crystals for healing, meditation or any another spiritual work, cleanse them after every session or they may hold energy from that session and impart it onto the next.

"Most crystals can be cleansed by holding them under running water or immersing them in salt water or pure rainwater. If using salt, ensure it is natural sea salt, not the sodium chloride table salt you may use in your cooking. As you bathe the crystals, hold in your mind the intention that all negativity will be washed away and the crystal re-energised. Most clusters can be left in sea salt water overnight, but gently brush or rinse every speck of salt off afterwards as this could damage the crystal, especially in a damp atmosphere.

"Be careful, though, as some crystals are water soluble (e.g. Selenite) and so could disintegrate if put in or under water. For those, there are other methods of cleansing, such as placing the crystal in the light of the sun or moon for a few hours to re-charge it. Be careful with stones that fade in sunlight (e.g. Amethyst); do not leave these out in the sun for any length of time, or the beautiful depth of colour you initially loved will fade away. Also, do take care where you place your crystals so that they will not amplify the sun's rays and cause a fire. If you read a book on crystals, you will find many different ways to care for and cleanse these precious gems.

"A few crystals never need cleansing, Citrine, Kyanite and Azeztulite are self-cleaning stones, but I still cleanse them now and again to refresh and renew their energy.

"Clear Quartz and Carnelian may be used as a platform to cleanse other crystals, especially delicate and friable ones (those that shatter easily), or those which cannot be put in water – but you must remember to cleanse the Quartz or Carnelian afterwards.

"A Dowsing Crystal may also be held over any crystal, to be cleansed, while you ask for all negativity to be removed, and for the crystal to be re-energised for its intended purpose. Your dowser will do the work for you by spinning to clear and amplify the energy of the chosen stone.

"Just remember that crystals are very powerful instruments, and need tender loving care to ensure that they continue to work for you in the way they should."

Olivia is still taking in all this information when Jane starts on another train of thought. "Whilst on the subject of crystals, do you know that the California Institute of Technology has discovered microscopic magnets in the human brain? These are little biological bar magnets made of crystals of the iron mineral, magnetite. These crystals are strongly magnetic, unlike other iron compounds in the body. Homing pigeons, whales, salmon, honeybees and some shell fish also have these microscopic magnets, which help them navigate or migrate by the use of the Earth's magnetic field. However, there is no evidence, at this time, that humans have this same inborn sense of direction.

"There is a chance that electromagnetic fields – which are invisible electric and magnetic force fields generated by power lines, appliances and anything electrical, such as 5G mobile phones – may react with these tiny magnets, to increase the risk of certain cancers and imbalances in humans and animals. Technicians and designers need to be careful to check how technology is affecting us all.

Jane stops and offers Olivia a chance to discuss some of the crystals in the house, explaining how important each one has been for her since she first obtained them. It fascinates her to see which ones her granddaughter is particularly drawn to.

"The best crystal," she says, "is the one given as a present because, as I have said before, it brings with it the love of the person who gave it to you. So you can choose one for me to give to you as a present, if you would like that Livvy?"

"That would be brilliant, thank you so much! I shall be spoilt for choice. Perhaps I'll use my Dowsing Crystal and let it choose?" Olivia exclaims.

They both smile.

CHAPTER ELEVEN

IONA

Olivia goes home late Sunday afternoon, elated from her chat with her grandmother, and carrying a huge Amethyst that she had coveted as a child, the purple so deep and calming. It had been in her bedroom at Jane's then, and it would be in her own bedroom now. A most generous gift!

As morning dawns, the winter sun struggles to shine its light through the barren trees in the garden. Nothing is growing, nothing is moving forward, everything is waiting and marking time until the thaw, when tiny shoots will raise their heads through the earth to herald the first signs of spring.

A bitter wind chills to the bone. The snow has dusted the tree tops and only a stray robin brings his vibrant song to the barren wilderness. The garden still lays desolate and unkempt, for Jane has other things to do at this time of year.

Jane decides she has time to write about her trip to Iona, the experience of which had been quite profound. She knows Olivia will be fascinated, so she makes a note of all her memories of the trip so she won't forget any detail.

Olivia arrives a few days later on a still, frosty morning. Jane has finished writing her Iona memoir, and on hearing this, Olivia wants to know all about the trip.

"One Spring a few years ago," Jane begins, "my friend Margaret and I decided to travel to Iona in the Inner Hebrides. We had been told by Spirit that this island would be an ideal place to visit to perform some Earth Healing. We had a long journey north, stopping *en route* in the Lake District for lunch. The views were spectacular, the landscape changing from the relative flatness and urbanisation of the south of the country to the huge open spaces and rolling hills of the north, expanding into a cloudless sky.

"We passed through the giant sprawl of Glasgow, then the woodlands of the Trossachs National Park, finally reaching Oban, where we broke our journey at a B&B.

"Our room had an amazing view of the setting sun, throwing a glittering cascade of pink on the water over the Sound of Mull, to the distant islands."

"It sounds lovely." Olivia interjects.

"The next morning we rose early, Shomas wanted to tell me where to find our final destination. As you know Shomas writes such beautiful words and these made my heart sing and set me up for the day." Jane reflects.

"We caught an early ferry across the Sound of Mull (the waterway between Mull and the main land). Tiny islands rose out of the water like giant turtles nestling in the waves and the gentle sound of water lapping against the boat was so soothing. We arrived on Mull with its incredible scenery, snow capped the mountain tops and waterfalls trickled down the hillsides, it was stunning! The road meanders across the island, weaving between the hills like a snake to the tiny harbour jetty of Fionnphort between Mull and Iona. No cars are allowed on Iona (unless you are one of the island's permanent inhabitants) so we left our car on Mull and hopped onto the little ferry for the ten minute crossing to our destination. I couldn't believe how clear the water was around the landing jetty, you can see every grain of sand, and it was such an incredible shade of the purest turquoise blue.

"The farmhouse B&B where we intended to stay proved to be cold, cramped and very dirty – so we made our way down a country lane in the pouring rain to a hotel nearby, the St. Columba, where we were given a warm welcome and a room that was clean, bright and warm. We slept like logs!

"The island of Iona itself is only three by one-and-a-half miles in size. It is a tiny speck in the amazingly turquoise sea. There are only two roads, north-to-south and east to half way across the island west. On such a tiny island it would seem impossible to get lost but apparently you can, in the copious amount of marshland, so you have to inform the hotel of your outward journey each day. At night there are no street lights to pollute the night sky, so the moon and a myriad of stars twinkle in the heavens to light your way.

"We had been advised by Spirit to visit a specific part of the Island, so on our very first day we made the journey south. We walked and walked. In the distance was St. Columba Bay, named after the Patron Saint of the Island who, according to legend, came to Iona from Ireland and fell in love with a mermaid. On the beaches are tiny green crystals/stones which folklore says are the tears of St. Columba and his mermaid, who cried because they couldn't be together. To find one is a treasure, I found three!

"After walking for a long while, I stopped to do some Writing with Shomas – who assured me we were on the right path, and said that the place we were trying to find would be lit up for us to see! We kept walking, ending up in marshland where suction sounds accompanied every footstep. While Margaret squelched her way back to the main path, I sat on a stone to catch my breath – and suddenly the hill behind me glowed gold in the light of the sun. I couldn't get closer, as the land was too boggy, but the sight alone was worth the wait. We did however find a spot close by, and our Quest was fulfilled.

"Each subsequent walk we went on was another voyage of discovery: steep hills, beautiful beaches, marshland. Much of the island was covered with sheep, most of whom were lambing then, and the bouncy gait and wiggling tails of baby lambs bleating for their mothers was adorable.

"The rock at the north of the Island is a Gneiss, the oldest rock in the world, dating back to the time of Earth's beginning. The Archaean rocks underlying Iona and the Hebrides were formed at the bottom of the sea, and those on Iona are a little older than the sea from which they rise. They are hard, rugged, twisted, and their marbling developed by vast heat and pressure during the Earth's formation. No living creature existed at that primaeval time, so they don't contain any fossils.

"Iona has a charisma of its own, all you want to do is sit and ponder. To sit on that rock and look out to the purest turquoise blue sea has a timeless quality. The white sand of the beaches consists of tiny snail shells, which drop to the sea bottom or blow onto the crops where their oil enriches the soil. The south of the Island is comprised mainly of Serpentine, which is a Healing stone. This could be why Iona has long been known as an island of pilgrimage and healing.

"The Abbey near the centre of the island is striking. Once a ruin, it has now been rebuilt but has lost none of its magic. The Cloisters are adorned with different carvings on every post: the breaking of bread, the taking of wine, Noah and the Dove, Lazarus, and flowers and birds of every type. Around the walls of the Cloisters are the coffin tops of the ancient Bishops of Iona, some going back to the times of the Vikings. To sit in the cloister courtyard in the sun and watched the doves (a symbol of Iona) flit mesmerisingly in and out of the Abbey bell tower is magical. Just to be in and around the Abbey, in prayer, in silence, or singing, brings an inner peace.

"The Ecumenical Iona Community runs the Abbey. They are volunteers from all over the world who come together on this holy island to pray. Some stay a week, others up to three years, holding services in the Abbey and running the Community Shop. Communion at the Abbey is a very long service, but the singing raises the roof, making a good start to any day. The hymns of this community are different to any I know, but I found myself humming one afterwards as I strolled down the Abbey path.

"Near the Abbey's front door is a tiny chapel dedicated to St. Oran, a companion of St. Columba and the first Christian to be buried on Iona. One day Margaret and I met a man there who told us that no matter what the weather, the cross on the altar can be seen glowing from the road outside. We went outside to look for ourselves and, sure enough, despite the Ionian rain, the golden cross could be seen glowing from the road, over a hundred yards away.

"Another evening we went to Evensong at the Abbey and were caught in a downpour and soaked to the skin. On leaving, we realised we had created a lake around the seats where we sat! No-one seemed to mind, thankfully. The stone floor will absorb the rain, as the island absorbs any feelings of hurt and pain as it spits you back out into the world a changed person, a better person, more caring, more spiritual, more at peace and in harmony with the Earth.

"The countryside is rugged and the weather is wild; it can change in an instant, full sun can be replaced by a whirling dervish of a storm in minutes. The wind can whisk up a flurry of white horses which toss about on the crest of the waves around the shore. The Isle of Mull, across the Sound from the Abbey, is formed of pink granite – and as the sun sets, that island seems to glow with a soft pink radiance. One day, to add to this miracle we saw a rainbow atop the mountains of Mull, stretching into the sea.

"There is a ruined Nunnery near the Iona slipway, and it was here that I had a profound experience. The building, which dates to before 1200 AD, was built on top of another building, dating back to the 8th century. Most of the Nuns were buried in a row outside the old stone walls, fenced off by a low iron railing – but one grave-stone is in the Sacristy, and it was there I saw an Angel, a huge 'pink' Angel – the same pink of the marble of Mull. She gently wrapped her wings around me and held me tight, it was glorious, I have never felt so enveloped in love."

"That must have been wonderful," Olivia responds, her eyes shining.

"It was," Jane admits. "I then felt inspired to walk into the Nun's Chapel, where I sat on a bench on which was the inscription: *The walls may crumble, but the spirit lives on.* And it does, Olivia, it does. Amidst the daffodils and chirping birds of that chapel you can sit and bare your soul. Closing my eyes, I could feel my heart opening. I was filled with love and an inner warmth, despite the biting cold. The Augustine Nuns must still be in those walls, holding you in suspended animation, whilst they heal your heart. I had a vision of my mum and dad, and burst into tears. My friend found me there, a soggy mess, rain and tears blending on my face."

The look on Olivia's face shows that she feels her grandmother's emotions.

"At the North end of the island, you can sit on a bench amidst the dunes, and look out at the other *Eilean's* (islands) of the Inner Hebrides. I felt such an affinity with them, and I am sure my mum, whose name was Eileen, was with me the whole time. I watched in trance-like curiosity as tiny blue orbs of light seemed to dance in and out of the waves near one of the islands closest to the beach.

"In the distance I could see the dark island of Staffa, and its Fingle's Cave which has been naturally created from hexagonal black basalt stones. The Cave is known for its natural acoustics as the sea flows in and out of the rocks, creating melodies which people travel far and wide just to hear. Mendelssohn visited Staffa in 1829 where he wrote his overture named after this famous Cave.

"Clouds flew by whilst I sat above the beach, but it seemed to me that the world stood still. There's no rush to be anywhere, to do anything, just stroll or sit, take in the essence of the place, the pure joy and tranquillity that Iona brings to your heart. The whole of Iona gets into your soul. There are not enough hours in the day to be at one with the place; the island opens your heart in a way I wouldn't have thought possible. I didn't care what was going on out in the world; I had the sea, bird song and the sound of the flute as the wind whistled through cracks in the rocks. Iona is known as an island is a pilgrimage, but it is more than that: there is a unique tranquillity there. You can hear the Angels sing: the sweetest and purest voices, a calm softness nurtures your soul. I found an inner peace on Iona that I haven't known since childhood, and a feeling of being complete in my own space.

"I have never known a place like it. People say that the island will call you back once it owns part of your heart, part of your soul. The winds there are biting, the rain torrential, but somehow it doesn't matter, the wild elements are all part of the journey. They say the veil between Heaven and Earth is thinnest on Iona, and I feel it is true. Angels embrace you, and your heart swells in your chest at the sheer beauty of the place. You want to sit, just sit, and be at one with the Earth, with the stone, with Heaven.

"I knew when I returned home I would be a different person. The world would keep spinning, the rat race would be back, but my heart would remain in Iona's peace and tranquillity for my lifetime and beyond. There is a magic, a real magic on the island. It takes the sad, the lonely, the heartbroken, the screwed-up oddballs, and puts them all in a melting pot, simmering them to calm, peace and joy.

"Iona reached into my heart like nowhere else."

"Oh Granny, will you take me there?" Olivia asks eagerly

"I will darling, I would love to go there with you," Jane agrees.

They smile at each other, sealing the promise.

CHAPTER TWELVE
MANKIND'S SPIRITUAL QUEST

Again Olivia has been caught up with work and many weeks have passed since she has been able to visit her grandmother. After a long, wet and wind-swept winter, spring has finally arrived and the weather is at last pleasant enough to go outside.

Olivia helps Jane to dig up and move a large plant at the end of the garden. Nothing is more grounding than working with the earth. All around the garden crystals are placed in strategic places to encourage and enhance the growing season. Whether it is their influence or not, the garden is full of colour, even so early in the year. Golden daffodils, tulips and hyacinths bring a well needed vibrancy to an over-wintered garden, and the birds are filling the spring air with their melodious songs.

Jane goes inside and gets them both a warming drink, then they sit and relax on the swing chair, enjoying the kind of serenity only a spring day in the country can bring. Later, as a cold wind blows across the garden, Jane suggests returning inside.

"It's starting to get chilly out here now. Do you want to go upstairs to see if Shomas will visit today?"

The house is warm, and upstairs the sun is creeping across the window sill, enlivening the room and their spirits. Jane hands Olivia a small piece of Apophylite: a crystal that brings universal love, and will attune her mind to Spirit. Then Jane leaves the room so Olivia can be enveloped by the peace and calm of her surroundings. Olivia knows the routine: she slowly allows her whole body to relax and goes into a deep meditation where, before long, Shomas appears.

"Good afternoon, Shomas," Olivia projects to the beautiful being before her. "It is lovely to speak to you today."

"Good afternoon, Olivia," he responds. "It is lovely to speak to you, too. Today I would like to tell you about Spiritual Quests.

"Everyone who has lost someone from their life needs something to believe in, or else they often need someone to blame. Perhaps they think that it is not fair that God has taken their loved one, or they need to know the reason why. This leads them to look deeper into the mystery of death, and it becomes their Spiritual Quest.

"If they go deep enough they will come to the realisation that the person they have lost has fulfilled their contract with the Earth plane and everything on it, and gone home. But some people will not relate to these findings, and will continue to mourn.

"Life is one huge puzzle. Each person's Spiritual Quest is to place the pieces in the right order to achieve the best possible life plan they can. As each of you delves deeper into your Quest, you will understand more and more why you are on Earth at this time. You will realise that everything is preordained, and everything in your life is part of the plan chosen before you were born. Each one of you, at some time in your pre-life state, decided how long you would remain on the Earth, how many lives you would touch with your presence, and to what depth. The aim is to fulfil your learning agreements, as much as possible, before returning home to the peace and tranquillity of a higher vibration, or, as you call it, 'Heaven'.

"Everyone is put on Earth to learn the lessons they need, in order to progress on the Spiritual Plane. You make a contract, before birth, to do a set number of tasks, to learn and progress, both spiritually and mentally. You promise yourself that you will not stray from your chosen path so that your learning experience will be completed. Unfortunately, maybe, you forget all this by the time you arrive on Earth. I say 'unfortunately', as you may stray so far from your chosen path that it can be a hard struggle to fulfil your contract. Some of you go so very far off the path that it cannot be fulfilled in one lifetime and, if this is the case, you will wonder why life is so hard. But each event is a lesson, each situation brings with it knowledge and understanding, so nothing is wasted.

"We know life is full of the unpredictable, full of trials and tribulations; and through that you are striving for more, for excellence. Whether you obtain it or not is irrelevant, as you continually learn and grow. Each experience, good or bad, teaches you a valuable lesson. All highs and lows are of equal importance in your development. Some days you win, some days you think you lose, but if you stop and reflect, you will find that even losing is a winning situation, it can work in your favour, because you learnt something from it. Turn it to the positive, and don't let it get you down. Every cloud has a silver lining. If you did know exactly what your path was and how to complete your learning agreement, you would never experience these highs and lows which allow you to live your life to the full.

"We would love you to have all highs, but what a boring life it would be if you never experienced a low point and the ecstasy of rising from it. Life is a roller coaster ride, to be taken as best you can throughout your time on Earth. You may at times need to retrace your steps to see which lessons were learnt on your pathway. Then take a large step forward and look back to reflect on the learning experience and the knowledge you have gleaned. This will help you to understand the purpose of life, and to see and feel that there is so much more than the everyday. The meaning of life is so complex that '42' is a good answer! (Your grandmother will explain this joke).

"Think of the wealth of knowledge you accumulate through every event in your life: from every meeting on your path, from every lesson you learn. Some lessons are learnt and some are not. Earth is only a schoolhouse, and you learn what you need for growth, both physically and spiritually.

"Acknowledge all the people who would not have come into your life if it had always been untroubled, and think how those people have touched and coloured your life because they did. Think of the places you would have missed, which you may not have chosen on your itinerary for this lifetime. Think of the sights you have seen, and the joy they have given you – and how you might have missed out on these beautiful sights if you had known, and stuck to, your plan. This is part of life's glorious tapestry, the adventure of the unknown.

"Some of the times when you felt down, you may have been taking on the troubles of someone else in order to help them in some way, and they may have drained you in order to replenish their own energies. Neither of you will have recognised this, but they will have felt so well in your company. You will often emanate an essence of well-being wherever you walk, and this wafts in and out of the lives of those you touch each day – be they friends, relatives or complete strangers – and it will uplift them in ways only we understand.

"You cannot only like the easy path through your lifetime; this is not always the right path to take. Tread the harder path; make an effort to like those who do not even like themselves. Make a point of speaking to those to whom it is difficult to speak. Talk with those who bore you and for whom you have little time. Spread these words to all, and this will help your development. Take time with those you would otherwise ignore. If a person is particularly obstructive, and you cannot get through the negativity, leave him to his own path or he will bring you down. But try first, try to understand why, in order to help him see the light in his life.

"There are times in your life, when you say you can't be bothered, but do bother. Take time to care; take time to be there for someone you don't really know, who needs you and your expressions of concern. Put yourself out for others – not to the detriment of your own health and happiness, but to bring Light and love into everyone's lives, to uplift them and bring them closer to the truth. We know it is hard to give of your spiritual self to all those around you, as everyone has bad thoughts come to the fore at times – but release these, let them go free, so that you can put your best foot forward in every situation. You can make a difference in your world you know. If everyone was to think positively, if everyone was to find no fault in friend or foe, life would be better for the whole of humankind.

"This is when your Spiritual Quest will come to the fore. You will have a need, a need to find something more, something in your life which makes more sense than the humdrum and the day to day. Some people find it in religion; they need to have something to look up to, to love, respect and revere. Others find it in themselves, in their inner thoughts, dreams and meditations, which show we are all part of God, and an infinitesimal part of the whole.

"Each and every one of you has a Light which shines within, showing the way to the truth and to peace, hope and love. Your Quest is to find your destiny, understand it, and to know the reason why: why you are on Earth in the first place, why you are so connected to other souls, and why they leave before you do, or you before them. Why you chose a particular lifestyle, and what the future may bring.

"Always use thought positively. Never use it to hate, or to bring anyone else down, as there is tremendous power in thought forms, far more than you could ever imagine. We need mankind to know about The Power of Thought. There is a leaden weight in the atmosphere between Heaven and Earth and this is caused by so much negative thinking around the globe. No-one realises the immense power of thought and how it is possible to manifest so many problems in one's lives, just by thought.

"You need to learn how to live a life with others: mixed nationalities, colours and creeds, and to diversify your thoughts and deeds in order to learn and understand their needs. You have been placed on the planet to develop awareness, and skills, which will be of use to you both on Earth, and on our side of the veil[6].

"We need you to raise your vibration, each and every one of you, so that the planet will rise automatically, bringing those in darkness into the Light. Think positively, think only of good, and this beautiful planet of yours will be raised to a higher level, bringing it back to its rightful place in space and time. One small word of positivity in each ear will set off a chain of events throughout the world, and your world will be a better place. No more wars or complacency, just joy, happiness and love, as it was designed to be.

"Mankind as a whole is a good race of people. You care for each other and for the world you live on – but there are the few who are so self centred. These few need to recognise that their lives destroy the idyll, and it is time for them to change. It fills us with sadness to see the destruction of a beautiful world by a few who have little in mind except their own progression. If you have a lack of respect for life, then this will be a barrier to progress on your spiritual path. Bring Light to the shadows, may peace reign on Earth, and may the Light of the Creator follow you always.

"Listen to your heart. Live your life to the full, helping each other to create a better world for all. Care for each other and for every living thing on the planet, no matter how small and seemingly insignificant. Everything is there for the betterment of everything else. Think before you do something, take a step back and think how it will affect others: if it helps, do it, if it doesn't, don't. Bring peace to the Earth and goodwill to all men. May joy and love always be with you."

"I promise I'll try Shomas," Olivia tells him solemnly.

"As you grow and develop," Shomas continues, "little events may happen: a psychic experience, a feeling of *deja-vu*, thoughts thrown at random into your head so that in conversation you think, 'Did I say that?' or 'Where did that come from?'...these are all signs that we are helping you on your path.

"It is very good for everyone to develop skills with which to connect to us more, improving and enhancing your abilities in channelling, clairvoyance and healing. Everyone has these abilities. It is just a matter of realising it and understanding how to do it properly. We wish for you all to continue our work.

"Let Spirit guide you one step at a time. For most of you this spiritual path has built up over many lifetimes: a strengthening of the link with the other side[6], as it is often called. In this lifetime just be sure you know what you are doing before you step onto a platform and metaphorically fall flat on your face.

"Gradually, your pathway will lead you to others of like mind, others who understand what is happening to you and who will help you to explore your skills. Take things slowly, and like a flowering lotus you will blossom into full spirituality and fulfil your destiny to do our work."

"I am so lucky to have you and Granny to guide me, aren't I?" Olivia says gratefully.

"We will always guide you," Shomas confirms. "We know the future is a scary place, full of the unknown – but take one step at a time and trust your Guides won't let you fall. Everything is part of the plan which will unfold before you, like a carpet of sweetly smelling blooms.

"Tread confidently towards your goal, we are here to clear the path. Hold your head high and don't look down; we won't let you fall. The future is there for all to see, happy and full of joy. If you doubt, then you won't achieve your goals. Trust, hold out your hand to us and ask for our guidance, and we won't let you down. Your true path is planned, most that befalls is chosen, so take confident steps to the future in the true knowledge that this is all for the good.

"I wish there was a way to let every soul in the world know that we are here, to tell them of the way their lives should really be. No-one truly looks into themselves for the real source of God and the all-knowing eye of their soul, but it is there if you look deep within yourself. You will see all you want to see, hear all you need to hear to propel yourself forward for the rest of your lifetime.

"Sadly, the dictates of power often destroy the real reason for life. The governments and religious powers of your world do not reveal the freedom you were born to have in order to discover your real future, your real reason for living, and to help each other to a brighter future. We send Light and love via corridors of Light to raise the consciousness of all mankind of every colour and creed, whether rich, poor, young, old, weak, or strong, to lift every one of you to an awareness of your true direction.

"Man has travelled a long and lonely pathway for too long. We have always been on hand to pick up the pieces...but he has not listened to his intuition, to his innermost thoughts, to help him keep to his chosen path. Only now, as the consciousness of the planet is rising, are you all starting to realise there is more to life and happiness than material wealth brings.

"We recognise your worth and bless you all for everything you do for everyone around you, and we give you many blessings for a peaceful life."

Olivia is dumbstruck. There is so much to take in that she does not know what questions to ask. Shomas knows her quandary and realises she needs time to absorb all that he has told her before she will be ready to talk to him again. He quietly withdraws and leaves her sitting in the chair, deep in contemplation.

Olivia exhales with a deep slow breath. Minutes pass as she sits in silence, pondering all that she has been told. Then she hears the door opening as Jane enters the room.

"How did you get on this time?" Jane asks.

"It was fascinating. Every time Shomas talks to me, there is so much to absorb, so much to think about, that I don't know where to start asking questions. But I do know one thing you must tell me: what is 42?!"

Jane laughs, "Oh, that's our little joke. Shomas and I have often spoken of the meaning of life, and I told him about the book *The Hitchhikers Guide to the Galaxy* by Douglas Adams. In the book, everyone has been waiting for millions of years to be told the meaning of life. They are finally called to hear the answer, waiting with bated breath, only to be told it is '42'! Very silly but funny. I didn't think Shomas would have remembered it, but perhaps I should have known he would, he has such a sense of fun."

"I have to read that book!" Olivia exclaims. Growing serious again, she has another question... "Shomas spoke about the Power of Thought. Do you really believe we can change things with our minds?"

"Yes, I do," Jane tells her, "and what is more, scientists do too. There are studies in which medical researchers have discovered that positive emotions such as joy, hope and gratitude all have beneficial effects on health. Serotonin is a chemical neurotransmitter in the human body which contributes to feelings of well-being and happiness. Research shows that when someone receives a gift their serotonin level increases, and that the person giving the gift will also see a rise in their serotonin, which seems logical. But what researchers also noticed was that anyone watching this exchange *also* had a rise in their serotonin levels – which proves that experiencing kindness, or even just seeing it has a positive physical effect on the body.

"In contrast, test subjects who witnessed animosity, anger and aggression showed decreased levels of serotonin, and research has proven that a deficit of serotonin can lead to depression. So you must be careful about watching aggressive films or depressing news as this will lower your levels of serotonin and, subsequently, your levels of happiness and well-being."

"That's interesting." Olivia says, "I must admit I often find the news so depressing. Shomas told me that research is being made into the mind's influence on health and disease, and that must be related."

Jane nods. "The Power of Thought is powerful indeed, and medical science is finally starting to understand this. What else did Shomas talk about today?"

"Oh, so many things! And I have so many questions, that my head is spinning!"

Jane sits down in the other big chair, making herself comfortable. "I am glad to see you're so interested in this. But relax, darling, we have plenty of time. I'm happy to answer all your questions, so let's take them one by one...."

CHAPTER THIRTEEN
MAN'S ROLE ON EARTH

When the time comes for Olivia's next session with Shomas, she finds it becoming easier to slip into a receptive state. She is quickly transported to the tranquil Crystal Cave with its beautiful crystal chair, where she sits and waits for Shomas to reappear. It isn't long until the gentle soul appears before her, dressed in his Tibetan robes.

"Good evening, Olivia. It is lovely to see you again. This time, I would like to give you a little more information about mankind's role on Earth.

"Human beings were put on Earth to care for one another, to help one another, and to bring peace and calm to the planet, to the wildlife, to the trees and plants and to themselves. They were put on Earth to enjoy the tranquillity and beauty of the planet: the greens and blues of land, sky and sea. Sadly, there have always been those who want more, those whose greed makes them want to take more from the planet; and in this taking, they have destroyed the idyll, not just for themselves but for everyone else. In the process they have corrupted the minds of others, dragging them down to their level, and changed the whole future well-being of the planet, ruining the peace and beauty of the paradise they were given.

"There is so much we want to say. We have information pertinent to man's role on that Earth of yours, regarding the part he has to play to bring it back from the brink and piece the planet back together, bit by bit. Man's job is to reinstate harmony; to bring Earth back in line with her lineage and her place in space; and to bring back her Light and the love she has for mankind.

"Man, for the most part, has taken a wrong pathway; but he can turn around, not go backwards but sideways and upwards instead, up to a raising of consciousness, up to a brighter future. He can choose a life full of love, joy and happiness, where there will be no more wars, no more sadness, no more hatred, homes for the homeless, food for the children of the world, peace for the shattered lives of so many. Let mankind know that we are here watching and waiting, holding our breath, in anticipation of the change of attitude that a lifetime can bring.

"Man is a complex creature; myriad thoughts and actions pave the way to his future. He was designed to clear past karma and follow a path to right all wrongs in his quest for fulfilment. Modern-day man has so many distractions, so many offers of change and chance, that it is hard for him to keep on the straight and narrow.

"Teach each person that if all seems to be going wrong, he or she must look inside for the cause, not to outside influences. Teach them to see how their lives can be changed by re-routing, by taking a fresh path, rather than continuing on the wrong path for this lifetime. Life is short, 'four score years and ten', so fill it to the brim with kindness and love for your fellow man, which will open paths of adventure and excitement as life is filled with joy. The kinder you are to others, the more fulfilling your own life will be.

"So many people at this time breed negativity as an essential element of their lives. This must stop as it has a bearing on their lives and the future of generations to come. *The Bible* says: 'A joyful heart is good medicine, but a crushed spirit saps one's strength'. Do not crush another's spirit. Let all have a joyful heart to bring them good health and good fortune.

"Man needs to realise he must jump-start his life on planet Earth. So much anger and negativity is not good for him, for his environment, or for his future. Cultivate a positive attitude; leave jealousy and anger behind and focus with cheerful determination.

"We want you to realise that some do not choose an easy path for their lives, some chose dilemmas and hardships in order to learn lessons which will clear karma from previous lifetimes spent in penitence and worry. Never judge others by your own standards; never make another feel 'wrong'. It is their path to tread and their choice, so let everyone fulfil their lives in their own way, to bring you all, eventually, to a state of bliss here in 'Heaven'.

"Take a hand and lead the weary; take a hand and lift the sad. If your life is full, give to those who are empty; if empty do not begrudge those whose lives are full. Many have worked hard to achieve the status of a successful life and have not been given it on a plate. But no matter how lowly, any job done with right intent gives status to its owner and allows that person self respect; and, with hard work and perseverance, everyone can achieve a 'glass half full'.

"Man is a fickle beast. He stands proud upon his land and maintains dignity in his own space and time – but if something or someone comes along to disrupt his idyll, he turns into a bear with claws and teeth, his dignity shattered by his anger and tenacity, which is not a pretty sight. It only takes the slightest derailment of his idyll for man to create havoc for himself and all in his vicinity; then he takes it for granted that someone else will sort out his mess, as he goes on his merry way without a thought for the poor souls that do.

"To sit back and expect others to pull you out of the mire is not the way. You were put on this planet to find your own path to fulfilment, to sort out your own issues. Do not take from others who appear more fortunate; this is not the way. Build your own future and hold your own joy by putting yourself in a position to achieve the best you can. We are looking forward to your achieving a state of equanimity in which you can develop your skills working for us, and help this planet of yours get back to how it was meant to be: an idyll to be enjoyed, not mastered.

"The youth of today are a new breed, for the most part they care about their home, the planet they live on, and the flora and fauna thereupon. Talk to the young about their planet and they are into far greener issues than their fathers and forefathers. They do not want to destroy, they want to build a better home for each one of you.

"We love you all. We cherish you all. We are here to hold your hands on the path to peace and wholeness, in harmony and righteousness, for your own sake and for the sake of others – not only for those closest to you, but also for the homeless, the persecuted, the battle weary, the hungry and the destitute, bringing joy to the hearts of all on the planet and to the planet herself."

Olivia feels the warmth of his words like a caress.

Then Shomas's speech takes a different direction. "Man was put on Earth to help his fellow man; to live in harmony with the beasts of land, sea and air; and to bring harmony to the planet. Many are realising their purpose – but there are still a few who have total disregard for anyone or anything but themselves and their own material gain. The small pockets of darkness will see the Light, and those who destroy will be taught to repair and put back all that is good in your world for the benefit of all.

"There has been so much cruelty perpetrated by man in your world, be it to animals or fellow human beings. In the 13th century the Cathars, a very spiritual race of people, were tortured during the Inquisition by men who believed them to be Heretics and so condemned them to death. In the Second World War, the Jews and Gypsies were tortured and put to death by the Nazis. And even now there are too many who spend their lives destroying the lives of others, no matter what colour, creed, age or discipline.

"There are still those who are led like lambs to slaughter by regimes which dictate and destroy in the name of their God, and who profess that this is for the benefit of the planet. These small, disaffected groups erroneously believe it is their right to destroy man, beast and property, but they are in the minority. They have lost their way, they don't know what to believe in, and so have joined an anarchic cause which brings them into the public eye where their infamy gives them joy.

"What need is there to inflict this pain? What hatred must there be in the hearts of men who want to hurt and maim others? Innocent bystanders are being destroyed before their time in the name of Gods and Masters who would never condone this sort of persecution. And although these deaths are becoming a unifying force across the globe, these innocent lives should not be lost in the first place, or lose their chance of a golden future.

"God, or similar names for the same entity, would never condone their actions. They will see this on their return 'home'. A slide-show of their negativity will allow them to see the hurt and despair they inflicted on fellow mortals: men, women and children who were merely going about their work and play, doing no harm to anyone. One day warmongers will review their beliefs and realise that war and destruction are not the way.

"When you watch the news it is so sad. There is very little uplifting and happy; there are mainly heart-rending stories of sorrow and malevolence. We are horrified at the continual bombardment on your broadcasting systems of everything negative about mankind.

"God only wants peace. All Gods are the one God, the God of all, in different guises, in different forms: one benign entity who only wants the best for his people, and what is righteous and peaceful for all mankind. God wants you to live in harmony with each other, to live in peace with your brethren no matter what race or creed, and to live in peace with the animals, birds, plants and marine life on this wonderful planet of yours.

"We need peace to prevail; we need to know we have put the planet in the right hands for its continuance. We aim to work to help your planet heal itself from the inside to out.

"Your Earth is a beautiful planet. From space, it glows with colour and vibrancy against a black sky, green and blue with diaphanous white clouds which hover and float above the surface. At night, your street lights sparkle like a million stars, and from space the Earth hangs like a beacon of hope in an infinity of orbs of light.

"Earth was created as a haven of tranquillity in an otherwise turbulent Universe. It was created as a focal point of Light, to herald peace across the cosmos. But this beautiful orb, this dalliance of Light, holds so much anger these days which darkens the skylines of cities across the world.

"Lift your eyes to the heavens. See the Light in the stars, which will show you the way to goodness and the Light in your own lives. See the galaxies, and realise how small a speck you are in the Universe. Realise there is a wealth of opportunity for each and every one of you to help the Earth as it moves forward to stand proud in its rightful place in the cosmos.

"If everyone looks up and realises how tiny a part they are in the whole, then they will want to grow and spread their wings. They will want to offer their lives in service to the planet which holds them dear. They will start to put their own needs after the needs and hopes of others, replacing their ego with compassion. We know there are many who put their lives at risk to protect and heal life on Earth itself. Humility and compassion should be the game word for life in this century.

"As we have said, many on your planet already put others first: man, the plant kingdom, animals, sea-life and, of course, the Earth herself. They take the time and effort to ensure that all living creatures receive the best possible care, giving their all in their quest. For this we thank them, and offer them our help to further their dedicated work.

"There are more and more people these days aware of the Earth, aware of the damage that has been done. More and more people are putting their hands in their pockets and lifting their hearts to help resurrect the planet and all upon her, to bring the Earth back to a state of harmony and peace.

"Humankind showed its caring side when saving a pod of whales stranded on a beach: many volunteers came to help them get back to the sea. Their navigational system went awry and they could not re-navigate out of the area on which they were beached. Sadly, this is quite common these days, as man's navigational sonar affects the natural sonar of these beautiful creatures. We thank all those who helped to 're-sail' these beautiful ships of the sea, who took time out of their busy schedules to encourage a helpless mammal to live a normal life within the ocean.

"We love all those who help to put others first, who still love life but not to the detriment of others. All mankind will follow this path in time, will show they care and receive the accolades they deserve for their kindness, either on Earth or when they return home. They will be recognised for the care and love they have given to life itself.

"Your planet is moving forward at a fast pace at this time in the Earth's evolution, to heal the veils between good and evil. No-one on your plane can see or feel the differences; they are infinitesimal, but they are there nonetheless, and suddenly it will seem to happen at once.

"You can make a difference, you know. You can all make a difference in your world. If everyone was to think positively, if everyone was to find no fault in friend or foe, life would be better for the whole of humankind. We only need you to raise your vibration: to lift your thoughts away from ego and materialism and to think how each and every one of you can help the planet to rise and bring those who live in darkness into the Light. Think positively, think only of good, and this beautiful planet of yours will be saved.

"We cannot understand how man, living on a planet which breathes such complexities of life, can betray the trust given to him to keep the land and seas safe, and to hold them in reverence for the place they occupy in mankind's ecology.

Without all living things on land, and in the sea, mankind could not survive. Without plants, trees, water and the creatures who inhabit the Earth, mankind would not exist. Yet despite this, despite being offered the best planet in the cosmos, many treat it, and everything else that lives on it, with contempt or disregard. Not all, we know, but many men and women of industry, of the corporate world, have only their own best interest at heart. These people do not honour the Earth, do not respect the paradise they have been given but, take, pillage and rape their Earth of all its goodness."

Olivia has been listening silently, but now she feels moved to tell Shomas about volunteers in her village who clear the beach each week to remove plastic and rubbish from the water's edge.

Shomas is pleased to hear this. "Individuals often feel they have no say in the world," he tells her, "but little acts of kindness like this mean a lot and multiply the positivity in the world". He then continues to tell his story.

"Environmental degradation is like a cancer, spreading silently, unseen, through the body of your planet. It is time to gaze anew at the sea, at the seashells clogged with garbage at your feet, and to envision the magic and power of the water which gives you life. If you continue to imperil the ocean, you continue to imperil yourselves. Ask everyone to care, ask them to put the planet first. It is a beautiful land with wondrous seas. All the planet needs is respect and it will continue to feed and house mankind for many lifetimes to come.

"We need you all to raise voices in peace, in harmony, to bring the Earth back from the edge – returning it to the glorious planet it should be, where man respects his fellow man and tends and cares for all. Let everyone raise their voices, let them all know our words and chant them together for a better future.

"Remember: 'One drop of water does not a pool make, but a hundred drops will create enough water to sustain life'. You can all have an effect on your world by adding your one small voice, which alone, like that single drop of water, when added to many voices, will make enough drops to create a pool, which can breed a multitude of organisms and create life.

"If you add your voice to many other voices singing the same song, then all your voices can have a powerful affect on the world you live in. When people say there is no point in their one voice, tell them they all count; tell them to add theirs to all the other voices all over the world, rising and singing for the future of the planet. A single voice may be nothing, but in harmony with others it is a choir – and the people in power have to take notice if the song is sung loudly enough. So add your voice to that choir. Sing with all your heart and see how that song resonates around the world, picking up momentum as in every country another voice joins the throng. You *can* do something: not as a single unit, but in unison with others your voice will be heard. Sing strong and loud! We look forward to hearing you like a heavenly choir.

"There are many in your world today who speak out for their beliefs, despite ridicule, expressing their concern for the planet and bringing forward others of like minds to speak with them of the truth. World leaders work mainly in the shadows. They need the reflective Light of many who can help them to live within their heart space in order to see where their decisions lead, and the repercussions thereof.

"There are some of those in power who already work for the Light. They are helping to build an infrastructure which will enhance the outlook for all nations, and bring fresh drinking water and nutritious food to even the poorest countries. They look beneath the facade of the richest nations to see the underbelly of sadness and degradation which needs to be turned around in order to lift the lives of all to a decent standard of living. Now is a time of the people, a time for everyone to help everyone else, a time to be there for your brothers and sisters and heal the world. It is time to pour Light and love into the planet to rebuild her strength for the future.

"You are all complex souls, with hearts of gold, minds full of clutter, dogma, rules, regulations and directives. Your hearts need to rule your heads – not totally, not in a soppy way, but to overcome the self-fulfilling prophecies of governments and leaders who direct your minds through an everyday minefield of issues. They have put man on a treadmill where he works for his basic needs, and for the benefit and greed of those in power, but, sadly, not for his own peace of mind."

Shomas pauses to allow Olivia to absorb this information. He can see that it has been a lot to take in, but her mind is as quick as her grandmother's, and soon she is ready for more. Now he continues in a different vein.

"Open your eyes," he urges. "Try to see the world through a new focus, encapsulating each minute of every day and seeing the magic that lies within. Watch in wonder as a flock of birds takes flight, as a pod of whales opens their blowholes to create fountains in the sea, and stare in awe as a bud unfurls its petals, opening its face to the sun.

"Have you ever truly looked at a flower? Each one is full of magic: the colours, the pollen, the blends of shades, all hold the magic of the Creator in their very essence. Stop and look at the intricacies of petals, stem, stamen, leaves, pollen and nectar, each part intrinsically linked to its partner, its family. It relies on insects to pollinate and proliferate its seed, expand its growth, and create more beauty across the land. Each petal unfurls to release an abundance of colour and aroma unique to each individual species. The leaves absorb light and moisture; the roots give it strength and sustenance; and the stem is the artery within which all life travels and nurtures from seed to flower. Study the form, the structure, the layout of each petal. See the labyrinth of complexity which invites insects to enter and extract the pollen to propagate the species. Flowers are so complex, so exquisite, and yet who takes the time to sit and ponder and absorb all that they offer?

"Take time to see the magic of a snowflake, or feel the relaxing warmth of a shower of summer rain; take a moment to see the glints of gold in a single raindrop; or breathe in the air of a forest of pine.

"Humankind is in such a hurry, rushing from here to there in a quest for materialistic gain, that the opportunity is missed to fully grasp the magic and beauty laid before you. Take time out. Take a while to relax and enjoy this planet of yours, to actually see what is offered and to appreciate the Creator's design. Take the time to see a prism in a dewdrop captured within a cobweb, and to marvel at the concentric circles of the web itself; to breathe sea air and catch the scent of the ocean; to watch a rainbow fall to the ground in a cascade of colour, and to see pictures in a near cloudless sky as wisps of cloud drift on the breeze. Slow down and truly experience the magic of a new dawn and the glory of a sunset at the completion of a fulfilling day. Take time, dear ones, to appreciate all that has been given to you for free. No money could buy the riches your planet offers to anyone who stops to see – riches worth far more than anything money could buy.

"Where is the magic in concrete? Where is the marvel in plastic? Look to nature for beauty; it is offered to you every day of your lives. Take time to see and appreciate all there is to see, feel, hear, touch and absorb. Take delight in it all.

"Nature is a wonderful thing, and you are all creatures of nature. We want you to enjoy your time on planet Earth. You need to grasp every opportunity to share the thrill of a bud unfurling, a snowflake on your tongue or the sparkles of sunlight on water. Take advantage of everything, and destroy nothing. This is for your enjoyment, and for the enjoyment of generations to come. Many other races, such as the Hopi Indians and Aborigines, believe in the philosophy that God is in everything. He is the Creator, the Life-force, the Source of everything: man, animals, plants, stones, and the very planet itself. Hold your hand out in peace, to lead others to this joy we offer you today, and every day of your life. We offer magic of the finest type: real magic, natural beauty at your fingertips, enjoy!!

"Appreciate your world, dear one. See, hear and touch everything in a new way, with gratitude for all you have been given. Do not ignore the crystalline structure of every single part of your homeland. You have been given the planet to enjoy, to relish in the magic of every thunderstorm, every rainbow. Open your eyes to see the world around you and then so much else will follow. Instead of drudging through everyday life, you will be open to helping others, to bringing love into the very heart of their lives, and to recognising that we are here to help and support you in this venture.

Take care and be confident in the knowledge that we love you, all of you, and we hold the safety net for your lives. You cannot fall, not once you look within yourself and acknowledge your true purpose. Be at one with all life, and offer help and solace to those less fortunate than yourself.

"All men and women are beings of pure Light and love. Throw off the shackles of hate, throw off the shackles of distrust and open your hearts to the possibilities your world has to offer in love, peace and healing.

"You are all our children and we want you to smile. We long for you to hold your heads up high, confident you are doing the right thing, in casting off materialism for a store of human kindness and happiness. We love you and want you all to be happy, and to pass to this side in the rightful knowledge that all will be well for generations to come. Bring peace to the Earth and goodwill to all men. May joy and love always be with you."

With that, Shomas departs as suddenly as he arrived. Olivia is unable to utter a sound as she has been enthralled by all he has had to say. The Crystal Cave slowly fades around her, and she is back in her grandmother's comfortable chair. It is only then that Olivia realises that her cheeks are wet with tears.

Tired, but exhilarated from everything she has heard, Olivia closes herself down carefully before she goes in search of Jane. She descends the stairs slowly, taking time to notice and appreciate the beauty in everything she passes.

CHAPTER FOURTEEN
HELPING THE PLANET

When Olivia appears at Jane's house the following week, she finds her grandmother in the garden as usual – but this time Jane only pauses for a moment of greeting; before Olivia enters the house, eager to visit with Shomas again.

As Olivia settles into her usual chair, she's amazed by how normal this has become. She is proud that her grandmother recognises she can meet Shomas on her own – although she is also grateful for the 'de-brief' she always has with Jane afterwards. This helps her reflect on Shomas's teachings, and gives her further information to absorb.

After a few minutes meditation, Shomas appears to Olivia readily, and he, too, is eager to start her lessons for the day.

"Man was put on your planet to breed," he begins, "and in that breeding to rear his children and his children's children in a way which would benefit Earth itself: as a caretaker of the land, the seas, the forests, and the animals which roamed the plains.

"When the planet was first formed, it glowed with colour and was vibrant with life. Everything was bright and delightful, so when man first arrived he found a green and glorious land full of life and vitality. Vividly-coloured flowers danced in the breeze and streams trickled melodiously throughout the countryside.

"Now, the rainforests worldwide which have stood sentinel for millions of years, are being destroyed by deforestation. This affects the balance of oxygen and carbon dioxide that creates your planet's life force. We are concerned that so many trees are being destroyed across the world for they help to keep the balance of oxygen and CO_2. No trees, plants or phytoplankton, no oxygen. No oxygen, no life on Earth. You all have to do something about this.

"Many problems in the world, health-wise, are caused by too much carbon dioxide, and there are not enough plants and trees to reprocess it to oxygen. Every tree is important, everywhere on the planet. *All* plants are essential to life. Do not let developers destroy more trees! The planet is losing its ecosystem. You need plants (crops, flowers, trees) and clear seas to maintain the lungs of the planet.

"Plant trees, so that your world can breathe fresh air again. Cars, planes and boats all bring with them congestion – not only of roads, skies and seas, but congestion of your lungs due to the emissions with which they fill your air and water. More trees and more fresh algae eases this congestion, eases the destruction of the ozone layer. Be mindful of what you put into the atmosphere as it is the lungs of the planet and affects you all. Do not cause impoverishment of the world's biological status. Enormous numbers of species are harmed or made homeless by deforestation and subsequent damage to soils and nutrient supplies.

"Pesticides and bad farming methods are affecting crops. Plants are being 'created' which do not produce fertile seed. All seeds should allow fruition; governments and scientists have no right to take this birthright away.

"Bees are dying by the millions. They are the lifeblood of the food chain, but few seem to care about their demise. No pollination means no plants, no flowers, no trees, and no vegetables for your table. Encourage bees in your garden, and give them the material to expand their hives.

"Mankind is already heading towards the precipice predicted by Nostradamus in his Quatrains. We feel much sadness at seeing man destroying his idyll; he has taken a jewel in the crown of the Universe and laid it bare to the elements. He has not protected and maintained the land, the seas and all the living organisms which make it so rich and full of life.

"Man needs to go back to basics. He has laid barren large expanses of woodland; clearing it as grazing land for cattle which will be slaughtered for fast food chains. The cattle on the way to the slaughter house know where they are going and why. They are afraid, and that fear transfers itself into toxins in the meat, which you then eat. As the years pass more and more people on the planet will come to realise that this is not the way. Live and let live, God has put so many wonderful things on the planet for man to eat, treat animals as you would treat yourself, with gentleness and kindness.

"Take life a little at a time. Take what you need and no more, and then there will be plenty for others who follow you – for generations who will need the resources just as much as you. Whenever possible, safeguard the world for the future."

Shomas stops: he can see Olivia is deeply troubled at the pain inflicted on these animals.

"We watch your world in its busy turmoil of activity, no-one knowing whether they are coming or going, no-one sure of their destiny, and we ask you all to listen to the voice within. Listen to the chords of reason, to the glimmer of hope and fulfilment which lies within you all to improve your world.

"In your world today, there are so many different levels of awareness: different natures, cultures, creeds, religions and colours all with different perspectives. There will always be the rich and the poor, the haves and have-nots in your world as long as there is a greedy culture to rule and control.

"Mankind was put on the planet to have free will, but some are freer than others! Some use their wisdom wisely and help others less fortunate. Others pocket their proceeds and build their own castles in the air, looking down in pity on the down and out. Turn that pity into charity: take a little less, give a little more.

"Man must learn to look to itself for a wealth of purpose and fulfilment. It is time to help raise the vibrations of the Earth, to lift the hearts and minds of all on the planet, and to think of more than just yourselves. It is time to take a stand, to take notice, and to encourage the world to be a better and safer place for all.

"Life on Earth is a conundrum. It is a strange fruit. In this day and age, an age of eloquence and good fortune, there are still millions suffering for want of aid. This is not right. When will man realise his life will be so much richer if only he would share? Give a little every day: give time, give money, or give a toy to a child and watch them smile. Those with little to give are often the most generous and the kindest to others.

"You have been given a beautiful world to live on, vibrant with colour and life: don't take it for granted. Give back to the soil; give back to the Earth all the goodness taken over the centuries. Replenish the fields of corn, the trees, the flowers, the diversity of wildlife. See the Earth transform from the beauty you have now to a glorious planet without disease, without hardship, without loss.

"We wish for man to prosper on his planet, we wish for him to grow and thrive. But he won't if he takes all the resources now, all the oil, minerals, goodness and nutrients from the Earth. The Earth needs a future for all the generations to come. Try to instil this in the minds of the young. Instil it in their thought patterns. The future can be very bright if mankind will let it be.

"Now, as the consciousness of the planet is rising, man is realising that there is more to life and happiness than material wealth can bring; realising everyone can contribute and plan for the future.

"We need you all to herald our messages to the world. We need people to try as a group consciousness, to stop war, want and waste. This is part of a huge plan to raise the consciousness of the planet, and you can heal the world with our words. Our plan for the future is to bring joy to those who are suffering. Tell everyone all will be well if all of you raise your consciousness now.

"The Earth is passing through a long orbit that brings it closer to the centre of Universal Truth. This is awakening people, who are spiritually aware, to the reality of one world, one Creator, one truth: that life is eternal and love is the unifying force of the cosmic world. Such an attitude will help you all to overcome your fears and reach out in helpfulness to others – especially when the Earth undergoes periods of famine, flood, earthquake, pestilence and warfare.

"During the past 2,000 years, the Piscean Age, man harnessed water and steam for power. He made great technological and medical advances, explored outer space and landed men on the moon. Now, with entry into the Age of Aquarius, human knowledge is delving into attitudes, emotions, the power of thought, meditation and prayer. This coming age will be one of greater spiritual and psychic awareness.

"Humanity will understand and live by the principles of love, helpfulness and the law of karma; and will also understand that life is eternal. The Age of Aquarius heralds in an age of peace and plenty, of love and joy. Your beautiful planet is desperately in need of love, peace and joy. It will come in the form of a prophet: a teacher who will walk amongst you to herald these messages."

Olivia has heard of the Age of Aquarius and looks forward to its coming.

"Many children of the Earth need help at this time, as they are so vulnerable and easily led." Shomas continues, "They have a spiritual awareness, but are not sure how to use it, they get dragged down by the negative forces which yearn to win their souls. Help them to see the Light; help them to grow spiritually and not be led into temptation. They are on Earth now to help the planet – they just need to be shown the right path to take, which will help them on their way."

As Shomas speaks, Olivia realises she is one of the children of Earth that he has been talking about: the younger generation entrusted to help the planet survive and heal. She has only just become spiritually aware, but he is here to guide her onto the right path. How much she has learned in the past few months! Now it is her task to disseminate this information to all those who want to know more. Vowing to do her best, she listens carefully as Shomas continues.

"Many Governments are letting their populace down. They are not doing their job of governance. Man has been led like a sheep to slaughter for years, turning to a power which lessens his own resonance upon the Earth. God, the Creator, is the only power, humankind should revere; he has the destiny of mankind at his finger tips and he only wants the best for every one of you. He fills your hearts with love, and if you can keep that love alight, your life will always be at peace.

"This is a time for everyone to help everyone else, a time to be there for your brother or sister and help to heal the world. It is time to pour Light and love into the planet to rebuild her strength to move forward into the future.

"You need to send more Light to dark places on the Earth, bathe them in Light, flood them with Light, pour it down through the corridors of power, pour it over the top of cities. Just ask your Guides and the Angels for the Light to be poured as though it is rainfall, poured into the hearts of the people in charge. Pour Light over the Halls of Power and wrap them in pink light. It helps, wrapping places in pink; it is a gentle Light, full of love. You can do this individually with just a thought. Close your eyes and envisage it: a watering can is good, sprinkling the Light like water... beautiful, bright, clear water...all over the Halls of Power, filling them with love and caring.

"Man must put his hand up and be counted as an armistice rules the world and people realise the worth of peace. In your own small way, make peace happen in your world, in your home, your street, your village. Offer the hand of friendship and harmony, and see faces lighten at your touch, your words, your smile, your help.

"Take the load off those on the breadline and lift their hearts and souls with your generosity of spirit. We want peace, harmony and a true life for all. This is a tough time, but it will resolve, we have it all in hand.

"You can offer friendship and kindness and touch the hearts of many in your vicinity. This is like ripples in a stream: it will flow on through your town, your county, your country, to the hearts and minds of others less fortunate than yourself. Spread cheer no matter how small. Open your heart to the world. Offer solace and warmth to the coldest soul, and it will warm and hold that warmth, melting the ice that holds that soul in stasis keeping it from the Light. Fan a small spark in every soul. Encourage others to lift their eyes to the heavens and realise their full potential.

"It is time. The darkness, unfortunately, has been creeping in for a long while now, trying to win over the Light, as it penetrates a lot of areas. All of you now who are raising the consciousness on the Earth are helping considerably, because there are less and less dark areas. There are pockets of Light all over the world, and gradually the darkness will realise that it won't win – as it thought it would at one point. But no, the consciousness of the planet is rising, and the planet itself will rise through the vibrations and the darkness and negativity will be vanquished. We have right on our side. We have the Light on our side. We will win.

"Mother Earth or Gaia[18] as you may wish to call her, wants to raise herself above this. She hates the negativity and darkness which has surrounded her for so long and wishes to raise herself out of it, to pull herself out of the mire, and you are the ones who are helping to improve your world.

"War is not the answer. Violence is not the result of unrest, it is the cause. With violence comes the resentment and hurt of all those on the sidelines. Remove all weapons; trade them in for a plough of peace. Plant crops and feed the starving millions. Use the money allocated for war to improve the health and welfare of all the nations across the globe instead. It is incongruous that in the 21st century there are still people dying of malnutrition or pollution from stagnant water. The money spent on warfare could clothe and house the children of the world who live like rats in the sewers of countries far wealthier than they appear.

"Life on Earth has been hard, but there will be Light at the end of the tunnel. There will be joy to be had in the future once we have cleared this negativity, anger and despair. It was prophesied that Earth would be led into extreme darkness, with mankind full of sloth, hate and anger – but now is the time to repair and reconcile your planet.

"Man is beginning to look back and realise what he has done to damage the planet and life upon it. So much harm has been done in the name of progress and advanced technology, but the planet is fighting back, she has no choice. If she stands back and lets it all continue, Earth will not survive and mankind will perish with her.

"Give back, give life back to the oceans by not over-fishing. If you eat all the fish, then the sea creatures which rely on these fish for their food will also not survive. What a sad planet it will be when there are no sea creatures, and when there are no animals left on the land except those reared for food."

Olivia's face has clouded, and Shomas stops to allow her to collect her thoughts. She says to Shomas "What can I do to help all of this?"

He gives her a look of great compassion. "Look to the future, look to the Light. It is hard now, but times will be better. The status of the planet will improve, and when it does, your life will be at one with your planet, the trees, the animals, and the other planets. It will be joyous again. Send your energy to the centre of the Earth so that myriad blessings will scatter across the planet to ease the pain and heartache of the many nations.

"There are a million blessings in the world, from the humblest insect to the glory of your God. Be thankful for the many blessings in your life, and your life will be blessed. Feel low and you will be low; feel bright and full of life and you will see the world through those eyes, and it will be transformed. Open your hearts to the planet. Do something positive today, something selfless to help others, to help the planet. You will feel better, and gradually the world will feel better too.

"When you feel low, think of all the things you can be thankful for, all the good things in your life – be it the love of your family, your friends, the roof over your head, the love of your animals. The security of closing your front door and feeling the warmth therein. The sun kissing your face, the wind in your hair, the sound of a robin singing, the beauty of a garden, the scent of a rose, the shelter of trees. Or the guidance of Spirit, its support and love.

"As we watch you today, the sun is shining and the spring is in full swing. The trees are in bud and the daffodils have lifted their cheery heads along the roadsides. Open your eyes, appreciate the beauty that has been given to you. Don't just drive blandly through the countryside – appreciate it, appreciate all it has to offer you. The freedom of being alive. Even in the most rundown cities, there is beauty. Even in the darkest industrial sites you can find Light, be it a flower, a bud, a tree, a mouse scurrying to find its next meal. There is beauty in the land wherever you are.

"If each and every person opened their eyes to see beauty and helped one another, put out their hands to lift a child or help an elderly person to their feet, then all would be enriched. A simple smile of appreciation would lift each heart and make it sing.

"If you could all do a random act of kindness every day for someone you don't know, it would make the world a far nicer place – and maybe, just maybe, the warring factions of the world would lay down their arms and smile with you. Maybe they would forget their anger, forget the angst, forget the reason they hate the world and everyone on it, and realise they were put on Earth for a purpose. They were put on Earth to nurture the planet, to care for everything on it; to be caretakers of all life, not just their own.

"We love you all, from the tiniest babe in arms to the wisest old man rocking in his chair on the veranda; from the most innocent of children to, yes, even the greediest and most malevolent of your governments. We love you, and we hope that with love, everyone will grow and change for the better. As you open your eyes to see and feel that love, your world will improve. When you all love each other, as we love you, peace will prevail and your planet will be a far better place on which to live.

"Give it time. It has taken thousands of years for the Earth to get to this desolate place and it will take a good many years to put it right. It *will* be put right, it will become the jewel in the crown of the Universe again. Man will live in peace and harmony with his fellow man, and with all the flora and fauna across the planet. Trust us, it will happen if you start this NOW!

"Open your eyes to see and appreciate all that is around you. Just one smile to a stranger starts a ripple effect which will surround your town, your country, the world. Start your charm offensive today. The sooner it starts, the sooner you will see a difference in your world and in the worlds of others.

"Hold out your hand and offer friendship. Open your heart and offer love. Not a greedy love, not an erotic or sensuous love but a love of friendship, a love of family, a love of pets and flowers and beauty. Take time to review your life and celebrate all your achievements. Recognise your own magnificence, not in an egotistical way but with humility. Move forward with a skip in your step and a song in your heart.

"Your planet needs you. We need you, to be our Messengers of Light, bringing Light to even the darkest corners of your world. Open your eyes and see the world as you have never seen it before. See everything with fresh eyes."

Shomas smiles as he says this and Olivia smiles back. "Yes," she tells him. "I so want to do that."

"We hope you will grow to love us," Shomas responds, "and realise we only have your welfare at heart. If you ask for our help we shall always be there, no matter what the situation, no matter where. We shall be there with love, support and kindness to help you on your path to a better future.

"As times become more troubled, people turn to us for answers to their questions. Many people are genuinely interested to stand up and be counted. We talk to them and assure them of their God's goodness. The young people of today chose to be on Earth at this time, as they are far more aware and willing to accept their rightful path than their elders have been.

"We will impart messages to you, and to all who ask, showing ways to look at what has been done and how it can be corrected. We offer a plan for the future to help all to see how good life can be if you all raise your consciousness and do what is right. All who wish to help the planet must walk the Earth helping people to understand this, putting our words into simple language so everyone knows what is happening. There is so much to come, so much to see and do. The world will be a wonderful place again, full of love, light, joy, peace, happiness and creativity and we need you all to show the way.

"What we tell you now will take place over thousands of years. It is a record of all that is to happen on Earth for the rest of this millennia and beyond – a record of Earth and all she stands for, a record of mankind and all it will achieve. So much potential has been lost in the aeons of time, so many chances to recompense destroyed. But now is the time to repair.

"Look to your future, and look inside yourself for your happiness. Take the wealth of the soul and expand it to gain your true riches. Nothing materialistic on Earth will give you what you need to progress on this plane. Nothing you can wish for will give you the immense happiness you deserve and have earned by just being who you are today.

"The future for mankind is bright, the future is full of promise. The world you know now will transform into a brighter, rosier future. Hostilities will cease, evil will fade away, and man will care about his fellow man. All will be done for the good of all, in unity, in companionship, in love. Life will be full of joy, children will see a future filled with love and happiness. They will be raised in peace and harmony and will understand the lighter side of life.

"Lift your hearts and follow the Light. Shine the way like a star to be followed leading to peace and harmony. Don't hide your Light: show it, glow with it and build on it, until all can see it and follow your guidance.

"We need Lightworkers now as Heralds, as Messengers, as Ambassadors of love and peace leading the way to harmony and respect. Help everyone to find the Light in their lives; help them to see it can lead to a future where everyone will be happy and joyful. Show the world the Light of our love, and bring everyone together as a whole to make life beautiful again. The future, which is coming, is full of hope. Life will be as it was in the beginning, as it is meant to be. Open your arms, embrace it, and lead the world on its happy path. Lift your head, show your Light like a beacon, and lead on!

"Ask all those who work for the Light to raise the consciousness of the planet, to take it up and away for the 21st century – up out of the darkness and negativity, away from despair and into the light of joy, love and peace. Live your life to the full, fill every moment with happiness. Dance in the sunshine, sing in the rain and enjoy life to the fullest.

"Look to the future, not the past. The past is gone. Do not grieve loss or departures, look to the future, to new beginnings and new life, each footfall fresh on dewy grass leading who knows where, an adventure into the unknown. The future will be filled with love, Light and joy if you let us into your hearts. We will not let you fall.

"Be of the Light, be of the spring and the summer, show this warmth and this sense of new beginnings to others. Help them to open their eyes and see that the beauty of the planet is there for the asking. So endeth our lecture for today."

With that, Shomas says his goodbye and leaves. Olivia sits for a while, stunned by his words. She knows she needs to help to change the future, but she feels so new at this, and there is still so much she doesn't know. Shomas has complete faith in her – but what if she is just not up to the task? She thinks about Jane, who has worked with the Light for many years. She will go and ask her for guidance.

She finds her grandmother relaxing in the conservatory overlooking her beloved garden. Jane puts down the book she has been reading and pats the cushion of the chair beside her. "You are looking a little dazed, Livvy. Come sit. How was your session today?"

Olivia sinks into the chair, exhilarated but exhausted, and tells Jane all about it.

When she is done, Jane gives her a thoughtful look, remembering her own early sessions with Shomas. She recalls being just the same: awed and overwhelmed, bursting with questions, anxious to know everything at once. She smiles to herself, remembering how hard it was to be patient back then. Olivia will learn.

"I am glad you are developing your own relationship with Shomas," she says. "He has such a lovely way of expressing himself doesn't he?"

Olivia agrees. "When he explains things, he does it with so much love that I can feel the emotions and 'see' what he means. Now I understand how badly the Earth has been treated, and why we must all help to heal it."

"I read, Livvy, that it takes an acre of growing trees to produce enough oxygen for sixteen people every day – as trees are cut down they need to be replaced with new growth! We have to remind ourselves how vital to our survival wild plants and animals are. Everything exists by courtesy of everything else. Every hour a unique species of plant or creature disappears from the face of the Earth. Millions of species are extinct – and, as the posters and T-shirts say: *Extinct is Forever*. I worry whether your children's children will ever see the millions of species which we know and love. Or will they just be myths and memories like the Dodo?"

"I often wonder what is going to happen. For thousands of years there have been prophesies (in the the Bible and by people like Nostradamus in the 15th century) that the planet is due for a cataclysmic shake-up which will turn all that we know upside-down."

Jane looks out of the window at her garden, whose vegetables have filled her larder, whose herbs have stocked her medicine cabinet, and whose flowers have given her such joy.

She suddenly says: "You probably have not heard of Sun Bear. He was a native American of Chippewa descent, a very wise man. He stated before his death that the Earth changes long prophesied by his people, are now here and are necessary for the survival of the planet. To the Chippewa, the Earth is a living, intelligent being who is capable of making the necessary changes for her own survival. These changes may not be convenient for humans but the Earth will make them anyway. There may be climatic changes, earthquakes and volcanic eruptions, economic and political problems and other issues which humans have caused for themselves. But he said he could see that the planet would survive and thrive and grow.

"Sun Bear also advised that it was time for every individual to take real responsibility for his or her own life. He felt the purpose of humanity now was for each of us to grow to our highest level of consciousness and power, and then to use that knowledge to help others and the Earth in these times. He also advised that to do so you have to develop a philosophy that '*grows corn*' – by which he meant it has to work here and now, every day of your life. It has to help you walk in a sacred manner, and give you the back-up power that you need for your survival on the planet. If it doesn't, he said, then you'd better 're-check your circuits'."

"I like that" says Olivia.

"As you know," Jane adds, "I used to teach in a college and was very impressed when one of my students wrote a lovely summary in an essay for a project. I can still remember it.

'I owe an allegiance to the planet which has made me possible, and to all the life on that planet, whether friendly or not. I also owe an allegiance to the 3.5 billion years of life that made it possible for me to be here and all the rest of you too. We have a responsibility to the largest population of all - the hundreds of billions of people who have not yet been born, who have a right to be. Who deserve a world at least a beautiful as ours, whose genes are now in our custody and no-one else's.'"

"That's beautiful and so profound!" says Olivia.

"I agree, I was so impressed that one of my young students should think about her world in that way. All our lives could be so much better if we just remembered to think before we act, and to put Mother Earth before ourselves."

The two women fall silent, contemplating how they can help planet Earth for the future.

CHAPTER FIFTEEN
FREE WILL & KARMA

Spring has made way for summer, and the glorious multi-petalled varieties of peonies and roses of every hue stand sentinel beside all the smaller, daintier flowers in Jane's garden. This really is a wonderful time of year for enjoying the outdoors, Olivia reflects. A light breeze stirs the leaves of the fruit trees and falling blossoms, like snow flakes, create a carpet of white on the soft green grass.

She has fallen into an easy routine when visiting Jane: normally a session with Shomas first, and then a follow-up talk with her grandmother, often over tea or a meal. Sometimes she stays for the whole weekend, as there is always something interesting to do: helping out in the garden, studying crystals, or curling up with a book from Jane's shelves (many of them rare and fascinating). Her chats with Shomas have become a highlight in her week, a chance to understand more about her own life and the lives of everyone else on the planet. She has grown in confidence and isn't afraid to ask questions of Shomas and her grandmother. She is keen to learn, and is eager to raise her awareness of everything around her.

Today, she asks Jane expectantly: "Can you tell me about free will and karma, please?"

"Well," Jane starts, thinking for a moment, "Shomas says that even though we chose our life path before we were born, every person also has the free will to do as they please with their life: to make up their own mind about any part of it, and to make their own mistakes. No-one is forced to comply with advice or information from their Guides – but as you can imagine, this free will can sometimes get us into trouble!

"Our Guides and Spirit Helpers are not allowed to interfere in any aspect of our lives – unless, of course, we ask for their help, when they will instantly come to our aid. Sometimes they will also come when we don't ask but only if they see us about to take a wrong step; when they will give us gentle nudges, in the form of a gut feeling or a sense of 'knowing', to help us to take the right course of action, as they have a better understanding of what is about to happen along our path and can see round the corners that we can't.

"What you have to realise, Livvy, is that your Guides are only advising you. Whether you listen or not is up to you. If you don't want to listen, then you can go your own sweet way and there is nothing they can do – but then you have to accept the consequences. If you pay attention and trust when you get a 'gut feeling' about something or someone, and realise that this comes from the Guides, who are just trying to help, then you will find your path runs a lot smoother.

"For example, have you ever felt suddenly compelled to do something – or conversely, *not* to do something, such as not to go down a certain road? You suddenly 'know' that it is the wrong path to take; you don't know why, but that feeling in the pit of your stomach tells you to go another way. This feeling comes from your Guide's, attempting to keep you safe from harm.

"Or, maybe you are running for a train and you trip, dropping everything, and by the time you gather all your belongings, the train has gone. What you need to realise is that you were not meant to catch that train – perhaps because it would befall disaster, or lead to some other form of harm or heartache. You didn't listen to the small quiet 'voice' in your head, so your Guides had to use another means of stopping you, not to hurt you, but to protect you, as they always have your best interests at heart.

"In some people, this innate sense of being guided is stronger than in others, and they understand that their Guides are telling them exactly where to go and what to do, helping them along their path. Some people call it premonition, or intuition. It is something everyone has – although many will not recognise it as a sign to help them and they block it out."

"I've definitely had that 'knowing' feeling," says Olivia, "but I could never quite put her finger on why I had it."

"You can strengthen this capability, and it will help to guide you throughout live. Why don't you go and ask Shomas about it?" Jane suggests. "We can have another chat afterwards."

Olivia agrees and climbs the stairs with heightened anticipation. Settling herself comfortably in the chair, she makes her link with Shomas almost instantly.

"Good morning," he says. "I understand you wish to know about free will and karma today."

"Yes, please," Olivia confirms, and Shomas begins.

"Complete free will was given to man when he first set foot on planet Earth, as from the outset it was deemed that free will would be utilised to wield the might of God on Earth. This was something of an experiment. Earth was designed as the planet of choice, where man could decide for himself the path he would take through his lifetime, choosing his own destiny. Unfortunately, it was not fully understood where giving man free rein would lead.

"Sadly, man took this free will and moulded it to fit his own desire, whether it led to the Light or the darkness. Some souls would find their way to their proper path and succeed in fulfilling their life's plan, but, alas, many would not!

"It is due to man's free will that the planet is in the mess it is in now – so it is up to man, using that same free will, to help Earth out of the mire and back onto the path of Light and love it is destined to follow. Free will is a wonderful gift, if used properly: for the benefit of others, rather than for self-gratification and self-destruction.

"Many souls have been swayed by the material opportunities offered to them by dark forces, and this has gradually brought the vibration of the planet down. Free will, unfortunately makes it easy for man to be tempted by the dark with offers of power, money and opportunity. The darkness has been winning many souls who are greedy and opportunistic, wanting everything for themselves, and seeking the power to rule.

"Working for the Light is harder. You may not benefit in the material sense during your time on Earth, nor have all the luxuries, but you will benefit spiritually and in many other ways. But some cannot see these rewards, and want something more tangible.

"We are pleased to say that an increasing number of you are now utilising free will in the service of the Light. You have incarnated on Earth to help the Light, to heal the Earth, and to clear the darkness and ignorance from around your planet. We, your Guides and Helpers, are here to enable you do this.

"Earth is a very popular planet on which to reincarnate because of free choice, which gives you the opportunity to clear karma, or even to build more karma. You have your path etched out for you when you arrive, but you can be inclined to deviate and go off at tangents as your life progresses. Other planets are structured not to have free choice. They don't necessarily have a strict regime, but the free will element is not there, the inhabitants know the path their life will take, know their destiny and everyone works towards advancing themselves.

"This is why Earth is surrounded by beings who wish to re-incarnate on the planet, because it really is an amazing opportunity for them to clear karma, fulfil their destiny, and enjoy the freedom that is not available anywhere else in the Universe. You may have experienced the lifestyle of other planets in previous lifetimes, but in this lifetime you have chosen to have the freedom available on planet Earth – to help to raise the vibrations of yourself and the planet. It is a wonderful place to be, especially at this time in Earth's evolution.

"Because you have free will, your personal future cannot be dictated precisely, as you may or may not follow your designated path. The global future, however, is slightly more predicable – although the free will of the populace can intervene and alter an otherwise destined course of events. Wars may be averted and situations may change, which is why you all have such power to help the Earth."

Shomas pauses, and Olivia concentrates, determined to understand and remember his words.

"Although you choose your path before birth," he explains, "you do not retain a conscious memory of that knowledge during your time on Earth. Remember that I told you life on your planet is a schoolhouse. If you knew your path at the outset, you would not learn anything by your mistakes. Although it is sad when you detour from your path, you do still learn.

"If you go to a medium or clairvoyant, you could find that the reading you receive may not always turn out exactly as predicted. This is because the people who they pick up in the reading have free will, yourself included, and may end up taking a different path to the one envisaged at that time. We can see from this side what your path should be, without any deviation – but free will can change the best laid of plans.

"From the Guides' vantage point on the spiritual plane, we can see beyond the bend in the river of life which you on Earth are travelling. We can foresee the obstacles which will confront you, but we cannot predict your final choices, only what will come to pass if you follow your true path.

"The Spiritual view of life is as an eternal cycle, found throughout the Universe in the creation of stars and galaxies, molecules and atoms. Man is just a part of that cycle. He is Spirit encased in flesh. Spirit is free and unrestricted, but to learn vital lessons a Spirit soul needs to impose restrictions upon itself – restrictions which limit perspective and abilities, hence being incarnated on Earth is simply a learning experience. It is a process which a soul will undergo many times, until it has learned enough lessons to return home to the world of Spirit for the final time.

"Free will on Earth gives you the ability to choose any path you desire – but in the end all paths return to the Source, by which time you will at least have achieved part, if not all, of the contract which has been created for your soul's growth. If only part of your contract has been fulfilled then you can elect to return to Earth to work on the rest in another lifetime, and another, until you have achieved your goals, and can move on through higher and higher vibrations in a spiral of never ending love, peace and learning.

"That is all I want to say about free will right now. You also asked about karma, so let us move on to that subject.

"Karma operates on every level of life, from people, to countries, to planets. It balances all experiences for your evolutionary benefit. Being put on Earth gives a soul the opportunity to learn the lessons which are needed in order to progress on to the spirit plane. Some lessons are learnt, and some are not. With some, more problems can be created, needing even more lessons to be learnt in the future.

"During this learning process known as lifetimes, you may make mistakes or even transgress the laws of nature, or of God, which incurs a debt known as karma, or the law of cause and effect. It is then essential to clear this karma before you can get the opportunity to develop and progress personally. By making recompense for past hurt and caring for, and sharing with, others. The Bible states, 'As you sow, so shall you reap', this is the law of karma, where every thought and deed creates a positive or negative energy. Karma is a way to balance these energies.

"If you do an ill deed toward someone, or think an ill thought, it is all kept on record. If you do not make recompense in one lifetime, then you will return to pay your debt in another lifetime. This is not designed as retribution, as many would think, but just to make amends and balance the books, so the speak. We offer karma to entice man to learn lessons to progress on his path to Light, not as any form of chastisement.

"Life is at one with nature. All that you see, hear and feel are part of your life, with you as an infinitesimal part, adding your portion to the whole. With each physical incarnation, you create a life plan designed to give both the positive and negative energies needed for balanced growth. You need both of these influences in your lives, but not to extremes. Too much positivity can send you in a haze of worship and idolatry, and too much negativity can surround you with anger and hatred. Try not to be negative about anyone in word or deed; these slings and arrows boomerang back, you know! Do good to others and good will come to you."

Olivia sits pensively thinking about this as Shomas continues.

"No-one can say that they have gone through their life without a bad thought or deed toward someone else – but beware, you are likely to meet that someone again, maybe in another lifetime. They will not necessarily be the same. A man could be a woman, a woman could be man, black could be white, white could be yellow – but you will owe them a debt, however small, which you will need to repay in some way.

"It is so silly to have hatred for another race or creed as you may have been one of that race or creed in a previous life. Or, you may come back as such in order to learn tolerance in your next lifetime. If someone in one lifetime was a very rich landowner, and not very kind to the people in his employ, then in his next lifetime he may have very little money and spend his life making sure that his fellow man is well cared for. This would be his karma, his lesson for a lifetime.

"We know you would never intentionally harm anyone, but try to be kind to everyone you meet and try really hard not to have bad thoughts about anyone, no matter who they are. As we have said before, these thoughts are like boomerangs and will always come back and 'bite you'.

"Your thoughts are just as effective as saying something out loud, for example: being derogatory about someone because we feel jealous, envious or cross, due to something they have done. This manifestation of your thoughts, ideas or emotions go across the ether to the person you are thinking about and hooks into them like a barb, and these barbs can cause all sorts of problems for the recipient. Each negative thought form sent out can bounce back, causing the sender distress – not always straight away, but eventually. So do be very careful of all your thoughts.

"This is why unconditional love is so important. To quote another old adage, 'Do unto others as you would have them do unto you'. In order to overcome negativity, it is vital to always give out unconditional love to all, making sure this comes from the heart in the form of a beautiful pink ray. Not in a soppy sentimental way, but to offer your best to everyone you meet.

"You all get your egos hurt at times – sometimes because another person's ego strikes out to take control, other times your hurt ego is caused by a loss of dignity. Let it go, turn the other cheek, be kind and not resentful.

"No-one here sits in judgement of your life; you are your own judge and jury. Everyone is accepted on our side, with open arms and love. No recriminations, no anger; those emotions aren't known here. There is no hell: this idea has been designed in order to rule with fear. If anything, Earth is where many nasty things happen. It is on Earth where it is possible to learn the lessons needed to progress to the Light and joy beyond, to make your path home easier.

"Once you reach our side, you will realise that we never stop learning. We know the Earth is a schoolhouse, but our side has Halls of Learning too, so that your souls can continue to progress. These are like your Universities, but far advanced of the education given there. Personal development here allows a soul to progress on an etheric level, to further their learning and understanding of life, unhampered by the restrictions of the physical body.

"When you pass on to our side, and look back on your life, you will decide what you still need to learn from the experiences you've had. You will choose your future path in order to experience situations which will balance events from your current lifetime and repay debts, which will help you progress. It is not a punishment, it is a balancing, and it will offer both pleasant as well as not-so-pleasant experiences, for future lifetimes.

"It would be difficult to explain to you what we learn here on our side, but part of this is to help your progression on the Earth plane. Every lesson will ensure you will be more advanced on your return, to be prepared to work for the Light there on Earth, to help others for a better future.

"Now, I think that is enough for one day. We will talk again soon."

Shomas and Olivia smile at each other. She thanks him very much for his insights, and he makes his exit, leaving her to think about what he has said today.

Jane, as usual, is waiting in the conservatory, a pot of tea on the table. She allows Olivia to come downstairs and 'chill' before asking her about the session with Shomas. It is always very tiring talking to Spirit, and Olivia finds these quiet, companionable moments with her grandmother restorative.

They take the tea into the garden, enjoying the fading glow of a glorious sunny day. As Olivia grounds herself in the physical world, she slowly relaxes and tells Jane all Shomas has had to say.

CHAPTER SIXTEEN

LOVE

Summer is now turning to autumn. The russets and golds of the leaves, as they tumble from the trees, add a different dimension to the garden, their colours scattering splashes of sunbeams across the lawn.

Jane is planting winter pansies as Olivia arrives, adding vibrant colour to the autumn focus of the flower beds. Olivia picks up a trowel and helps to create the holes for the tiny plants to fill. The companionable ease between the two women is palpable in the cooling air. No words need to be spoken. The only sounds disturbing the silence are the glorious song of a robin in a distant tree and Jane's cat, Chloe, softly purring as she nudges Olivia's hand for attention.

It has been quite a few weeks since Olivia last visited her grandmother, but their love is so secure that there is no awkwardness; they lapse into their usual relationship as though no time has passed. The planting finished, they go inside, have a warming drink and then go upstairs together, where Jane places an exquisite piece of Rhodochrosite crystal in Olivia's hands.

"Why this crystal today?" Olivia enquires.

"This stone is encompassed by heavenly energies; it is a stone of Love," Jane advises. "It expands consciousness and attracts lightness into life. It seems a very good stone for the lessons Shomas has told me he wishes to impart today."

Olivia sits in her usual chair, and Jane takes her into a deep meditation. This time, she meets Shomas on a path near a babbling stream. He leads her to a glade, where she sits on sun-warmed grass next to the water.

"I really look forward to our visits, Olivia," he says, "I have so much more to share with you."

"I enjoy them too," she tells him truthfully. "May I ask our topic for today?"

He smiles. "We would like to speak with you of Love."

Olivia then realises why her Grandmother had chosen the crystal she is holding.

"Love is the cog on which the whole of life turns," he begins. "Love is the best tool anyone can use to bring Light onto the planet. Love is the unifying force of the cosmic world. Love is the most precious thing that mankind has been given.

"Man was put on the Earth to love his fellow man, to care for all the creatures and cherish the plant and mineral kingdoms thereon. True unconditional love is the greatest thing man can give to man. (When we say 'man', we also mean 'woman', of course. It is just an easier figure of speech.)

"Life is hardly worth living without love, in some form or other. Over the centuries, man has sadly lost this ability to love unconditionally. He thinks he is superior to animals and fishes, and he has little respect for plants or minerals. If mankind could only love all creatures, great and small, from the largest bear to the tiniest insect, the balance of the planet would be restored. Help nature to heal the planet, and give joy to all who live in harmony upon the Earth. Take time to think of others, not just of yourself, and help one another to a better life and a healthier future.

"Love is not just an expression of lust. It is a way of making someone feel special – to make your friends, family, loved ones and all the world feel you care about their well-being, their future, their lives. Love is the balance for all eternity, without love the world is a sad and lonely place.

"Love makes the world go round. It gives you a strength of purpose; it gives you the will to carry on when all seems forsaken. Give love everywhere you go, to everyone you meet, rich or poor, sad or happy, sick or well. Love can cure so many ills.

"Take the world by the hand, give our love to all, and spread it around the globe. Show love, compassion and thoughtfulness to everyone: especially to the sad, the lonely, the lost, the bereaved, the angry, the diseased, and the desolate. Show the entire world the Light of our love and bring everyone upon the planet together as a whole. Give everyone a chance to experience the joy of love, the delight of knowing someone cares unreservedly for them, and that no matter what they do there is someone who can see a glimmer of Light in their soul.

"Love is not an easy thing to achieve, especially unconditional love for all, but it is worth it if you try. There will be times when you feel you cannot love a person at all, but make an effort. Somewhere in their being is the slightest glimmer of Light, which is the kernel of a good soul, and if you nurture that kernel it will grow, and the Light will expand to fill his or her whole being.

"There is so much negativity in the world today, and a lot of people build up a wall of it around themselves – but deep in their hearts, there is a glimmer of hope. Give them love and they will respond. Like attracts like, remember. Give everyone the benefit of the doubt and see how they grow. Life is too short to bear grudges. Give love, Light and a smile to show people you care. Help everyone to understand about love, care and compassion.

"You are beautiful beings. Your Light shines from within you and your hearts are filled with love. Let everyone feel that love, and they will spill over with it in their lives, then they will start to show love to others. Love is an infectious thing: it traverses the world linking all colours, cultures, attitudes and temperaments. Love can conquer all. It can build hope and confidence. It can take away desolation and despair. Just a kind word, a smile, a thoughtful deed is all anyone needs to ignite that spark within themselves, giving them a purpose, a reason to live and make use of their lives for the future.

"Take the hands of the bereaved and show that love continues after life has ended. Show that it doesn't stop there, that it goes on into eternity. Love is not a relationship, it is a state of being. Love is a tremendously powerful force and everyone can show it, hold it and give it. It brings a smile to the saddest of souls. Go forth and show love to the world, and you will get it returned sevenfold.

"Help the world to be a better place. We would like you to visualise placing your hands and heart on the planet's trouble spots to heal their ills. Wherever you go, give of yourself: in your work, in your personal life, and in your home life. Give your all to everyone so they can feel the Light and the love emanating from your very being; then they will be encouraged to pass that feeling on to others in their own way. Love can traverse the world. Smile and the world smiles with you. Take your smile to the lives of all. Give everyone your smile and help them to feel that someone cares and there is hope for a better future.

"Life is for living: for living, loving and filling people's hearts with joy. Whoever you touch in your lifetime will feel the joy and Light from your being, and it will transform them. You are magical people. You are people of great Light and love. I know you may not realise this, but the Light of your higher self manifests in your smile and your embrace, so give them both to the world and help to heal its ills."

"So that is why Granny smiles at everyone!" Olivia interrupts.

"Your grandmother has a Healing smile, and so do you," he tells her, and continues.

"You all shine with a Light of love and caring – a Light which makes others feel special. You give them your best, so they glow and feel good about themselves. Love and light, that is what we are about, and it is now felt through you, and not just you, but a million like you. Wherever you go, it is spiralling outwardly and people know it is pure Light and joy.

"Everyone in the world needs to feel loved and cared for. Everyone in the world needs to feel needed and wanted, and you have the ability to make everyone feel special, as though they are the only person in the world who matters. Every single person will feel like that as you all link with each other. Our way is to love everyone: all races, creeds, intellects. No-one is too lowly to receive love: everyone has a Light within which shines when ignited by love. Take our Light to all corners of the Earth. We have enough Light to fill the world and you can carry this forward.

"The more that people raise their consciousness on the Earth and show that they care for their fellow man and beast, the sooner peace will reign supreme. We love you all, large and small, rich and poor, ill and well and wish for a brighter future for each and every one of you, a future filled with love. The smile of joy on the face of an innocent child is the smile we want to see on every one of you as you reawaken to the knowledge that life is great, and designed for you to live and enjoy.

"The world is a newspaper and every person a page. You have to read the whole page, even the small print, to understand that person completely. No-one does that: no-one reads anyone completely. They scan over the page, read the parts they like the look of, and walk away. There are so many facets to each person's character and so much is missed by not waiting, looking and taking the time to see all there is to see. Read *all* the pages, and you will understand so much more about everyone you meet."

Olivia likes that analogy.

Shomas looks at her tenderly. "You, on planet Earth, are all our children. We want you all to smile. We want you to hold your heads up high in the confidence that you know you are doing the right thing, casting off material wealth for a store of human kindness and happiness. We want you all to be happy, and to pass to this side in the rightful knowledge that all will be well for generations to come. Be confident in the knowledge that we hold the safety net for your life; you cannot fall once you look within and acknowledge your true purpose.

"Love is so profound; it is a beautiful thing given to man to blend his soul with another. Sadly, there are those who cannot love. They have brought with them the anger and decay of previous lifetimes of hurt and distress, which leave them in a void where they cannot be touched by love or compassion. They drag their ego around with them, hiding behind it in order to stop others from giving them kindness and love. Their ego is a metal shield of ill will; it encompasses their every thought. Such sadness and neglect destroys a soul. Some never clear their resentments, which cling to them like a disease though lifetime upon lifetime. The cycle needs to be broken in order to release them from this void. There are many souls who need to learn how to show and share unconditional love, opening their eyes to see the true path that will eventually take them home.

"All creatures were put on Earth to love each other – not just in a physical way to procreate, but in a gentle way, full of kindness and sincerity for every being on Earth. We need you to remember this.

"The world is your oyster, so to speak. You can have anything you like, as long as it is not to the detriment of another living being. You just have to wish it, and it is there, because this is the way things are, and always have been. Love is always there for you; it is just a case of opening your mind to it. Remember: peace and the Light of love is with you at all times."

Shomas sits down on the grass beside her. "Have you ever seen a dolphin?"

"Only in photographs and films," she answers, puzzled.

"You must try to go to see them," he advises. "Dolphins are very ancient souls who chose to come back to your Earth to reach the masses with their love and cheerfulness, in order to earn their 'wings' and a chance on our plane. They are wonderfully intelligent beings, as you probably know. If they could speak, they could tell you a thing or two about the world, the Universe and the power of love. Anyone who has swum with a dolphin will tell you of the affinity they have with human beings, and how healing it is to touch them, and share their love of fun and play. Dolphins help fishermen and swimmers, and care for the deep and all within it. Their goal is to show mankind how to love unconditionally.

"We love you all, with all our hearts, and hope you will grow to love us in return. You are always in our arms, and we hold you in much reverence. We care only for your welfare, and if you ask for our help we shall always be there. No matter what the situation, we shall be there with love, support and kindness to help you on your path to a better future.

"We hold your hand, leading you to better and greater things. We show you the way to walk with your head held high, confident that life is for living, loving and sharing. Comfort those less fortune, and make the world a better place for each person, in every land."

Shomas pauses for a moment as a group of beings come to the glade to add to the conversation.

"We treasure you all, and want you to know how much we care for your livelihood. Just trust us. Hold out your hand for us to help you. Think positive thoughts, have positive actions, and your life will be a dream come true, lived to the fullest potential you can muster. Bless you, our children of Light, bless you and we thank you for all you do in our name." *(The Elohim)*

Shomas takes over the conversation again. "Bring our love to your planet, Livvy, to show mankind just how glorious life can be with a little kindness and thoughtfulness towards others. The more love one gives, the more is received. If the world was full of love, it would be a much better place than it is now. So clear the negativity and put forward your love to heal and help the world and see what a difference it will make."

With that, Shomas rises to his feet, and makes a small bow of blessing.

"Oh Shomas, that was beautiful," Olivia tells him, deeply moved. "I felt the warmth of all the love whilst you were talking. It was just so powerful. You have given me a lot to think about, and to talk over with my grandmother."

Shomas smiles, he is pleased he is having an impact with his words. He then turns and vanishes from sight.

Olivia knows that all she is hearing now will affect how she lives the rest of her life. She now knows why her grandmother always seems so peaceful and so loving. Jane hardly ever has a bad word to say about anyone, and she smiles and chats to complete strangers. It all begins to fall into place.

Coming out of the meditation, Olivia returns to the room. Jane has come back in, and is standing by the window, deep in thought. The younger woman crosses the room and hugs her tightly.

"Hello darling, that was lovely, what has prompted this?" Jane enquires.

"Shomas's talk about Love made me realise how you live your life by his words, and just how much I love you. I now know why you chose that beautiful pink stone for me today."

They stand at the window wrapped in each others arms, enjoying the peace of the moment. It has been a really bonding experience, one Olivia will not forget in a hurry.

It has rained while Olivia was visiting with Shomas, but now the sun is breaking through the clouds and a rainbow arcs across the sky. Raindrops stand like jewels on a cobweb which has been spun across the window frame.

Remembering Shomas's words about slowing down and paying attention, she absorbs the beauty of the cobweb, the shifting clouds and the rain-soaked hills beyond. She sees a world filled with love and Light, and sighs with appreciation.

A small noise stirs them both, and they turn to see Chloe has managed to push open the door and is now sitting methodically washing herself within a ray of sunshine which has penetrated the clouds and is shining onto the carpet where the cat is basking in its warmth.

CHAPTER SEVENTEEN

RELIGION

Snow is falling, and the village is held in the still white hush of winter. There is a gentle dance of snowflakes and an eerie silence which is palpable as the layer of fallen snow muffles all sound. Most people are wrapped up warm indoors, quieting the normal rush of life.

Olivia elects to go to Jane's by train as the roads are icy and hazardous. By the time she arrives she looks like an Eskimo; her boots are encrusted in white and her face is hidden inside the folds of fur on the edge of her hood. Jane welcomes her, ushering her in to sit by the warmth of the hearth; she rushes off to make a warming pot of soup, with fresh bread straight from the oven.

Over the meal, they discuss family life and events of the past weeks. Then, once warm, Olivia is keen to go upstairs to speak to Shomas, as it has been quite a while since she last had the chance. The heating is on, so the room is nice and cosy. Jane comes up just long enough to make sure Olivia is comfortably settled, and hands her a large crystal to hold, which will amplify her link with Spirit. As Jane creeps quietly out of the room, Chloe trailing behind her, Olivia begins her meditation.

Shomas appears before her within moments and greets her warmly. "Today, we would like to talk to you of ancient religions, of writings handed down from generation to generation.

"King Constantine, a Roman Emperor in the 4th Century AD, is renowned as the person who brought Christianity to the masses, making it one of the major religions in the world today. He called the Council of Nicaea to decree what was acceptable, or not, to the Christian orthodoxy. The Romans of the time wanted to maintain their beliefs in their own Gods, so Constantine chose to change all the Pagan festivals into Christian ones in order to incorporate the new festivals into the lives of his people without disrupting the dates that they held dear. Many of the Christian religious festivals you know now originated in Pagan times. Easter, for example, derives from the earlier celebration of the Spring Equinox and the name taken from the Spring Goddess 'Eastre'."

Olivia had not known this, and asks Shomas to tell her more.

"If you could see beneath many of the churches in England," he responds, "you would find the remains of earlier Christian structures. These were often built upon the foundations of Roman temples, which themselves could have replaced Celtic Holy Places. In all probability, the history of such sites would date back thousands of years. You may also find that many of these buildings are built on the crossing of leylines, as man's earlier ancestors recognised these as a source of power.

"Churches were built to specific dimensions, and orientated to face the direction of the rising and setting sun in order to obtain the greatest sources of power and energy. Just as the pyramids were shaped to preserve life, so the churches' dimensions were designed to increase the energy within. Over the centuries, the reason for these specific dimensions has been lost to man, and the churches have become mere buildings for worship, instead of the power-houses for which they were designed. Restoring that power could raise the consciousness of the planet and lift the souls of all those who attend services in these buildings, to a greater state of awareness.

"Religion was originally designed to help man to have an understanding of creation and all it entailed, to help man understand his path through life, and to encourage him to work for the betterment of all. These days, however, differing faiths are so often the cause of conflict, and so much strife has been created in the world in the name of religion.

"When is mankind going to realise that you all come from the same source. You were all made in the same way, and it is high time you all got on together. Let the religions of the world merge into one belief system. If there was but one religion there would be very few wars, and that one path could lead the way to a better world.

"Some religions are trying to stem the flow of evil, but are unwilling to listen to New Age philosophy which aims to do the same. They group all 'alternative' religions together, not realising these all want the same things that they do: a better, more peaceful life for all, filled with Light and love. There is such a misguided element between religion and spirituality. Those who have taken religion into their lives believe that those who work with Spirit are the devil's workers, but nothing could be further from the truth.

"The main difference between religion and spirituality is that religion was made in the likeness of those who wished for mankind to believe in their one God and no other. It consists of a range of organised beliefs, practices and rules that are shared within each individual religion or church group.

"Spirituality, on the other hand, is more of an individual practice. It is a means of sensing a connection to something bigger than yourselves, along with a belief in a supernatural realm beyond the known and observable world. Recognising that life is more than the every-day, spirituality offers a chance to gain perspective on all aspects of life in every form, to pursue a quest for a sacred meaning and greater purpose to life, to relieve dependence on material things, and to find a sense of peace and a real interconnection to others of like minds.

"You all have an innate love of your God and of his ministries. In essence, those who carry spiritual love in their hearts are caring and loving to all lifeforms. All those who have found either religion or spirituality pray or find comfort in their own personal relationship with God, or their higher power. What you have to realise is that there is only one God, one Heavenly source, one Creator, one infinite power, with his Angels and Masters speaking to you all, giving you his messages of love and hope.

"Let the religions of the world unite in one voice. Let them raise that voice to heal the ills of the world, and to help the planet come to a time of great joy and peace. This is what religion is really for: to weld hearts and souls together in one united force for the betterment of all. Not to divide in fractious rebellion against one another. It is for all to believe in one God, one Creator, and the power of his will, for the good of every living thing.

"Now, I am going to speak specifically about Christianity," Shomas tells Olivia, "but as you study and read spiritual books, you will find similar stories within other religions.

"The writings of the Old Testament of the Bible pre-date the time of the Early Christians. They are the writings of the Emperors of the five kingdoms in place at the beginning of time on Earth. The Bible is essential reading as the words have a resonance, and if read correctly, impart a blessing as they interact with the reader's very being. The Bible is a record of a place in time where magic happened: where the principal players were blessed, and their words carried a reverence which has lasted to this day, and shall last beyond. Certain aspects of the Bible are written in a form of code, telling many truths to help man at this time. Read and re-read certain sections in depth. Study the Creation story, for example, and there you will gather a wealth of knowledge. This sounds extraordinary and it will take a leap of faith to understand. We have to acknowledge that the Bible has been written and rewritten over the centuries, and so some of it now is a document of the editors – but still, beneath the words lies an essence of truth that will last forever.

"The books of the Gospels of The Essenes and The Dead Sea Scrolls were very important; they told a lot of the story of Jesus as he was during his time on Earth. The Bible does not show much of the time between his birth and a few years before his death: what he did, the places he visited. But the truth is out there and the time is ripe for this to be known.

"The date given for the birth of Jesus, set to align with pagan winter festivals, was not the honest date of the birth of a major element in your biblical story. His birth was so nondescript: in a manger, in a lowly place; but his coming has stayed in the hearts and minds of millions through the ages and into this new millennium. His birth was divine law and his mother was pure as driven snow, gentle, tender and kind.

"The story of Jesus is an enigma. He was of humble birth, he was bought up as most boys of the time, in a lowly place, but he knew from the outset he was different, he knew he could help and heal others. If his brothers fell, he healed their cuts and bruises, and for him this was normal. His brothers accepted he could do this, so turned to him for help in all things.

"Jesus came to Earth as a man, an ordinary man – no airs and graces, with a humility all his own. But his coming was heralded by a star, and gifts, which were brought to his crib. He was a pilgrim whose lineage went back to the start of time. As a child he played, just as other children played – but on occasion he was drawn to hold court to his elders, as he saw the error of their ways. He lived a frugal life. His followers served at his feet, but never held him in awe. He never wanted that.

"Mary, his Mother, was blessed with more sons, and she brought them all up the same. They all ate the same bread, drank the same wine, and prayed to the same God in Heaven. But she knew her first born son was different. He was destined for great things – but she was scared he would upset the apple cart, stir up emotions in the powers of the time.

"When Jesus travelled to far-off lands, although she was fraught with worry and despair, she knew it was for the best. She heard nothing for years until stories of his work started to filter through the towns and cities. People spoke of his miracles, and she was quietly proud. She did not wave banners or sing songs in his name, but she held his magic in her heart with pride, as he traversed the world helping all in his path to grow and develop spiritually in his name.

"Man needed a role model, someone he could look up to – so Jesus chose to come to Earth, knowing his life would be short, but hoping to affect the lives of many. Little did he know, at that time, how his life would affect millions into the 21st century and beyond.

"At the time of his birth, pure Light was brought into his physical body. He was the chosen one, the one who would show man how to live a good life in the eyes of God. He was chosen as a beacon of Light and goodness, to represent all that is pure from our side. He hoped to affect mankind for a thousand years. Beyond that curve in the river, time is as invisible to us as it is to you. We delight in the longevity of the Bible and its stories: it is there forever now, etched in stone as a catalyst. It has rolled through the ages and will continue to do so.

"He vanished from the history books for many years, travelling the world offering his blessings to those who had never heard of his birth. He had never enjoyed such freedom before, a chance to be 'real', not an icon. He preferred the simple things of life: the enjoyment of good company, a nice warm welcome and a full stomach. After his travels, he knew he had to show his face and be repelled by those who had feared his coming. He wanted to be seen as a simple man, with simple tastes, who had only wanted to help others. Sadly, he was persecuted beyond reason by foolish men who had no respect for his humility.

"His time on the cross brought his name to everyone's lips. His tales of help and Healing became legend, showing that all he ever wanted was to help others, which was the best path to take. So now mankind can follow that path, or the path of his persecutors, and see which leads to Heaven!

"Jesus was the son of God, but what everyone has to realise is that all humankind are sons and daughters of God. The Second Coming will not be a physical coming, it will be a re-harmonising of the planet, bringing it back into resonance with our world and God himself.

"Jesus still walks the Spiritual path, and he still keeps a ministry for his followers. Some see him, some don't, but they feel his love and understanding in their lives every day. He has not returned to Earth for two thousand years, and is delighted that his teachings are still so much a part of life for so many at this time. He will one day tell everyone the truth of his life, but until then he keeps quiet. We thank you for all your trust and belief in everything we do to help humanity, and we want you to know Jesus is always with you all."

"The way you describe him really brings him to life for me Shomas!" exclaims Olivia.

The beautiful being smiles, pleased that his words have had this effect.

"On this very night in 2019," he adds, "there will be a light shining in the sky as brightly as that early star marking Jesus' birth, and this will herald a new beginning: the start of a move to enlighten and envision a better future for all mankind. Blessed be all of those who work in the Light and carry our strength through to mankind."

Shomas bows, preparing to leave, but Olivia doesn't want to let him go. She is thinking about the Easter story, and asks why this happened.

"Jesus wants you to know that he gave his life for the betterment of man," says Shomas. "He gave his life that man may be free of darkness and hatred. But, sadly, the purpose of his passing has been long forgotten by those who now only work in the name of the dark Lord.

"He is pleased you have thought of him, but asks that you do not feel sorrow. He wants you to know he is in the Realms of Light with his Father and watches over you all with Love. Those who did this to him have all long passed and been forgiven.

"Always remember to forgive. This is important. Do not bear grudges or let resentment fester, for this is not his way. Forgive and forget is the way of our Lord. Forgive and forget all transgressions, all slights and hurts. 'They know not what they do'."

Shomas decides to stay and speak a little longer.

"Many of those whose atrocities are playing out across the world believe they are doing this in the name of their God. Some are even giving up their own lives to take the lives of other innocent people, in the belief they will go straight to Heaven.

"Everyone comes to Heaven eventually, but not all come immediately. Heaven is a state of mind. It is a journey through the afterlife to realms of purity and love, where Angels bless you all and keep you safe. And Heaven isn't only for the Earth, it is for the Universe.

"If anyone has their own cross to bear, they often have to go to penitence first to make right all they did wrong. All the perpetrators of evil need to be brought into the Light and shown the true path to goodness and mercy so they may return to Earth and work to make recompense for their sins.

"Those of you working in the Light have chosen to return to Earth and put yourselves through the rigours of life in order to help others less knowledgeable to understand our work so that they may return to their true path.

"We want you all to work together to save mankind from the evil influences which are attempting to control the Earth, trying to win minds and souls for evil purposes. We need you all to pray for protection and give out emanations of love.

"Jesus loves you all, no matter what religion, what race. He is a symbol of Light and Love in every religious book. You will find his name changes from book to book, but his essence and his message is carried through all beliefs.

"Take time today to praise your God in his glory. To take a few minutes out of your day to thank him for the flowers, for the trees, for the blue skies and the rain. Thank him for the wind which blows away the cobwebs of life, bringing fresh air in readiness for spring. Realise that everything has a purpose, be it good or bad; everything has a reason, which makes itself clear in time. Only the Creator knows the purpose at this time, only he can see what is to come. There is peace in the wings, waiting to show its face: a thousand years of peace for mankind. A peace so close and so profound that it is tangible."

"Now we have talked long enough and I must take my leave for today."

"Thank you so much Shomas!" Olivia calls as the gentle soul departs.

When she goes downstairs to talk to Jane, her grandmother recalls a programme she saw on television in which members of different religions were brought together to see if they believed in the same God. The older members of the panel insisted that 'their God' was unique, whilst the younger members believed that, despite the cultural variations, it was all the same God. These younger people were more at ease with neighbours from all the different religions, recognising that we are all brothers and sisters in the eyes of one God.

"Maybe the youth of today will sort out the problem at long last," adds Jane. "My Guides tell me that all religions need to realise that there are many paths to the top of the mountain. Some are winding and some are straight, but they all lead to the same place: to God, the Creator, the One all-seeing, all-hearing entity, or power over all, who apparently has a 'plan' for the way life has been created and how it will be better again."

As Jane and Olivia settle into an interesting discussion about religion in all its different guises, the light starts to fade and the snow keeps falling. Olivia isn't worried about the weather as she had already planned to stay the night. She will have a good night's sleep under Jane's warm quilts...and then tomorrow she will see Shomas again.

CHAPTER EIGHTEEN
SPIRITUAL HIERARCHY

Early the next morning, Jane and Olivia sit by a re-laid fire in the lounge, still wrapped in snugly warm dressing gowns. It is still bitterly cold and snow has settled on the window panes like an classic Dickensian image from *A Christmas Carol*. Neither of them feel the inclination to move, as the fire is so warming and the view out of the window is quite picturesque. Chloe is purring on Olivia's lap as Jane begins to read the magnificent writings from Shomas on Angels and Archangels.

"'Angels are always around you, no matter what your beliefs may be. Even if you do not believe in Angels, they are always there. They are non-denominational beings of pure energy and love, carrying a spark of the Divine within. It is the same Divine spark that you carry within you, the same part of the God/Goddess essence which you were given when your soul was created, which is why you and the Angels have a strong connection at a deep energetic level. There are thousands of Angels, some of whom are Guides. Everyone has Angels and Guides watching over them, and if you meditate you may sense them around you.

"'Sadly, for many, their ego, thoughts, and beliefs may tell them there is no such thing as Angels, or that they could never communicate with them. But, believe me, Angels are around to help protect you and to serve as messengers from God at all times. They are part of a team of spiritual help and support who are always on hand, whenever you ask.

"'We speak of the Hierarchy of Angels working with Earth, but there is no actual hierarchy. Angels exist on all different levels, but none is superior to another. Our world doesn't need the power echelons that your world thrives on; our figurehead and source of all is the Creator, by whatever name you know him, he oversees everything. He built the Halls of Wisdom and created the paradise we call home.'"

"But what is the Hierarchy of Angels?" Olivia asks Jane.

"Well," her grandmother replies, "there's the Cherubim, Seraphim and Thrones, all of whom work closest to God. And Dominions, Virtues and Powers who are each assigned to specific planets and work with the Angels below them. Then there is also the Heavenly choir, the Principalities who watch over cities and nations, and the Archangels who all have specific roles there and with mankind. But Shomas can explain this better than I. Why don't you go and ask him?"

Olivia goes upstairs, gets dressed, and is soon ready to speak to Shomas. Settling in her usual chair, her meditation takes her to the Crystal Cave, where the beautiful being is waiting for her.

"Good morning Olivia, it is lovely to speak with you," he says. "Today, we wish to talk to you of life in heaven. We need you to be able to explain it to non-believers, to allow them the peace and tranquillity of knowing that the transition that you call 'death' has a purpose and a happy ending.

"We have so much to share! It is all waiting like a tap to pour out to you, a wealth of knowledge and quantifiable facts which will prove the existence of our world, and that life exists after death and on other planets across the cosmos. We have so much to tell you, so much information to share with you and the world. We shall, over time, prove that life exists elsewhere in the Universe, and that we watch over you all. It will be fact-driven and accountable, so you will be proven right in believing in us. We have an extraordinary range of spiritual information that you can access from here. But firstly, we would like to tell you about The Masters.

"Above the Angelic realms are the realms of the Masters: those who attain to higher knowledge but still maintain links with all humanity. At this level, they are able to see the wider view of your world's past and future, and links with other worlds. The Masters are very knowledgeable beings who love to make contact with the Earth and impart their teachings. They are a race of beings of remarkable gentleness and calm, and they always bring their love, their Light and their blessings to all of you who work for us.

"Some Masters have had lifetimes in many Universes including yours. They are a delight to work with, and a delight to hear when they impart their knowledge. They are Guides of tremendous power, and help mankind enormously. They love their links with the spiritual beings on Earth who wish for contact with them.

"The Masters of the Universal Light, who have never been on Earth, are eternal Spirits growing and developing in their field. Their power is phenomenal. Although they are not from the Earth, they know of it and of all its peoples.

"The White Brotherhood and the Elohim are singularly wonderful groups of souls who work solely for the benefit of man. Both groups see all, hear all, and do their best to lead mankind away from the brink of destruction.

"The White Brotherhood are highly evolved beings who lived on Earth at one time and are part of the Spiritual Hierarchy overseeing the Earth and other planes. Many Ascended Masters belong to the White Brotherhood and the Order of Melchizedek, and bring Light into the hearts and minds of humanity to further their development. They guide, protect, inspire, heal and assist in the progress of mankind.

"These advanced Spiritual beings of Light also assist humanity in its evolution. They are supernatural beings of great power who spread spiritual teachings and are often known as the Masters of the Ancient Wisdom, or Ascended Masters. They are in charge of renewing or reawakening creation.

"The Elohim are mighty Beings of Love and Light who use the creative powers of thought, feeling and word to help mankind and planet Earth. They carry the highest vibration of Light that you can comprehend in your state of evolution. They are the most powerful aspect of the Consciousness of God. Jesus' teachings were in a large part sent from them. They have access to those who want to work with them on Earth. They are Supreme Celestial beings, part of the planetary logos. Lord St. Germain and Jesus are their ambassadors.

"Angels and Archangels fill our world with joy and love for each other and for mankind as a whole. Angels are those closest to humankind, responsible for each single living being. Angels, especially, keep a watchful eye on those of you on the Earth plane who are working for the Light in order to help and guide you. They also watch all mankind, in the hope they will be recognised and called upon for help in times of need. Angels have a glow which attracts new visitors, to our level upon their demise, where these souls will be led and directed in order to help them settle into their new home.

"Angels were placed in Heaven to be heralds or messengers on high, letting man know about the glory of the Creator. Over the aeons, Angels have matured and grown in stature and ability, reining supreme over all the Guides and Helpers who now work for mankind as a whole. Angels guide and direct, like a conductor of a musical orchestra, to ensure every person on Earth has the help they need to follow a safe and true path throughout their lives.

"Angels can see all. They appear to those in danger and guide them to safety. They collect souls and take them home, showing the pathway to the Light. There are an infinite number of Angels, all with their own personalities and divine qualities, each designated to help those in need. And above the Angels are the Archangels, who can help man in so many different ways if he will only ask.

"Take Archangel Michael, for example, who carries a mighty sword. If you wish to sever your link to an uncomfortable situation, you can ask him to 'cut the ties that bind': just visualise his sword cutting the umbilical cord connecting your solar plexus to the antagonist. As Archangel Michael smites the connection with his sword in your mind's eye, you will see the cord break and the link between you and the other person involved will sever. This is a good thing to do after the break up of a relationship, as it frees you and the other person involved from any unwanted baggage which may have grown between you. It sets you both free to move on with your lives.

"Archangel Raphael can be called upon to help with Healing, especially in war-torn parts of the world. Just ask him to lay his hands on the land to heal it, and to heal its people, giving them the gift of safe passage to the future.

"Melchizedek was an instigator of settling life on Earth in the beginning. He brings his Light back now to lift the energy of the planet and all upon her back to its original blueprint.

"We suggest you read a good book about Angels to learn more about what they do to help you in your daily work on Earth; and also how they help other beings on other planets across the cosmos."

"I will," Olivia promises, and Shomas continues.

"The Spiritual Realm is unseen by human eyes, but you are all connected to it – and what goes on in the Spiritual Realm directly affects your physical world. Spirit Guides are non-physical beings who are assigned to you, often before you are born, to help nudge and guide you through your life. You are more than physical entities: you possess a soul, a Spirit destined to exist for eternity. Spirit Guides help that soul to traverse its Earthly path before returning home.

"There is no hierarchy in our world, just levels of existence and knowledge. There is no kudos in being higher up the ladder; it is just a different level for different knowledge.

"Once you, who live in the light, come home, you will move beyond the basic levels of existence presented to the rest of mankind and be swiftly elevated to places of special interest to your ancestry. Dependant upon how spiritually advanced you are on Earth, you may enter at a level which will progress your learning. You will be delighted to go straight to work – unlike those who have had no contact with us and must ascend slowly through the veils. There are so many different ways of working with Spirit, and we shall show you many variations of our work, as we would like you to learn and advance in more fields than one. You may be offered the opportunity to become a Guide and watch over a soul on Earth, or you may want to teach in the Halls of Learning to offer wisdom to others, who wish to further develop their spiritual growth.

"All Spirit Guides working with humanity are evolved souls who devote their time to helping each individual one of you during each lifetime. These Guides are at varying levels of consciousness themselves. Some may be highly-evolved Ascended Masters, and others might be Spirits who happen to be Masters in certain areas. Angels or Spirit Guides may appear to have male or female energy, though in reality there is no distinction: they are neither, just energy. They may have had physical incarnations, may even have had lives on Earth at some time in their history, or they may never have taken human form. You may be the only person they are guiding, or they may be helping other people as well. Your Guide might even be a deceased relative who wishes to help your life progress – although such souls do not normally act as Guides, but, rather as non-physical champions, looking out for you in the best way possible.

"Before birth, you choose the Spirit Guides who will best help you on your path: those who are selected, are willing and able to guide you through the events and experiences you are expecting to undertake during this specific lifetime.

"As your soul never incarnates completely, whilst you are in an Earthly body you also exist in higher dimensions, this is your Higher Self. Your Higher Self helps to select the Guides, who will have access to all the levels of information which will be of benefit to you in the life you are about to begin.

"You may have many Guides around you at one time. Some will stay with you throughout your entire life, and some are transient, popping in every now and again, only staying whilst needed to help you with specific areas of your life, or specific goals you are trying to achieve. Once the task or goal is complete, they will move on to help someone else. When your Spirit Guides help you, they tune in to your energy to direct you to fulfil your Earthly mission. They see the full perspective of your life, and can help you stay on track to learn this life's lessons.

"Spirit Guides tend to work together, with each one performing their individual role as a part of a team. They are obviously pure spirit, but if you are to see them, they will take on an appearance with which you can resonate. You may have a Power Animal too, which will stay to guide and protect you. Again, there are books you can read to learn about these wonderful creatures."

Olivia nods. Jane has talked about Power Animals before.

"Spirit Guides are available at all times, so remember to ask them for their help," Shomas advises. "Neither they, nor the Angels, can do anything without your asking first. As we have discussed before, you have been given free will to do as you please throughout your time on Earth, and the Angels and Guides cannot interfere or make decisions for you. But if you turn to them for help they will be there instantly, delighted to aid you in any way they can, to bring comfort and protection.

"For those who are not confident speaking directly to their Spirit Guides, dowsing with a pendulum is another way to ask for advice. Pendulums answer 'yes', 'no' or 'neither', so be precise, with no ambiguity in your query. As your grandmother explained to you: ask simple questions initially, in order to gain insight as to how the pendulum swings for each option. It is useful to carry your pendulum with you so that you can use it at any time. Don't forget to cleanse it regularly to ensure the clarity of the answers. Also, trust your intuition, your first instinct, as it is sent from here."

Olivia is pleased to hear this as she has been practising with her pendulum and is beginning to recognise her natural intuition.

Shomas continues, "A Guardian Angel is a Guide who will always help you to follow your true path to your destiny. You may or may not know intuitively that they are there – but if you can listen to the small, quiet voice they place in your soul, you will find that it can warn you to detour from a perilous path which will keep you safe from harm. We need you all to learn to listen to the inner voice warning you of peril. Then you will become accustomed to asking for our help in other life matters too.

"Everyone has a Guardian Angel, with no exceptions, although many people do not know it. Sometimes you may even have more than one. This Angel's role is to protect you physically, emotionally and spiritually, and to offer comfort. Guardian Angels all have their own specific souls to care for, coming into your life to watch over you and to help whenever needed. Your Guardian Angel will constantly stay with you from birth until your transition back home, with a love that is unconditional. This Angel offers guidance, protection and nurturing for your individual soul throughout your travail on Earth, and can warn you of any impending danger.

"Over the ages, man has, for the most part, lost his ability to talk directly with his Guardian Angel. This was once a normal conversation, but you lost this ability to communicate freely such a very long time ago. Yet your Guardian Angels are always there to answer any prayer or a plea for help and assistance, instantly. They are often on a higher vibration than the other Spirit Guides surrounding you.

"We wish that you could all be aware of the beauty of the Angelic Realm! Choirs of Angels sing to your glory, bringing our world to yours for just a second of light and joy. Our lives here resonate to the sound of Angels, and harps of purest gold create our song of Love for all Creation. It is true Manna from Heaven.

"From our vantage point, we can see all worlds, all galaxies, all universes, and the billions of life forms created therein. Our world is infinite and there are no boundaries. We exist on so many different levels[8]; every person being an infinitesimal part of a much bigger system than you realise, and once you arrive here you can learn so much more than you can on Earth.

"Life is beautiful on this plane, but we worry so about all of you that we spend most of our time on the lower dimensions[7] instilling the knowledge which will help to allay problems for the consciousness of your world.

"Watchtowers were put in place for man at the beginning of time, as it was seen at the start he would need protection. Now these watchtowers are evolving: all the Archangels of Light are holding mankind encircled in their wings for added protection. Once darkness has fallen from grace, these Archangels will return to work for the betterment of humanity instead of just protecting it."

Suddenly, Shomas takes a step back as a huge being of bright Light steps forward. Olivia gasps, but she is not afraid, and Shomas is proud of her quiet courage.

"I am Lord Metatron," he says, his very being pulsing with radiance. "I am a pure soul of little worth in the great scheme of things – but my name, with the names of others of similar worth, has long be known to humankind, for we wield the web of the Ancients to hold the Light on Earth. As a united group we are All. We hold the energy of the Ancient world in your place on Earth. We bring our Light, our energy and our love to breathe life into your soul. Take this Light, this Love and this Energy out into the world; share it with enthusiasm and skill to ensure even those in the grey areas pick up on this Light.

"Light was extinguished from your planet many, many years ago – but thanks to all Lightworkers[3] currently incarnated on the Earth, the Light is back, and with a vengeance. All the Masters of Light wield swords of Light, and the might of the Lord our God, to smite the darkness across the globe. Resist all temptation of the dark-side in order to bring your worth to the people of Christ. Show the Light to all who wish to work under our wings of Love."

Metatron vanishes as quickly as he came, and before Olivia has even caught her breath, Shomas steps forward again. She meets his eyes, aware he is about to say something of great importance.

"You are a Lightworker," he tells the young woman, "as your grandmother has been before you. Lightworkers are those who work in the Light and for the Light on Earth – helping others to find their true path, to ease conflict in their lives, and endeavouring to bring mankind and Planet Earth to a place of peace. We are honoured to work with you in this way.

"You, dear one, are a daughter of the Light. You have been on our radar for millennia and have held the Light for many lifetimes as a High Priestess dedicated to our work. You were in the Temple of Isis at the time of the Pharaohs, so you have a place in our realm already; it is your birthright. Your true worth is far higher than you realise. We love and cherish you, and we want you to know we shall always be with you in your lifetime on the Earth and when you come home."

"I think I understand," she responds, trying to keep her voice steady. What he has just told her is extraordinary, yet deep within her she knows it is the truth.

Shomas gives her a look eloquent with love. "I shall take my leave of you now. We will talk again soon." His departure is slower than Metatron's, but soon Olivia is alone.

She pulls her consciousness back to the quiet room, before she rushes downstairs to speak to Jane. She wants to know so much more about Guides and Angels, and what it means to be a Lightworker.

Jane sits her granddaughter down in the alcove of the lounge where she keeps all her books, then searches for one on Angels in the overcrowded shelves. Finding the volume she wants at last, she passes it to Olivia; then she pulls up a chair and tells her what she has learnt over the years.

"Guardian Angels carry us through our darkest hours, and watch over us as we evolve and grow. I am lead to believe that the light in Heaven is infinitely brighter than the light on Earth. In this light, Spirits and Angels radiate in glorious colours so they may recognise one another and the work they share.

"Spiritual Guidance and its effects show in many ways throughout our daily lives: for example, a feeling of discomfort and ill ease are ways our bodies show they are out of balance with the outside world. When we follow proper guidance, it means we rest when we are tired, eat when we are hungry and take care of life's circumstances at all times. When we listen to our internal messages we will rarely find ourselves out of balance.

"Spiritual Guidance can be heard, seen or felt, and is unique to every single person here on Earth. It is guidance direct from our Higher Self, our soul, our spirit, our true essence, directed by the Angels and Guides.

"We are blessed with the connection to Spirit Guides throughout our lives," Jane adds. "Each Guide is a Light being who works for our highest good, connecting to us closely in each experience throughout our lifetime. They will leave us when we reached the level required for our own spiritual growth, allowing other Guides to come in to assist with the continuance of that human journey. Our Guides do a lot of positive work behind the scenes, and we are truly blessed to have them with us.

"Our Spirit Guides can see what is to come; they know the plan we each follow, as it is mapped out in advance. They can warn us when we are heading into trouble, but they cannot tell us too much in advance, for that would prevent us from learning the things we are here to learn."

Jane pauses. Olivia is looking quizzical, so she chooses her next words carefully, wanting her granddaughter to understand fully.

"The important thing to remember, Livvy, is not to let your imagination limit access to the Universe and all it offers. It is there for you to take all you require – not in a grabbing sense, but to be able to access anything that you need for your spiritual growth and development. There are Angels for everything and everyone. Just ask for an Angel's help, and they will be there to hold your hand and give you the support you need. They are always eager to assist us and never tire of our asking."

"Have Angels been around me all this time?" Olivia asks.

"Yes," Jane confirms, "though it is only now you are opening up to sensing their presence. Did I ever tell you of my visit to Greece, where I think I saw an Angel?" Olivia shakes her head, so Jane tells her the story.

"I was on the Island of Rhodes with my partner, and we had walked for miles up into the mountains to a monastery. There was a wood, near the top, which looked so quiet and peaceful until we disturbed the silence. Butterflies lay dormant on the trees, the brown backs to their wings merging with the tree bark, lying unseen until our movement caused them to fill the forest with colour. The air exploded with thousands of salmon tinted wings fluttering around us.

"It was quite a climb to the top of the hill, and I was exhausted by the time we arrived at the monastery. After stopping for a drink and freshly cooked doughnuts prepared by the monks, we tried to get a taxi back down to the beach – but the drivers were all waiting for other passengers they had brought up the hill and were not interested in taking us anywhere. We walked down to the coast, strolled along the sandy beach, then back uphill to our accommodation. In the evening, we took another walk to a local restaurant for a meal, but on the journey down I started to feel unwell, so we hailed a taxi back to our room.

"The next morning, we decided to go by bus into Rhodes town – but the bus was packed, so we had to stand. I was near the back, 'strap hanging', when my arm started to go numb. I swapped hands, but then the other arm went numb. I could feel a fizzy kind of numbness creeping across my forehead and down my nose. I must have shown my panic, as someone sitting near me stood up and let me have their seat. As soon as I sat down the numbness crept up my legs. The other passengers were beginning to worry about me – but they indicated to my partner not to take me off the bus until it reached the main town, which had a hospital where he could take me.

"I just sat on that bus getting increasingly panicked until we reached the terminal. By then, I was so paralysed that I couldn't speak. I had to be carried off the bus and placed on a seat by the roadside.

"My partner was about to go off to find a telephone and call for an ambulance when a man walked up to us. 'I recognise those symptoms,' he said in excellent English. 'She has sunstroke. Go and get me as much ice as you can'. My partner duly rushed off to the nearest bar and came back with buckets of ice. Then, apologising for putting his hands all over me, the man started to rub ice all over my body, legs, and arms, also putting ice cubes in my hands and on my feet. I was terrified. My mother had had a stroke many years before, at about the same age that I was then, and the symptoms seemed similar. This man said he lived in Lindos, which was the other end of the island; he had come to Rhodes Town to get his car tax renewed. He had just been passing by when he saw my predicament and decided to help.

"I couldn't move a muscle, so he just continued rubbing ice all over me. He did this for over two hours! He then sent my partner to get a glass of pure squeezed orange juice with a straw, and when it was obtained, he kept trying to open my mouth to accept the straw. Eventually I could open my mouth just slightly, and I started to swallow the refreshing drink. The man, whose name I never did get to know, advised us that the vitamin C would be very beneficial.

"About another hour later, when I could make small movements with my fingers, he said he knew I would be okay. Then, as quickly as he had arrived, he disappeared into the crowd, without giving me a chance to thank him properly for helping me. I am sure he must have been an Angel sent to help me: because of the time he arrived, just as the bus had dropped me off, and the way he just vanished hours later. He saved my life and I shall always be so grateful. A while later when I was well enough to walk into the town, we went to a local taverna and I had a few more large glasses of freshly squeezed orange juice. Then we returned to our accommodation, where I slept like a baby for hours. The next day I was up and about as usual, and able to continue our holiday without this event affecting me at all. It was so amazing – a true miracle!!

"You must have been terrified Granny. What an incredible story," Olivia exclaims.

"I know," Jane responds, smiling. "Remember, whenever you are travelling, always ask Angels to surround you and to guide your way. They will stay with you and protect you throughout your journey, I always take the time to do it now. And, I wear a hat and carry a bottle of water in the hot sun!"

Jane stops for a moment, thinking gratefully of the man who had helped her that day. He really was a saviour. Then she is reminded of another way that Angels can help in daily life.

"Have you heard of the 'Parking Angel'? Just ask for a space near where you have to be," Jane advises with a grin. "It seems cheeky, but they help you to find one every time, if they can. Either there will be a space waiting for you, or a car will pull out just as you arrive – its incredible. Also, it is said that if you find a white feather it is a sign that the Angels are watching over you, so do always watch for them. It is a real delight and honour to find one."

"Oh, I love that! I shall definitely watch for one," Olivia confirms.

Jane also has a little warning. "You also need to be aware that there are a lot of good spirits, but there are also bad spirits on the lower spiritual vibrations, who may affect your energy, so it is advisable for you to protect yourself with a quiet prayer, or by envisioning yourself encircled within an imaginary protective shield of Light and goodness. If your Guides are working well for you, they will protect you from any bad entities, but you need to protect yourself as well.

"After meditation or working with Spirit," Jane explains, "I am aware that my aura is very 'open' so, as I have said before, I always close all my chakras to protect myself. I do this by imagining a circle encompassing a cross of Light on each chakra, back and front, and then I put myself inside a protective bubble of Light before going outside into the everyday world." Jane demonstrates, and suggests Olivia does this after each visit with Shomas. "Linking to Spirit opens your Light for all to see, which may attract dubious energy. Aligning your chakras will bring your body into harmony with the Light."

"My, that's a lot to remember and a lot of effort," Olivia observes, "but if it keeps you safe, it must be worth it."

"There are so many different ways to close yourself down," Jane adds. "For example: putting on a purple cloak, zipping up your chakras, or visualising each one closing like a lotus. So many different ways, and none any better than the rest. Just use whichever you are most comfortable with, and which you feel will give you the best security. Now, let's practice together."

Olivia follows Jane's leave and closes herself down, then the two women leave the room. The snow has finally stopped falling, but it is still very cold outside. Jane makes a pot of tea, then they take their warm drinks back into the cosy lounge, settling by the fire to continue talking. Jane decides to discuss the Angelic Rays, sharing more information from Shomas.

"There are seven different light rays which are classified as the metaphysical system of colours, each corresponding to different Angels," she explains. "In the Bible, there is a description of seven Angels who stand before God. There are seven main chakras, which to my understanding is why there are seven colours. Shomas told me, 'The seven rays can be blended and sent across the Universe to enlighten and maintain Light within the hearts and minds of many, across the solar system. It is important to maintain and hold this Light in order to keep mankind on the straight and narrow towards world peace'.

"Shomas defines the rays like this: Pink is the Ray of Love and Peace. Blue is the Ray of Pure Spirit and Protection. Red is the Ray of Knowledge. Orange is the Ray of Emotion and Creativity. Green is the Healing Energy of the Cosmos. Purple is the Ray of Strength and Healing for Heart and Mind. Yellow is perfect for Wisdom and Initiations into Spiritual work; it holds the energy of the Light beings who perform the Initiation. Then there is White, which is created by the combination of all Rays; it brings the Light of generations of Healers, Soothsayers and Ancients into one – to be laid bare before the souls of all on Planet Earth and on other Planets of Life. The White Light is the one true Light. It is the Light of the One God, the True God, the Creator of all things. It is the be all and end or beginning of all Light: purest Harmony, Light, Love and Healing.

"Each Ray is modulated to shine at its optimum strength in order to blend, amalgamate and create magic. This is pure; this is something to fill the hearts and minds of all with Energy, Love and Light, making them purer and more attuned to their place in the Cosmos."

Olivia listens to the description of the different Rays in amazement. Each day brings new wonders to her life and new knowledge to absorb and retain. Then she remembers Shomas mentioning Power Animals, and she wants to know more.

Jane is happy to explain. "Animals have, since earliest times, been used as totems. For example, the lion represents strength or the lamb for purity. Animals can be found in the zodiac as well as in the Chinese calendar. They appear as symbols representing countries, and in many advertisements especially those for cars. Power Animals are used a lot in Shamanic rituals, but they also appear in our lives to represent the natural aspects of our soul.

"When we call for a Power Animal, Spirit provides us with whatever we need. The animal that is chosen for us may not be the one we would have chosen ourselves, but it represents an instinctive part of who we are becoming, so we need to recognise its worth. Your Power Animal may stay in your aura to guide and protect.

"My Power Animal is a kestrel," Jane adds. "I first met him in a meditation, where he and I became one; and as I flew, I could see and recognise the markings on his chest. It was the most amazing experience swooping, and flying like a bird.

"Once, when I was asked to do some Earth Healing, I went to my selected coastal path to find the exact place I needed to work on, and suddenly a kestrel flew over from the land to the side of me. He hovered over a particular spot, about a hundred yards in front of me, and did not move until I reached it. When I was precisely beneath him, he swooped and flew off. I could not have asked for a better indicator.

"Another time, I was working in a different area to heal the land, and as I drove away, a kestrel was sitting on a road sign right in the middle of the roundabout I had to use to get home – another indication that I must have been working in the right place."

"How amazing," Olivia says, her eyes wide. Her life has changed so much since she has been allowed to share in this magic. Would she have a Power Animal of her own one day? She has a million more questions, as usual, and she and Jane chat late into the night.

CHAPTER NINETEEN
DIFFERENT LEVELS OF EXISTENCE

Christmas has come and gone, the fuss and celebration short lived. Jane had spent a relaxing time with her family, thoroughly spoilt by their kindness and generosity, but she is back in her own home now, looking forward to Olivia spending a couple of days with her between Christmas and New Year.

She ensures that the house is lovely and warm, with a roaring fire in the hearth, on the day Olivia arrives. It is freezing outside, and a thick fog obscures the view. Jane hears Olivia's car moving very slowly and carefully into the drive, so rushes to the door to welcome her granddaughter in from the cold.

"Hi, darling. Do come and snuggle down by the fire. You look chilled to the bone!"

"What a scary drive! The fog is so thick that everyone was driving at a snail's pace," Olivia reports. "I am so glad to be here, Granny and it looks very cosy, thank you."

They take seats on either side of the hearth and chat while Olivia thaws. Neither is inclined to move for a while as it is so comfortable. Chloe has settled herself on the mat in front of the fire, licking her paws and relishing the warmth. Olivia's eyes are bright, and Jane knows she is ready for her next lesson.

"Shomas has asked me to talk to you today about the different levels of existence," Jane begins. "I learned about this a very long time ago, when I first started to get writing from him. He explained that the spiritual plane is here, sharing the same Earth space as us, just on a different vibration. Our planet is a three-dimensional object, with us as three-dimensional beings on this low vibratory level, living and working on its surface.

"All around us, unbound by the limitations of walls and boundaries, are Spirit beings at various levels of development. We cannot see them (unless we are psychic) as their vibratory speed is far higher than ours, but they can see and influence us – that is, if we want to listen. I shall read to you what he told me at that time," Jane offers, opening a book of the most exquisite writing. Her own handwriting is poor from years of scribbling teaching notes, but the writing from Shomas is distinctly different: the finest of scripts, delicately written onto each page.

She turns to the section she wants to share, and starts to read....

"'Here, there are so many levels of Light: and as your consciousness raises, so does your Spirit. Each level is lighter and more loving than the last, until you are pure Light and love, with wings of purest gold.

"'I wish to talk to you about the etheric body. This is a part of you; it is your essence; it is your whole being. The physical body is but a shell which keeps you in your three-dimensional world.

"'At the time of passing from your current life, the two parts of your body separate. The Light body leaves the material body, the three-dimensional image that has been 'yourself' for this lifetime. As the etheric body remoulds itself outside of the physical body, it is attached by a fine thread or cord of Light. This holds the two parts together as you begin to make your transitional journey from one life to another. It has been likened to a journey through a tunnel, and is, in fact, your journey down the lifeline which links your old life to your new. As you reach the end, there will be before you a beautiful Light, beckoning you to the joys beyond. At that moment, the moment you on earth call 'clinical death', the line will break and leave your shell behind to enable your spirit to go on its way to a new future: to a rebirth into our plane; a birthday on our side, if you like. The etheric body will then get a sense of lightness and freedom as it loses the three-dimensional suit of armour it has worn on the Earth plane. It will be free to return from whence it originally came.

"'When someone dies on the Earth plane, many religions counsel wearing black, and there is such sorrow felt for the passing of that soul. The grief isn't only for the one who has passed, but also for those who have been left behind. They grieve because they will miss the person they love. They grieve for lost moments, words left unsaid, a missed hug, a kiss or farewell embrace. Many do not get to say a last goodbye and this eats at their heart. But for the soul who has passed, there is no such sorrow; they are going on to pastures new, to a world long last remembered.

"'Do not grieve for those who have gone. Rejoice in their freedom; rejoice in the knowledge you will see them again – not in the physical realm but in the world of Spirit, the land beyond your present understanding. Your loved ones are in our arms, and their hearts will stay with you forever.

"'We know it is very hard, but try not to continue to grieve for months after your loved one has gone because it retards the progress of a newly-passed soul. Yes, that person will miss the people they left behind, but now they are free. They are no longer encumbered by the leaden body, which weighed them down to the Earth. They are light: they have no illness, no stress, no memories of any hurt and they are free to watch all the loved ones they have left behind. They are also able to see all those they thought gone forever: to be with souls they never thought they would see again, to meet with everyone that they have loved who has passed before. They are also free to learn at the feet of the Ancients, who have wisdom beyond imagining.

"'No-one should be afraid of dying. You need to understand that it is not a death, it is a rebirth. When you arrive in Heaven it is a 'coming home' to the realm of spirit, and you will recognise it as home as all the memories of your previous lives flood back.'"

Jane looks up and interjects, "This reminded me of two lines of a famous hymn which says something like 'How shall man learn to greet death, as a friend, as a new beginning not an end'. So apt."

She returns to Shomas's writing "'There is so much to do here, in the world of Spirit, and aeons of time to do it in, so there is no rush, no hurry, no stress, just the joy of knowing. You can look back in awe at the lives you have led, and the trials and tribulations you endured, relishing in the freedom that being in Spirit brings.

"'Friends and family here throw a party at your re-birth into the Spirit world. So whilst there is sorrow when a soul passes on Earth, we delight in greeting that soul back into the fold. So rejoice for those who pass to a better life, rejoice in their freedom and unfettered pleasure. Sing their praises, remember their accomplishments, and relish in the joy of having had them in your life. Relinquish sorrow and pain, for we do not have that here and wish you did not have it on your plane. We are alive and well here, and you will see us all again.

"'Many Middle Eastern religions have retained the knowledge that a life exists after death: that a person doesn't just fade away into nothing at the end of their time on Earth. There are many religions around your world in which people believe that the soul should be sent on its last journey with rejoicing. Practitioners of these religions understand that life is eternal, a continuing process where you learn from your mistakes and expand your awareness and knowledge. They understand that there is work to be done and lessons to be learned ready for your return to Earth, when you will further your development and grow within yourself for the betterment of yourselves and others.

"'We need you to realise that there is a place in time where all matter starts – but there will never be a time when it ends. Life is eternal, and the rules of reincarnation mean that your life will never end; it is one continuing circle of living and learning.

"'You are all God's creatures; you are all basically the same. You are all born, live your lives and die, and then you all go to 'Heaven' at the end. This is the known concept. Those who take a broader look at the hereafter realise that 'Heaven' is just another level – a vibration whose frequency is faster than yours, a frequency that you cannot see.

"'You haven't lost those friends and relatives who you feel are dead and buried, they have just passed from your three-dimensional world and are actually on another vibration, a different plane or level. They are still able to contact you if you learn to tune into them, in much the same way as tuning into a radio station. Some souls elect to stay on a vibration to watch over those they have left behind; not to cause any mischief, but to gently guide and hold out a helping hand. When possible, they will come through a medium to advise you.

"'Sometimes when someone passes into Spirit suddenly, they cannot accept that they have gone. They hang about the house trying to talk to their family and wonder why no-one is taking any notice of them. They cannot grasp the fact that they have moved into another dimension and that their family cannot see or hear them. They live in the same house, they share the same space, but because they are not in three-dimensional form they cannot be seen or heard – except by those who want to see or hear them, primarily mediums, clairvoyants, small children and animals. These souls may be too traumatised to realise that they should move into the Light and be free. They do not realise there are Guides and Helpers always available to show them the way home. Some souls refuse to acknowledge this help as they want to remain attached to the Earth plane, close to all they hold dear.

"'Most spirits who haunt your dimension are just souls who have not grasped the fact they can't be seen. They can see you, and expect you to see them, but most of you are not attuned to their vibrations and therefore cannot. They become frustrated when they are ignored, and this frustration can turn into mischief. As soon as these so called 'ghosts' realise where they are and grasp the fundamentals of life after death, they will move to a higher vibration, leaving their 'haunting' behind.

"'For souls who stay close to the Earth plane, your three-dimensional world holds no barriers. There are no material constraints. Physical objects have no boundaries, in the same way as there are no boundaries for radio waves. Think about all the ghost stories you have read, in which ghosts float through walls and doors with ease, or glide along passages that no longer exist. They are following pathways that existed in that place when they were on the Earth plane.

"'How many children do you know who have an invisible friend that they insist is in the house with them and must have a chair to sit on? You go along with it to appease the child, hoping it is just a phase they are going through – but often they really do have a friend, a friend from Spirit. Sometimes it is simply a lost child who hasn't yet accepted that they have passed, and therefore has not completely left the Earth plane. This will be a spirit friend that only the living child can see, as small children find this concept easier to accept, whilst adults mainly block their minds to anything of the kind.

"'Once a body has acknowledged the fact that it has passed into Spirit and freed itself of the shackles of its old three dimensional world, then there is a wonderful new world to explore, as on the return to Spirit there is no physical body to weigh you down. You will vibrate to a note specific to yourself, and you will glow with your own blend of colours which show your purity, your love, your compassion and your level of awareness. These colours and associated sounds will attract those who have shared your colour blends over many lifetimes. They will recognise you in an instant.

"'You will vibrate to the same note as your family and friends who are here. You will be pulled to those you loved the most and will instantly recognise each other on our side. Each lifetime you are brought together with souls of like minds who have shared your life before. There are an infinite number of possibilities but within each lifetime you share your path with a finite few, over and over again in different guises.

"'When you pass to the Spirit Realm, you can move away from your thoughts of the Earth and relax, or you can watch closely all that happens and help those who you have left behind. You will always be able to watch the Earth; you only have to ask and, like a big window, the landscape will scroll in front of you. You can see your family and friends and how they are getting on, and you will be able to send messages and advice to them via a clairvoyant or medium. Some mediums are attuned to the deceased, and others are more naturally attuned to Angels and Spirit Guides."

"On this side of the veil, the sky is always blue, and there are no boundaries, no walls – just freedom, peace and love," Shomas continues. "You will see glorious colours far brighter than on Earth – which only shows reflections of the true shades. The colours here are a beautiful hue, and the light radiates from everything, making you feel calm and at peace with all.

"'Life, at first, can be similar to that on Earth. There are flowers and trees and Halls of Learning for you to use. There are fields and forests, birds, flowers and animals. There are beautiful views and pretty gardens where you can sit and contemplate if you choose. Some people need to have possessions around them, because this is what they are used to. They will gradually relinquish these material needs as they rise through the vibrations.

"'There is no pressure to be anywhere or do anything; you can just sit and listen to the music, or watch your family on Earth, but eventually you will want to do something else, something more productive. You can study anything you like, anything you have always dreamed of doing. It is amazing how much people can learn here. There are many mansions, as the Bible says, and it all depends on what you need when you pass.

"'You may wish to learn academically, or perhaps you have always wanted to learn a musical instrument. There is such beautiful music playing here, which is so good for the soul.

"'We know this all sounds far-fetched to the layman. You will see on your arrival here that everyone works to get you settled, and once you have met family and friends and enjoyed relaxing for a while, you will want to do more. Then you will be shown the Halls of Learning and a plan can be made for whatever you want to do with your time whilst you are here in order to further your spiritual growth and soul development.'"

Jane pauses, wondering if she has read enough for Olivia to absorb – but her granddaughter is eager to hear more, so she continues.

"'Your Guides and Helpers can always see you on Earth. We have only to think ourselves beside you and there we are. We choose to guide and help you by staying close, but we can go off elsewhere if we need to. During your sleep state you sometimes come to join us, and we show you things you need to know when you return to your Earth state and awake. We often take enlightened souls out of their bodies at night to help us heal places and people in areas of conflict around your world.

"'There are so many souls in Spirit who wish to be able to contact mankind. If you are open and let them through to guide you, your path will be easier to bear, as they hold out a helping hand to lead, advise and explain.

"'There is no real concept of time over here; the days and months blend into one as there are no clocks to tell us the time and no seasons with which to gauge the year. So we cannot give you exact dates for any forthcoming event, just an awareness of what is to come in your destiny.

"'As your Guides, we know your every thought and your every move – but we are discreet enough to leave you alone at more personal times!'"

Olivia giggles and Jane smiles in return. Then she resumes reading.

"'As sources of energy we can move anywhere we please, within the Spirit Realm. We can visit anyone we please, on our vibration or below – but we are not allowed to progress to higher levels of awareness until we have earned our 'wings'.

"'We come from many levels of existence (dependent upon our knowledge and abilities) down to the level where we are able to chat with you. We can travel down through the vibrations towards you, no matter how fine ours is; but the third dimension, where you are now, is the most difficult for us to access due to its extreme density. We need mankind to understand the concept of us all working together, of man raising his vibration as high as possible in order to meet us half-way so to speak. This helps us to communicate, so that we can tell you all you need to know to help the planet for the future.

"'As we have said, you are on the third dimension. The astral is on the fourth, and the Astral level is nearly as base as yours. Not all souls relinquish the essence of their three-dimensional body on leaving your planet; they hold memories close and do not free themselves from bondage until they move through many portals of Light. The Astral level is where some souls currently go when they first leave the Earth, especially when it is unexpectedly through trauma. They go to this level in order to be close to the Earth and to be able to reincarnate quickly back to your world. One problem with this is that such souls will not have developed sufficiently to realise that there is more to life than being on planet Earth – and so, when they pass, they just stay close, awaiting an opportunity to quickly return to human form. Unfortunately, this can entail a running link with the past, bringing bad karma back with them from their previous existence.

"'Those on the fourth, or Astral level cannot channel, as mainly they have no knowledge of these matters, but sometimes they may gain access to the people on Earth through a medium or clairvoyant.

"'Channelling is normally done from the higher planes. You rise to a level equivalent to five of our veils, or levels, when you come to connect with us. This lifts your vibration and enables us to connect with you more easily, but it is still a struggle for us to slow our own vibrations down enough to link. Nonetheless, we do it with delight to help your growth, and our advancement.

"'After you have passed to this side of the veil, and after you have spent some time with us here, you will have the choice to either go back to an Earth life to fulfil karma, or to stay in Spirit and learn more lessons before your return. You don't have to learn if you don't want to, it is up to you. Your spiritual growth depends on how much you learn, and you can choose how many lifetimes you wish to take to learn it all. With a few lessons on this side, you can lessen the number of times you have to return to Earth, with all its trials and tribulations.

"'When you are ready to reincarnate, you can choose the parents you wish to have and how your life will be to ensure that you learn lessons which will increase your spiritual growth. The whole aim is to raise your levels of consciousness in order to get closer to the Source or Creator.

"'Once settled here, and when you wish to look back at the life you lived, there are computers, of a kind, on which are kept the Akashic Records. These contain an individual 'book of life' or blueprint for your character. Imagine this as a video recorder which has always existed from the beginning of time, and which will always exist, with an unlimited storage capacity. The Akashic Record records everything that has ever happened or will ever happen to everyone. You can look at these records, research the lives you have lived before and look toward the path you wish to take next to fulfil your karma. They are there for everyone to look at; they show what you have done from time immemorial, and what there is still to do in order to progress to a higher plane.

"'We are often asked why you cannot remember your previous lives when you are on the Earth plane, and why you need to start from scratch in each new life. We can only tell you that with each new life memories of the past must be forgotten so that you can start new lives of love and meaning with souls who choose to reconnect with you in this matrix of time. Each new life is like a sunrise on a new day, full of wonder and anticipation of the day to come.'"

"I like that analogy!" says Olivia, "please, continue."

"'You can return to Earth time and time again to get things right,'" Jane reads, "'to pay back any wrongs. You can plan your next lives to clear the record of karmic debt. It is all here like a map for you to work out your future.

"'Some souls, once they have settled here, elect to work in the hospitals and way stations, guiding newly arrived souls to their destinations. The hospitals do amazing work, allaying the fears of transit and helping each soul adjust to their new surroundings. Anyone who has been ill or had an accident will come to the hospitals for rest and recuperation, where they will be Healed of all that ails them before they progress. If someone has arrived due to trauma, their shattered nerves are calmed and if from a prolonged illness, all essence of this is removed. There are also convalescent homes where more Healing takes place, so each soul may pass on their way in health and happiness.

"'We spend our days learning new things about life in order to progress along our Spiritual Pathway. Our learning is a continual progression of stimulating discovery. When we are not watching over you, we are furthering our own spiritual awareness too. We are multifaceted, and so can be in many places at the same time.

"'Once here, you can see the people you want to see, do the things you want to do – but, if you don't learn, you don't progress. There is so much to learn, so much to see. The knowledge you have now is but an infinitesimal part of the whole. When you get here you will realise just how little you know; but as time passes, you will learn more and be able to pass this information on to others.

"'All life on Earth, and off it, is a learning process. The more you learn, the further you will progress. After some time on each dimension, if you have learnt enough you will pass to higher dimensions, where again there are more Halls of Learning.

"'Bodies on these higher vibrations are lighter and more diaphanous, with everyone having everyone else's progress at heart, helping each other to get higher and attain more knowledge. There are temples in these dimensions where the most evolved Spirits give lessons, in order that you may return to Earth with even more spiritual knowledge. The souls who return over the next millennium will be able to use that knowledge to its greatest capacity on the Earth plane, when the planet rises through the vibrations and as all upon her wish to become more spiritually aware.

"'You cannot, at the moment, comprehend what you will see here. Just get on with your life as usual on the Earth plane and work to help others – which will help your own spiritual growth.'"

Jane pauses again, flicking through the pages of the book to find the next section she wants to read. Shomas's teaching are quite deep, but Olivia seems to understand them nonetheless.

"'To help in the understanding of the Spiritual Realm,'" she reads, "'an interest in Quantum Physics may be useful. This is a study of four dimensions, which takes in the possibility of there being another dimension where life can exist, outside of our awareness, but within the same space. Multiple dimensions of reality are the buzz words of science fiction, but in essence are the truth.

"'Each life has many layers, and all aspects of reality change according to the layer in affect at that time. You feel the essence of all that is in your bodily matrix, but do not realise the power that this wields. Across the Universe there are many levels of awareness and of knowledge. On each level there are layers of consciousness, each appertaining to different aspects of time and space. On Earth, few sense the layers or see the opportunities to expand their consciousness in order to flow over many levels. There are time frames in space, and once you can sense the different levels you will be able to see and hear Spirit, and, in Healing, be able to see the working of the body like an x-ray. This is available to all, if you would only realise this.

"'Based on this, we need you to understand the vibrations a little better. Since the time of Atlantis, Planet Earth has fallen down through seven levels/veils/vibrations/ frequencies [see glossary for explanations], as the state of the planet and its peoples deteriorated.

"'The vibrations come at many levels. As we have mentioned before, Earth is on one of the lowest. This has come about due to warring factions through the ages, and through evil permeating into man's thought patterns. As more and more people become spiritually aware, they will raise the consciousness of the planet. The Earth is ready to rise up through these vibrations to a higher level of spiritual awareness and understanding, to a much higher frequency. This is not a physical/three dimensional move, it is a moving through time and space. It will be a raising of spiritual consciousness and awareness.

"'The higher your vibration is, the more in touch you are with your Higher Self, inner consciousness, or your true nature. High vibrations are generally associated with positive qualities and feelings, such as love, forgiveness, compassion and peace. Have you ever gone to a concert and felt a sense of lightness or elation? If so, you are 'tuning into' a different frequency of energy in your life.

"'The lower your vibration is, the more out of sync you are with your Higher Self, and the more conflict you may experience in life. Low vibrations are associated with darker qualities, such as hatred, fear, greed and depression.

"'As the vibrations on your planet rise, all the evil in the world will gradually be left behind and the Earth will become a far more gentle and peaceful place on which to reside. The planet will move, and all on her will move. Some will come here, but most will stay on the planet to see it through this roller coaster ride. This will take a long time, but it is long overdue; and with the rise in vibrations will come a greater awareness of the needs of the Earth, and man will have more consideration of her resources.

"'More and more people are becoming spiritually aware. They will raise the consciousness of the planet and therefore raise the vibrations of all upon her to such an extent that man will acquire a greater understanding, and become more aware of his potential to use his abilities to help others.

"'There are so many amazing things the brain is capable of but – these have been lost and forgotten due to man falling through the vibrations, and to so much evil clouding the issue. Natural healing, telepathy and astral travel are all within everyone's capabilities, but the knowledge for these has been lost in the deep recesses of the mind. Lost, that is, until the time is right for man to use them all again, in the name of good, not evil. If these abilities were to be used for evil, the mind would block them out again, and mankind would fall back down through the vibrations.

"'As man gets pulled deeper into the dark side, we need to show the Light as the saviour, the redeemer of life, and to make it more attractive and more viable than the darkness. The darkness is ignorance, neglect and in opposition to goodness, respect and wisdom.

"'We need to pull those born today into the Light from birth so that they will stay magnetised to the Light for life. We need to bring children into the soular matrix of life from the very start, which will hold their energy in this space throughout their lifetime, bringing peace and harmony to all.

"'Man must learn to look to himself for fulfilment, for his wealth of purpose. Man is a complex creature, so full of emotion and upheaval, so full of rage and compassion; he swings from happy to sad or angry at a whim. This will stop, once the Lords of Darkness let go of the planet; once they relinquish their hold on mankind, these mood swings will cease. There will be no more anger, no more frustration or sadness. Everyone will work for the benefit of their fellow man, to bring joy, love and peace to everything they touch. Man will meet his fullest potential again and rediscover the abilities which have lain dormant for thousands of years. There is so much for him to learn and do for the future: he will hold his head up high and be an integral part of the Universe again.

"'It has taken a long time for us to be able to regain control of planet Earth and lift man out of the darkness and back into the Light. As time passes, it will become obvious that people are lighter, more pleasant, more caring, as their vibrations rise through the levels of consciousness. You will notice a difference: people will smile more, be more courteous to one another. They will hold out their hands to help their fellow man instead of leaving him in the gutter. Many don't know what is happening; many don't know how this is affecting them; but soon they will realise that this is a lifting of vibrations and losing of density.

"'Take time today to thank your God for everything which is good, for everything which is filled with Light and Love, and trust us that all will be well in your world soon – not in weeks, or months, but in the future. All wrongs will be put right and your world will be a far happier place in which to live. The future is a wonderful place, your destiny lies there. Hold out your hand and we shall take you, and there you will find your dream.'"

With that Jane closes the book.

"Wow," is all Olivia can say at first after sitting silently for so long. The expression on her face tells Jane how much she has been moved by these words. "It does stop you being afraid of dying, doesn't it? I look forward to the future and seeing how, gradually, the planet and all the people on it will be at peace."

Jane agrees. "Yes, it does! Roll on the future – a future of peace and happiness! I hope I see it in this lifetime," she adds. "I apparently have had many, many lifetimes, I think they kept throwing me back to try again to get it right!"

The two women both laugh.

"Whilst we are on this topic," Jane adds, "I will tell you the differences between clairvoyants, mediums and psychics, who contact the other side. 'Psychic' just means someone who can develop their mind to see further than the confines of our normal 3D world. All of the other terms are forms of being psychic. Clairvoyants literally 'clearly see' images of Spirit, to varying degrees. They tune into the energy of people or objects. They can see those who wish to speak to anyone on Earth. Clairvoyants normally have a specific Spirit Guide who passes information on to them. They may validate things for you that have happened in the past or will happen in the present, but they will hesitate to give direction about what's ahead, because free will may change the future.

"Other aspects of clairvoyance include clauraudience, which means 'hearing' information from Spirit. The messages from the Spirit World are passed on aurally, and intended to bring you comfort. Clairsentience is the ability to tune into the energy around you, sensing different physical or emotional stimuli from other people or the environment around you. Claircognizance refers to the ability to know things instinctively, and clairgustance is the ability to sense a smell related to a Spirit, such as the scent of a certain perfume or tobacco, which brings back long-buried memories of loved ones.

"Mediums have the ability to receive and pass on messages from those who have died, as well as Spirit Guides, Angels, etc. They provide a communication link between the Spirit world and people on the Earth plane. Visit a medium if you wish to contact a loved one who has passed: they will tune into the Spirit energy surrounding you, conveying any personal messages.

"There are different kinds of mediums, each working in different ways. Trance mediums, for example, allow their bodies to be temporarily taken over, merging with someone from the Spirit world to allow communication between the living and those on the other side. Performance mediums give shows where they communicate with those who have passed, giving relevant information to members of their audience. Remember what Shomas said: mediums can bring messages from beyond the veil to comfort those who grieve."

"Channellers are in contact with higher Realms. They speak with the Angels, Messengers and Guides who give information of a pure quality on the state of mankind in this time frame. Channellers do not usually link with souls on the Astral plane, unless it is essential for the wellbeing of those left behind."

"Ah, that makes it clearer, thank you," Olivia responds. "I did wonder what the difference was between mediums and channellers."

"Is that enough for one day, or would you like to hear about the Elementals?" Jane enquires.

"Elementals? What are they?" Olivia asks, choosing to carry on.

CHAPTER TWENTY
ELEMENTALS

Stopping to get a warming drink, Jane and Olivia continue their conversation.

"Elementals are Nature beings serving directly under the Elohim, who are a powerful aspect of the Consciousness of the Creator," Jane begins.

"There are many elemental energy streams: elves, fairies, devas etc. – so many to learn from and bring back into the world consciousness. Fairies and elfin folk weave webs of magic. Devas are nature spirits. Unicorns bring love and Light. And dragons are horned serpents who repel the evil one and his armies. Sylphs control the air, gnomes control the earth, undines control the water, and salamanders control the fire element. I must admit that when I was first told about them all, I was very sceptical – but I have learnt they are real, and exist in our lives whether we believe in them or not and they have their own spiritual path to follow.

"A while ago, I received some writing about the Elements of Air, Water, Earth and Fire. I would like to share it with you." Jane picks up a journal and begins to read.

"'We know you wish to contact the beings who honour the Elements, they are tasked to connect with you to bring their Light into the work you do currently. They have a consciousness and intelligence in their own right.

"'There are four Archangels of Light who work with the four Elements. Archangel Michael: Fire, Archangel Gabriel: Water, Archangel Raphael: Air, Archangel Uriel: Earth. They honour and accept the Wisdom of the Elements.

"'Michael wields his sword of Light to expand the energy of his element of Fire across the Earth. He brings wisdom and the mentality of the Hierarchy of Angels into your lives, to lift you to a higher level universally.

"'Gabriel heralds his wisdom across the ages to bring forward ancient knowledge held in the Water for the betterment of mankind as a whole.

"'Raphael spreads his Light across the Earth to heal its trouble spots, and anchors the Light into the darkest recesses of every soul on their journey.

"'Uriel spreads the word of the Archangels that there is life beyond death, affirming that life continues to the four corners of the Universe and beyond. He pays the boatman to take all souls to safety who work for the Light.'"

Jane looks up to find Olivia enrapt, so she decides to share another piece of writing.

"One day Shomas wrote for Archangel Michael, as he wished to tell me about himself. Here is what he said....

"'I am Michael, I am the Lord Protector of the solar system. I wield my sword of Light to smite the dross of life away from Earth in a clean sweep, to purify and energise her love of life and for all in the Cosmos.

"'I work to help wipe the slate clean for all those who work in the Light. This will purify their energy systems, and purify their hearts to live life only for the benefit of Earth and all upon her. This will clear karma and show them the way to keep thoughts pure and hearts light; to always show their Light in the darkness; and to never be afraid, as my shield protects them from barbs of negativity and hatred.

"'I am Michael, I am the Light of God the Creator. I walk in the Jesuits' shoes to clear a path of Light for all those who walk in service for the Light. I am, I was and always will be a Protector of the Light on Earth. You need to know my presence and the force with which I can smite the damned.

"'I am pure Light, and as such can lighten the load of all who work for the Light, and in the Light, to purify their souls for their journey back from whence they came.

"'I smite my sword to adorn them with the blessings of the Lord our God, and to show them their wealth in the Realms of the Ancients. My Sword of Light and Shield of Light will protect their heart space and enlighten their soul.

"'I can express my will to bring Light back to Earth. I bring law and order to the Universe to rebuild the matrix of life itself for all time. I have might, and I have wrath, but my gentleness knows no bounds in my plan to show man how to create a purer and holier life than currently offered.

"'I am might, I am wrath. My will is linked to the will of God, and in his name I work and do only good. But I have my own will within this regime, to bend a little further to left or right, to bring Light closer to the Earth.'"

Olivia's face is glowing when Jane finishes reading. "An Archangel communicated with you! How wonderful to know he protects everyone who works for the Light!"

"The Elementals help us too, so let me tell you more about them. One day I channelled for a friend and this is the information we received:

"'We acknowledge the need for all on your Earth to understand the four Elements and the Elementals who work therein,'" she reads. "'We bring you the wisdom of the fairy folk, of the devas, the goblins and gnomes, the sylphs, the dragons, the unicorns, and all elementals of Air, Water, Earth and Fire, to light your life with their gentle yet powerful energies.'"

"I felt a shift in energy," Jane explains, "and then received:

"'I am the King of Water. I speak to thee to offer my guidance to you in your work for the Light. I offer my assistance to you to bring those with little knowledge forward to understand my will and my way. To understand the element of water, you need to flow with the energy of water itself. Water is fluid, all things shrink or expand in water.

"'As I say, water is fluid; it brings life to all beings on Earth, be they man, creatures of the sea, flora, fauna or minerals. Nothing exists without water. Water is the main element in the construction of man, and the major element across the planet. Water cannot be harnessed; it is the free flow of water which keeps its purity. Harness it and stagnation will occur.

"'Your structure is already seventy percent water and it is the utilising of that water which maintains its purity and life-giving properties. Drink plenty of water to keep the free flow of water through your body. Invoke the elemental beings of water to help you cleanse and purify it in your system, and to utilise and expand your heart, your brain, and your soul, to allow them to flow with the freedom of life itself.

"'You can see me reflected in your soul as it fills with the life-giving water of your Earth. I am crystal. I am ice. I can breathe as you breathe, and I allow you to fill but not to drown in my essence.

"'I thank you for calling on me to show my worth to you; to show you all that I am and can be, here to help you to flow through your life like the water in a stream. You may fall over rocky ground, but water smooths the way. I bless you with all that there is in my world.'"

"I was then passed to the Fire Elemental," says Jane, reading:

"'I am the King of Fire. I bring you the Light of the World, and I light your way on Earth. Beware my fury, as I flame and burn – but allow my gentleness to warm and light your way. I offer you my heart-strings, to show you the way of the Light. You are part of me and I am part of you. A fire burns in your soul for the knowledge you seek.

"'I breathe fire in the Earth, beneath the mantle of life, within the soil, to maintain life itself. The melody of life is sweet, and fire is the essence of the lifeblood of the Universe. The Light breathes its essence into our being.

"'I offer my services to you to heal the rift which has opened on your planet between good and evil. I can seal the door where evil dwells, and meld the rock to form a lock for eternity.

"'Everyone needs to understand my fury and my Light: a two sided sword. Be aware of both sides, and utilise these to help and heal the Earth. We hold the element of fire in abeyance in the Earth. To allow it to have full rein would destroy the planet, but its warmth springs life into the Universe, nurturing the plants and trees into life so they may show their colour and increase their benefit to mankind.

"'Man is slow, he can make fire, but I *am* fire. I am the fire in every human soul. You are made of fire; there is fire in your belly. I bring you warmth and love. I am the Light; I show the way. From man's early beginnings, I gave the soul warmth and showed the way of love. I can add passion to the Light of Life.

"'Fan the flames of life in your soul. Fan the flames to bring life forward out of the doldrums, out of the cold, into the sunlight and parade this life in the fulfilment of love and creativity. You need to fan the flames in your psyche to move forward a pace and to herald your coming into the New Age of Light.

"'You can use a candle to light your way and the gentle flame will flicker, but it needs air to ensure it doesn't die. But the fury of my anger can manifest as a volcano, which blocks light and smothers life. Do not invoke my anger, treat me with respect.

"'I, beloved of the Jesuit, offer my services to you in peace and love. Be aware that I can wield a tremendous force, but that water can extinguish me. Air is my ally, as it breathes force into my flames.

"'To bring the element of Fire to the fore, breathe air into my lungs to expand and quantify my value. To dampen my soul, bring water to my aid. I look forward to bringing fire to your belly and Light to your soul.

"'Cosmic fire brings an element of heat and Light to planets so far unseen in the cosmos. Those which lack life will come to fruition and be adorned with the Light of a million stars. This fire is the thread which holds all worlds together.

"'I am the wind that blows at your back as the flame flickers beneath your feet. Speed on, dear ones, speed on. I light your path; I herald your coming. The flame that beats in your heart progresses you through the dross of life on Earth, and creates a portal of Light to show you the way through the veils.

"'I want you to know of my love, and my passion for life. I need you to throw caution to the wind and flow with the passion of life to create a true way to move you through the portals of space and time to a higher dimension of Light and love; to heal and seal the planet in an orb of pure Light; to destroy the darkness. My blessing to you. Thank you for the work you do in my name.'"

"Next," Jane says, "I was addressed by the Air Elemental:

"'I am the King of Air, I blow the cobwebs from your mind and the dust from your soul. I am the air you breathe and the wings beneath your feet. I fill your lungs with my very essence and expand your breath with my soul. I am the element of Aquarius: I am the era of Light about to begin. I blow the trees and whisper through the grasses. I am your life force and, as such, essential to your very being. I am the air you breathe and the lungs of the planet. Without my element no life exists.

"'I wish you to blow my air through the Earth; to wield a force to batter those in darkness. A gale is air. A breeze is air. A tempest or a tornado can do their worst to unsettle the seas, lay waste to the land and forge a forest fire. I am the breath you take; inhale my positivity and exhale my negativity, to cleanse your body and your soul. I am air; I am the lightness of foot, the wil o' the wisp, the softness of a falling snow flake. Respect my Air. Air is life, air is good, air will fan the flame of life and lighten the load.

"'Air needs to be spun on threads of gold. Show everyone air as a tool and as a weapon of Light and love to breathe life into the planet on which they live. Air can flush the world with life and love. I am purity. I am lightness. Breathe me in and blow away the woes of the world. I show you my lack of stability: that air is transient, fickle and light. I do not stay in one place. I flow with the wind, I blow like a torrent. Feel me, taste me. I am yours always. Feel me at your back: I am the hand which guides your footsteps.'"

"Then last but not least, the Earth Elemental:

"'I am Lord of the Earth, I am the might and power that is Gaia. I bring solidity and strength to your soul matrix to let you feel the stability that is Earth. Earth is your planet; it is the glowing orb in your cosmos. I am the soil on which you walk. I am the ground on which you lie.

"'I am soil. I feed nutrients to the plants and trees, the life forms which wear my cloak. But I need water or I will dry and the soil will crack; I need the life-giving element of water to heal my wounds.

"'I am stability. You ground yourself at my feet. I will hold you safe on my surface to bring you into sunlight and rain to see the Earth in her beauty. I am the one who holds you dear. I do not burn or drown you; I do not blow you away. I am the solidity of mountains but also the lightness of the sand between your toes. Revere me for the place I hold in your hearts. I am the planet on which you live; without me you would be of the ether and not of the ground. I bless you for loving me and holding me dear, and for all you do to heal my wounds and keep me safe from harm.

"'Touch my lands. Feel my soil. Feel the sand and the rock and the minerals I form in my caves. I bring you colour and beauty. I am the soil on which all plants grow and fill your world with the beauty of nature.

"'I, as Lord of Earth, bless you and thank you for allowing me to help you shield and protect the Earth, by bringing in new souls to fill my army for truth and light.

"All Elements enter your heart space, and hold you dear. Please respect and revere us in return.'"

When Jane has finished, Olivia wants to know more. It has been fascinating to hear how the Elements interact with each other, and with the human race.

They sit and talk long into the afternoon. By the time they are done, the fog has lifted, but the roads are still hazardous.

Jane recommends Olivia stay for the night. Olivia quickly agrees. It is always a treat to stay, as her grandmother will delight in spoiling her and she has a chance for another day being part of the magic of her grandmother's world!!

CHAPTER TWENTY-ONE

EGYPT

Although still cold, the sun kisses the top of Olivia's head, bringing out a shimmer of copper tones in her dark hair, as she sits in the conservatory. The last threads of winter are still clinging to the earth as tiny white snowdrops raise their delicate heads to embrace the early sun. Although still battered by the winds, they stand strong and sentinel, proving that new life is just around the corner.

Olivia is all smiles. She knows today they are going to talk more about Jane's adventures, and she is excited to know more about her grandmother's life.

"Hi Granny," she says as Jane comes to join her.

"I thought I would tell you about my trip to Egypt, if you are interested," Jane says.

"That would be great," Olivia enthuses, she is fascinated by her grandmother's artefacts: ankhs, pyramids, scarabs and Buddhas, and she would like to know where they originated.

"From many ancient civilisations," says Jane. "The ankh, pyramids and scarabs come from Egypt of course. I went there with my friend Helen, for a cruise down the River Nile from Luxor to Abu Simbel. It was a fantastic trip, I had wanted to go for years and she suddenly arranged it.

"We started our cruise from Luxor and Karnak, two beautiful temples which are sited beside each other, on one side of the Nile. The architecture of both is phenomenal.

"The temple of Karnak is really a city of temples, which were built over a span of two thousand years and dedicated to Amun, one of the most powerful Gods in ancient Egypt, who was also called the 'King of the Gods'. Karnak was part of the monumental city of Thebes, and apparently over thirty Pharaohs contributed to its building.

"Karnak is one of the largest religious buildings ever made. The great temple, at the heart, is so big that St. Peter's Basilica, St. Paul's Cathedral and Notre Dame Cathedral would all fit within its walls. Inside the temple, the Hypostyle hall has one hundred and thirty four beautifully carved columns, many over ten metres tall! Outside the temple there is an avenue of Ram headed Sphinx, each protecting a small statue of a Pharaoh between their feet. They used to line a path all the way to Luxor temple, about a mile and a half to the south; but sadly, they are mainly broken and scattered now. Nonetheless those remaining are still impressive.

"Within the Luxor temple complex there are a further arrays of fascinating carvings and drawings; and there is also a statue of Tutankhamun and his wife Ankhesenamun, both of whom were so young to be king and queen of such a great land.

"Our guide on the trip was excellent: not just a guide but also an Egyptologist. He talked us through the story of each temple we visited by reading the images and hieroglyphics, explaining the world of the Egyptians at that time. He brought the whole era of the Pharaohs to life for us.

"On leaving Luxor and Karnak, we cruised down the Nile to Edfu. This is the Ptolemaic Temple of Horus, who was the son of Isis and Osiris. He is depicted as a man with the head of a great falcon with outstretched wings, whose right eye, it was said, was the sun and the left eye the moon. It is the most completely preserved temple along the river. The carvings and paintings are exquisite.

"From there we sailed on to Kom Ombo, which is a double temple dedicated to Sobek the Crocodile God and to falcon-headed Horus, and is quite unique in its symmetry. Its double design means all rooms were duplicated for the two separate Gods. The southern half of the temple is dedicated to Sobek, who was a god of fertility and the northern part is dedicated to Horus, a god of kingship and the sky.

"Everywhere we stopped we learnt so much about the people of the time. Both the Edfu and Kom Ombo temples were en route to Philae and the Temple of the Goddess Isis – which was one temple I really wanted to visit.

"It was so peaceful gliding down the Nile, seeing the people working in the fields on the river bank. It takes you back centuries. Children run along the tow paths, waving ecstatically to all the boats passing by.

"Philae is set upon a rocky island in the Nile, near the city of Aswan. The Temple of Isis is one of Egypt's most enigmatic temples, named after Isis the wife of Osiris, and mother of Horus. She is known as the giver of life and protector of kings, as she brought her husband back to life after he was murdered by his brother Seth.

"Shomas had told me: 'The Lineage of Osiris and Isis is the ground-root of the magic of life itself. Their story demonstrated that when life was torn asunder, it was reconstructed and formulated in truth for all time. Isis is the goddess of all that is good. She seals and repairs the lives of all who work in her name. She will endow those who wish it with her name and her honour in the Temples of the Gods. She brings freedom and life to the High Temples. She is the Goddess of Love, and as such she holds the central core of life in her hands, to maintain and protect it from harm. Isis offers those who wish to work in her name the Lamp to light their way to the Temples of Wisdom, to access the learning of the Ancients, and to bring this knowledge forward in time and space. She and all who work for her bring the energy of Love to the physical.'"

"No wonder you wanted to go to her Temple," Olivia says. "I'd like to go there too."

"On first arriving at Philae and the Temple of Isis, I was a little disappointed," Jane admits. "I knew that there had originally been two wells set inside the temple grounds: one in which the water rotated clockwise and the other anti-clockwise. In the 1960s the whole temple was raised from its original site to make way for the Aswan High Dam, and the area was flooded by what is now Lake Nasser. It is tragic that the wells, with all their magic, have been lost. The energy in the Temple did not seem to be as intense as I had expected...but I was oh, so wrong!

"One of my Spirit Guides is Mamoses. She had been a dancer in some of the temples of Egypt, especially Philae, and I had been told by Shomas that she would be travelling with me so that she could see her old homeland through my eyes.

"Helen and I walked all around the Temple, and it was beautiful. I then felt compelled to wander off on my own. I walked around the outside of the main Temple and there, painted on the outer walls, I saw a frieze of dancers all kneeling, side on, facing to the left.

"As I walked along the line searching for a clue as to which of them might be Mamoses, one of the heads turned out of the painted wall, faced me and smiled. Talk about shock! I just stood frozen to the spot as the head rotated back into its original position in the frieze. I ran back around the building to find Helen and show her – but it didn't happen again, and she really wasn't sure whether she believed me or not. I don't blame her as I was rather stunned myself."

Olivia sits spellbound.

"The next day we had the opportunity to fly to Abu Simbel. We couldn't sail, as the Nasser Dam blocks the river's route, and all tourists are encouraged not to drive or sail to that part of Egypt due to terrorists in the area. It is far quicker and safer to fly – the only issue being that we had to leave our cruise ship at 4 a.m. in order to get there, explore Abu Simbel, and then make it back to our ship before the heat of the midday sun.

"From the airport, we were taken by coach to what I thought was an empty piece of desert – but as we walked around a corner, there in front of us was the most awesome sight. Abu Simbel is enormous, and the two seated figures of the Pharaoh Rameses II which adorn the front of his Temple are colossal, I was hardly the height of his big toe!

"There are two temples on this particular site. A smaller temple built for Rameses' wife Nefertari is set beside her husband's more imposing edifice. As with Philae, both Temples had been lifted away from their original location because of the Aswan Dam and Lake Nasser, but much care and attention had been taken to ensure that these Temples were reconstructed to look exactly as they originally did. They were stunning.

"Everything inside Rameses' Temple is enormous. He was a great Pharaoh and it shows. Nefertari's temple is so much more dainty. We walked around both, and as we came along a corridor in the smaller temple, I saw a line of dancers similar to the frieze at Philae – and again Mamoses made herself known by turning her head and smiling at me. It was wonderful!"

Jane smiles to herself as she recollects the experience.

"All the temples we were lucky enough to visit were exquisite, Livvy. Every wall was painted in beautiful colours, with intricate detail telling the lives of the Pharaohs for whom they had been built.

"On our return journey up the Nile, we sailed in a Felucca, a native Egyptian sailing vessel, and we were taken to the Mortuary Temple of Queen Hatshepsut, the first Pharaoh Queen. This temple, is also colossal, and was said to be one of the most beautiful of ancient Egypt. It is located at Deir el-Bahari, or the Northern Monastery, on the west bank of the Nile, near the Valley of the Kings. It is also known as Djeser-Djeseru, or Holy of Holies. The Temple sits directly against the rock, which creates an amphitheatre around the building so that it appears to grow out of the cliff behind.

"The Valley of the Kings was built beneath cliffs that naturally form a peak resembling a pyramid. The tombs here are painted just as elaborately as the temples and some are so complex in design. We had the chance to explore quite a few of them, and they were beautiful – but the queue for Tutankhamun's tomb was so long we never had the chance to see inside.

"We were also taken to the Colossi of Memnon. These are two sixty-foot-high seated figures which originally guarded the Mortuary Temple of Amenhotep III. Due to their state of disrepair, (an earthquake shattered parts of them many years before), they create the most eerie sound as the wind weaves its way through the cracks in their structure. The locals used to be scared of them as they believed these statues 'sang'.

"When we took the trip, a few years ago, Egypt was a dangerous place to visit. Our boat had an armed guard, who watched everyone get on and off at every dock. Helen and I escaped from the ship one day and went into Luxor city to shop for outfits for a fancy dress ball. I bought some lovely items, including a tiny gold charm of the Goddess Isis. I still have it on my bracelet as a memory of 'meeting' Mamoses. Helen and I hired a pony and trap to ensure we arrived back at the ship before it sailed. The poor man and his horse had to rush to deliver us to the dock just in time! It was the most fantastic holiday, with memories I shall cherish forever."

"Would you go again?" Olivia asks.

"In a heartbeat," Jane says, smiling. "But that's enough about my travels for now. You should ask Shomas about ancient civilisations. I am sure you are eager to visit with him."

CHAPTER TWENTY-TWO
ANCIENT CIVILISATIONS

Olivia goes upstairs and as soon as she has settled and started to meditate, she finds herself back in the crystal cave. Shomas arrives, and immediately begins to tell his story, taking Olivia on a journey through time.

"There was, once upon a time, a highly evolved race of people known as the Lemurians," he says, "they were a peaceful nation of beautiful, ethereal and spiritually aware people with lives full of light, love and music. They helped each other and cared for the land on which they lived.

"These gentle beings could come to and go from Earth as they pleased. There was no death then, and no birth. They could travel directly to our realms and back again at will, nothing barred their way: they could visit us, and we them, as free as birds.

"But one day a passing super-nova fragment created a violent shift in the Earth's orbit. The land masses on the planet changed, and their beautiful island vanished under the sea. The Lemurian race descended into matter as their land fell, and they were no longer able to freely travel the realms as they did before. Some who were saved from the catastrophe mated with the indigenous peoples of Earth, and this started the cycle of birth and death as you know it today.

"Some Lemurians have elected to return to Earth at this time to help man as he rises through the veils to a more spiritual way of life. You will recognise them by their calm, peaceful, simplistic ways. Watch for them."

Olivia promises that she will.

"We also wish to talk about Atlantis today. Atlanteans were very tall and slim, with quite large eyes and slightly domed heads. The people of these early civilisations tended to be taller than people today because Earth's gravity was not as heavy as it is at present. Their bodies were more ethereal because the consciousness of the planet was much higher.

"In the beginning, Atlantis was very peaceful. These people were very kind and cared for their fellow man. They worked together and helped each other, creating a wonderful, harmonious community spirit. There were no laws; everyone was equal; and they had a very nice way of life. At that time, there was so much spiritual power on the Earth that the planet glowed with Light.

"The Atlanteans spent their days learning and developing new ideas. They meditated and worked towards a general goal where everything was developed to help their communities, in every way possible. They never did anything which was selfish, or materialistic.

"Atlantis was beautiful, and the main city was enormous. It was built on concentric circles with a temple at the centre. Encircling the temple was a ring of water, then the next ring contained housing and a market, another ring of water, and then an outer ring which held a race course (they enjoyed horse racing). Channels or moats ran between each ring, and palaces and pyramids preserved all that was good. The circular walls seen beneath the waves of the ocean are the encircling walls of the main city of Poseidon. The mountains around the city of Atlantis were extremely high, and are now part of what is known as the Azores.

"Technologically, the Atlanteans were far in advance of yourselves now. Crystals were used for power generation: there was one huge crystal which was the main energy source for the whole of Atlantis. They built ships and powerful aeroplanes of a sort, and these vehicles were powered using smaller crystals, similar to motors, each of which linked into the larger crystal for their energy.

"This nation never strayed far from their own land, as this was where all was good and where they felt safe. They could control the weather to a certain degree, calling on the rain when required by a form of electromagnetic force field. Much of the time their weather was idyllic.

"Originally, everyone worked for the good of all, but over time, a faction of priests attained an increased level of awareness and sought to isolate themselves from the rest. Initially this endeavour was well-meant, intended to encourage others to follow them into greater understanding of the meaning of life.

"As these priests, gained power, they created senior authoritarian positions, and began to think they were superior to, and of a higher spiritual level than, the rest of the Atlanteans. Before long they had formed a hierarchy in which the people who were in charge of the temples lived and ruled like lords. They made laws which the citizens were commanded to obey. More temples were built and monuments erected, and admission to the temples had to be earned rather than being freely open to all. This caused a lot of unrest, and ultimately led to widespread resentment, and to the start of the fall in the vibrational frequencies of the whole continent.

"The populace could not understand why these elders suddenly had such airs and graces, declaring that the Gods would send wrath upon the people if they did not do as they were told. Their wonderful lifestyle was suddenly changing.

"In the beginning, the Atlanteans had known how to astral travel, to levitate and teleport themselves, but over time they lost these skills. The peace and tranquillity which had been so marked in their society became a thing of the past. This was the start of a downward spiralling of the vibration on which they existed. The whole community continued to degenerate, and the civilisation of Atlantis became decadent and manipulative. As the Atlanteans fell down through the vibrations, their psychic abilities diminished.

"The Atlanteans could not fight a war when their civilisation began; there was nothing, absolutely nothing, in their society that would have caused any dissent. A huge protective dome of energy, love, peace and Light created a barrier around the entire land mass so nothing could get through. The whole continent was encompassed in Light and goodness, and no-one else could come into their sphere, or send their warriors there. But, of course, once there was dissent, this barrier, this dome broke down. There were little cracks in the armour, the defences were low and they feared that other beings would attack, they realised they needed weapons to protect the area in which they lived, and they developed warheads.

"There was another race on the planet at that time which was not so spiritually aware, and who became obsessed with science. They were great warmongers, and had mighty warships. They attacked Atlantis in order to win the land. Wars raged, and they blew themselves to pieces.

"All this came about because of a few men who thought they were superior, and wanted the power to rule over others. This has happened throughout mankind's history. It is like a small seed which grows inside certain people, taking over their hearts and souls and turning them into autocrats. They need to rule and be ever more powerful, wishing everyone else to be subservient. It is such a destructive force, as can be seen in the times of other dictators, almost from the beginning of time."

Olivia nods her head sadly in agreement as she thinks of all the dictators she has read about in history books.

"The Earth, rather than allow these once magnificent people to fall further and further down the vibratory levels, decided to take action to end their civilisation," says Shomas. "There was much geographical activity: earthquakes, volcanoes and tsunamis which affected the original land mass of the planet. It broke into pieces, causing the oceans to move, and the polar ice caps to melt. These Earth changes saw all trace of Atlantis erased from the planet's surface.

"Premonitions had warned some Atlanteans their civilisation was about to end. So they secreted their records in safe places in the Yucatan and Egypt, and established themselves across the globe by traversing between the tectonic plates before those parted, creating the different continents you recognise today.

"Many people nowadays have a fear of the unknown and the unexplained. Instead of looking into it further, they shut off their minds and disregard the idea of a city which, in all its splendour, vanished beneath the waves. Man can be so blinkered to anything which he does not understand and cannot quantify. Those who have a more open outlook to life recognise that there have been many civilisations before yours with knowledge of technology and psychic matters.

"When Atlantis fell into the sea, all was lost, including the huge crystal, most of which is still under the sea off the coast of Bermuda. This crystal is still very powerful – and when the planetary alignment is right, it is charged up to its full power, and can affect the navigational equipment of ships and aeroplanes in that area, moving some things through the vibrations."

Olivia's remembers her grandmother talking about the powerful ancient crystal that lies below the Bermuda Triangle. Now she realises how it could have got there.

Shomas finishes his story, "After the fall of Atlantis, as the Earth fell into denser and denser sub-planes of the physical dimension, gravity became extremely heavy and the people of the planet became shorter in height. Their DNA[15] mutated in order to adapt to the changing frequencies.

"But now, as the consciousness of the planet rises, your youth are growing taller again. Earth's scientists have already discovered two extra strands of DNA in many children currently on Earth. Humans are going through a leap in evolution, which will make man more intuitive and intelligent, perceptive and aware. Eventually, this will help to give a better understanding of the origins of life.

"Many good people escaped the destruction of Atlantis, but also some of the more nefarious ones who went to Egypt, created problems by ruling as very strict and powerful Pharaohs. Fortunately, they were eventually overpowered – and the better (that is the only word I can think of, better) more spiritual souls survived and as these benign, highly evolved souls came to prominence. They looked after Egypt in a wonderful and very peaceful way, nurturing and helping that land to grow and develop in harmony for many years.

"At that time, the consciousness of the people of Egypt was raised. It was they who built pyramids – not as temples to the Gods, nor solely as burial grounds for the Pharaohs, but to store information. These remarkable buildings were aligned with the particular planets that the Egyptians saw in their night sky, and were storehouses of enormous energy. The outsides of the pyramids were designed to be smooth and shiny because of the power they attracted, so anything put inside them was preserved.

"The pyramids were used for many things. They were tombs of the Kings; a library of knowledge of Atlantis and Lemuria; a record of the early times of the Egyptians. They also contain mathematical references on how to return to other planets from whence people came to the Earth as the ancient Egyptians revered the Gods who came from the stars to help their people. They held them in high esteem and respected them as Deities.

"Hidden under a great pyramid at Giza, there is a Hall of Records[22], with a great wealth of knowledge. It is not one of the three in line with Orion's belt, but a greater, more sophisticated pyramid which has lain dormant for aeons in the sands of time, protected from the climate and the marauding feet of visitors to that land. Some parchments will be found there which tell of man's true origins. The texts will be strange, but no stranger than the hieroglyphics which have been deciphered before. When these are found they will explain a million and one anomalies that have occurred within humanity's life-span

"In this place man will find signs of the provenance of the civilisations on your planet. He will find the truth: that the origins of man are not ape, nor amoeba, but alien life forms who are the mother and father of Earth's creation. This will shatter man's illusions that he is unique in the Universe. It will destroy man's arrogant assumption of superiority, and open his heart to other races, other creeds, and even other life forms on distant planets.

"There is so much information stored in the pyramid – but unfortunately, or maybe fortunately these records have not yet been accessed. If a lot of this information was to surface now, it would probably be dismissed, as the current consciousness of the planet is not quite sufficient for humanity to understand this depth of knowledge. We wait for your planet to raise its consciousness – and then these records will be found and recognised for the truth they hold."

"I hope I live to see that," says Olivia

"It is possible," Shomas confirms, and then continues his story. "The Egyptians had considerable help in building their pyramids and temples from people of other planets, who taught them different ways of building. The Atlanteans had not originally needed this help, due to their powers, but as their consciousness fell, so did their abilities. Man needed to be taught how to build large structures using machinery: how to place stones one on top of the other, held in place by a substance similar to cement.

"But then, as man's consciousness rose again, so did his psychic abilities. He learned how to levitate crystal energies by breaking down the molecular structure of the rocks (a little like in your science fiction films). He did not need pulleys and cranes, the stones could be deconstructed, lifted into position, and solidified again. This was a lot easier than the historians think. There is so much about the building of the great monuments, standing stones, tumuli, pyramids and churches which man still needs to understand in order to understand himself.

"There are so many remarkable sites around the world that you must go and see,

Olivia. Against the backdrop of the Peruvian desert near Nazca, for example, there are earth lines which, when viewed from the air, take the form of beautiful birds, animals and insects. They are enormous figures, accurately delineated in yellowish-white earth, but their origins and means are still unknown to man.

"The Incas built pyramids and many other wondrous buildings – but these, alas, have been destroyed or have crumbled over the centuries. Only the ruins remain. At some point we will talk to you of ancient writings handed down from generation to generation telling the history of the Inca civilisation.

"There is so much that was natural to these ancient civilisations which will be brought to the fore again in the times to come as the vibrations rise and humanity's consciousness rises with them.

"The ancient civilisations had many natural psychic abilities, as we have said before. They were natural Healers, and as such they were skilled in healing themselves and others. Some could open a person's aura and put their hands inside to heal, pushing the aura safely back together when they had finished. They had no need for drugs, or a surgeon's knife. Everyone on Earth right now has Healing abilities; they are latent in the human subconscious, where they wait be released. Life is a wondrous thing, dear one, and the capabilities of the mind are infinite – just tap the wisdom of the past to find it. When changes on Earth are complete, the vibrations of the planet will quicken again and many things which the ancient civilisations could do will become second nature to man once more.

"There are many on planet Earth today who originally came from these ancient civilisations. There are more and more of them choosing to come back to Earth now, to help mankind. They want to guide others in the old ways of understanding and gentleness for fellow creatures. As man goes up through the vibrations, the levels of awareness common to the ancients will be available once again; he will attain higher goals of peace and tranquillity for himself and all mankind.

"These ancient extremely spiritual souls are now returning to Earth to help the planet work through the darkness and raise it to the Light. Many of these good souls who are returning now have realised their origins, and are working for peace and harmony, to raise the consciousness of man. The Earth needs to be raised by many levels in order to clear the darkness, and that is why these souls have chosen to be on the planet right now. They will teach others how to unwrap their hidden talents and work to heal the world.

"Earth is an exciting place to be right now. It is a privilege to be incarnated on Earth at this most crucial time in her evolution. So many people want to be incarnated on the planet currently that your world is over-populated, and still there is a bottleneck of souls wishing to enter. Many are choosing to be there now to help the planet progress. Earth is the most popular planet on which to incarnate to ensure this 'Paradise', this 'Garden of Eden' stays that way.

"It is a fantastic opportunity to be on Earth, as man's level of consciousness expands. You chose this path and this karmic journey – not as a punishment, but as an experience for growth. Although this is going to be a tough time, it will help you clear much karma, and allow you to progress spiritually. You will have a chance to see the world change for the better and the planet refresh and replenish herself for the good of all.

"Do your part to bring everyone together as a whole, to support planet Earth in her hour of need. Help to heal her environment, and return her to glory, love and Light. Our aim for planet Earth is peace, and for it to be a wonderful place for all of you to live on for a very long time to come.

"Like the tarot card for the 21st century which depicts an Angel, so in this century you shall all be Angels metaphorically. There will be peace on Earth again and there will be freedom for all living creatures on the planet.

"Your history books don't go back thousands of years, so you have no way of knowing what happened before, but history is repeating itself. Twice before, man has been given his beautiful planet only to destroy what is good and pure. Man has yet again ruined what is potentially a lovely world, with his industry and pollution. But Earth is giving man yet another chance. This time, if man raises his consciousness enough, there will be no destructive industry, no pollution, no use of fossil fuels, no acid rain, no scars on the landscape. The planet will be beautiful.

"You are very fortunate, Olivia, to be able to watch this change-over, and the return to growing the purest crops and being self sufficient, as before."

"Will it really happen?" Olivia asks him.

"If you work together, with each one of you doing your part. You have free will, so I cannot promise; but the world's vibration has been steadily rising, which is a good sign. Now I think that is sufficient information for today," he tells her, bowing slightly and taking his leave.

She sits in silence, reflecting on his words.

Jane hearing movement pops her head around the door and seeing that Olivia is now 'alone', comes in and sits down in the other chair, Chloe at her feet.

When Olivia is ready to speak, she shares her latest lesson with Jane. Her grandmother, familiar with the information, adds a little more to it.

"We have had ancient civilisations in Britain too. Think about all our standing stones! Stonehenge, for example, is a legendary enigma. It is believed to be an astronomical clock which tells the days and marks the seasons. However, despite much archaeological research the real truth of its purpose is still unknown. The original earthworks for Stonehenge are believed to have been built as early as 2600 BC.

"The 'sarsens' (the huge blocks which make up the familiar uprights) and lintels are the epitome of a stone circle. They are believed to have been put into place around 1500BC, and were quarried about five miles away from where they now stand. The smaller 'bluestones' came from the Preseli Hills of South Wales, some two hundred miles from the site and were probably erected some centuries later. We used to think Neolithic man was savage, but now research shows that they may have had a very advanced culture, with a considerable knowledge of mathematics used to build this type of structure."

"I've always thought they must have been wise to have made such a stunning monument," Olivia comments. "It should be in our historical books."

"It probably will be one day," Jane says sagely, "The more research that is performed, the more we are learning about so many sites around the world, and the clearer it becomes that ancient civilisations have much to teach us."

Olivia then asks if Jane would guide her through another meditation. Her grandmother agrees, and Olivia prepares herself: feet flat on the floor, spine straight and shoulders relaxed.

"Now focus on your breath," Jane tells her. "Inhale positivity, exhale negativity. Remember the scent of honeysuckle, and let it take you back to the lane...."

This time, Jane leads Olivia to a quiet place in her mind and then leaves her there.

Almost immediately Olivia finds herself in the destruction of Atlantis. Everything is falling away, a boiling sea surges below, and she is pulled into a beam of white light, which turns into a vortex lifting her up. She sees a small boy cowering in a corner and, grabbing his hand, she pulls him into her arms and takes him with her. Thirteen crystal skulls encircle them as they rise, but the higher they get, they all fall away. She watches as they fall all over the world: Sri Lanka, Russia, Peru.

Hooded beings are looking down from above, welcoming her home. They are six high priests and six high priestesses of Atlantis, highly evolved cosmic beings, who take instruction directly from the Intergalactic Council. Each being in charge of one of the twelve climatic regions[26] of the Earth, these noble leaders work selflessly for the greatest good of the people. They pour Light and pure high-frequency energy down onto the populace to maintain the Light of Atlantis on Earth today.

Olivia sees an Egyptian pyramid where Mamoses, her grandmother's Spirit Guide, is dancing, joyous that she is there. Then Olivia is pulled further into the white light, drifting over to the Sahara where the wind blows the sand away from an enormous amber skull. It is absolutely huge, far bigger than real life, and Angels come to protect her from its intense energy. They lift her up and take her to the Halls of Learning, where etherial bodies lead her to the front of the lecture hall. The lecturer gives her a pen, like a quill, to take home and to use in the future. Then the gossamer beings take her back to the Angels, who return her to ancient Egypt, where she leans against the pyramid walls and writes using the quill. As she does this, she sees a beautiful green-faced being, with amazing amber eyes. He has long, curly blonde hair, and his mouth is open in song. He is wearing a jewelled and golden crown and deep blue robes. As he sings a long clear note he merges his energy with Olivia's. His name is Uriel, she is told: green of the Earth, with eyes the colour of amber tree resin. She can call on him to work with her on Earth energies, as he represents the solid element of Earth in nature.

Slowly the images fade away and Olivia hears her grandmother's voice, beckoning her back to the room. Jane waits until Olivia is fully present and then asks about her journey.

When Jane hears about the crystal and amber skulls, she tells Olivia the story of the thirteen crystal skulls. It is purported that they were carved by an ancient Mesoamerican civilisation tens of thousands of years ago. They were scattered around the globe, and are believed to have once been used for rituals and ceremonies. They are supposed to hold knowledge regarding the history of the human race and civilisation and have perceived supernatural powers. There have been claims of Healing and expanded psychic abilities from those who have been in the presence of these skulls.

"They may be relics from Atlantis, or be proof that extraterrestrials visited the makers," Jane says. "Both archaeologists and anthropologists are curious about their existence and purpose, as most of the crystal carvings are perfect replicas of a human skull. The carvings have been made out of rock crystal cut against the axis – which would normally shatter the crystal, but these skulls remain smooth and finely polished."

Olivia listens, fascinated, and decides to look up more information about these, on the Internet, when she gets home.

While they have been talking, the weather has taken a turn for the worse, and Jane doesn't want her granddaughter caught in a storm – so after a warming bowl of soup and home-made bread to restore her energy, Olivia wends her way home. She is already making plans for another trip into the 'unknown' very soon.

CHAPTER TWENTY-THREE
THE OTHER PLANETS

At long last the final dregs of winter are vanquished, and as it slowly ebbs away, the first faint murmurings of spring are sensed in the air. Jane waits anxiously at the door. Despite the clocks going forward it is still very cold, and she doesn't want Olivia standing on the doorstep long. Her son calls her a mother hen and he is probably right, but she cannot stop caring. It would be against her nature.

Once Olivia arrives, she and Jane sit toasting crumpets on the fire, chatting about their lives since the last time they were together. Olivia appreciates the way her spiritual journey has brought the two of them even closer.

Eventually, excusing herself and pushing a very sleepy Chloe off her lap, Olivia rises and heads for the stairs, wondering what gems of wisdom Shomas has in store for her today. Settled comfortably in the big armchair, she slides quickly into a deep meditative state to await Shomas's arrival. It is not long before the Guide appears, leading her to a secluded glade. Today, he advises Olivia, he wishes to talk to her about the Universe and beyond.

"I would like to tell you about your moon, that beautiful orb in the night sky which shines its silver light on the Earth...but the moon is so much more than that. It has an effect on your weather patterns, and on women's monthly cycle. Its' gravity controls your tides, pulling at the seas as it travels across the skies above your planet, forcing them to rise and fall twice a day. It can also have an affect on the emotions of every creature on the planet, from the wolf baying at the moon to man's lunacy, which was believed to related to phases of the moon.

"The moon was also once a home base for visitors from other planets, who traversed the skies to come and visit the inhabitants of Earth. You may be surprised to know, Olivia, that the moon holds valuable information, stored underground in base stations far superior to any known currently to man.

"On one of the other planets in your solar system, Mars, there are pyramids which were created to preserve life, and also to be habitats for beings from other planets to use when they visited your solar system. Travelling from their original home to Earth was a trip that took light years, so Mars provided a way station on their route. Inside the pyramids on Mars' surface are chambers which can sustain life. Messages to mankind are strewn across the walls, explaining how the pyramids were built and why. These messages will answer many questions in years to come, once man can explore their caverns."

Olivia is fascinated by the whole subject, and asks Shomas to tell her more.

"Life on Earth is but an infinitessimal part of the whole," he explains. "Humans are just one of millions of species which can walk, talk and communicate through voice. Mankind, in its arrogance, has lost all contact with its origins. Man thinks he is lord and master of his world, the stars and the Universe. This is not so, and he will be amazed to realise his history is not always accurate, and his world is a far different place to the one he thought he knew. He has believed for so long that his is the only intelligence in the Universe, but he is wrong; he has no idea of the complexities of the cosmos and all the beings who reside therein.

"Yours is not the only Universe. There are many universes, all interlinked by a grid of energy which criss-crosses between them. This sounds extraordinary we know, but Earth's scientists are exploring these same concepts as we write, and discovering the complexities of life outside your own solar system. Once visitors from other planets make themselves known, the information available will amplify a million fold.

"Matter outside of the sphere of your own planet's orbit is full of particles, protons, atoms, neutrons, all floating in space, all invisible to the human eye, but still an integral part of the planetary systems. In the black void between planets are a myriad of life forms which create the dense mass of the Universe itself. And there are many black holes, which are doorways to parallel universes, and these gateways or portals allow ships to pass between them.

"Millions of planets set in their own galaxies bear no life at all – but what you have to realise is that each galaxy has star systems scattered far and wide, each of them with their own sun, and many which do bear the fruits of life as you know it.

"There are literally hundreds of inhabited planets, with beings both inferior and superior in intelligence to man. Some visited your planet many years ago, manifesting themselves on Earth in order to experience the pain and loving which goes on in the hearts of its inhabitants. Man would have been able to travel through space too if he had not fallen through the vibrations and lost many of his abilities, but now he is far behind civilisations which have had space flight for thousands of years.

"There are a wide variety of species on these planets we speak of. Some are inhabited by tiny life forms which live and breathe on their surfaces, so small they are hardly seen, but still capable of procreating and maintaining the elements. Others have life forms similar to you, in looks and characteristics and some with the same intelligence as mankind, or some even better.

"The time is right for man to know the truth about the existence of other life forms and how they have influenced his past. It is time for man to forget his arrogance and open his arms to the stars and all their populations. It is time to chase the stars, follow their pathways, and learn about the past in order to herald the future. One day, man will find that there is life elsewhere – and a possible new home will be recognised as such, perhaps even within your lifetime."

Olivia sits with eyes open wide as Shomas continues:

"Man has waited a long time to find out if he is alone in the Universe, and now he will realise he is not. The Adam and Eve theory is a little off-beat, but it is in essence correct. When Earth was new and souls elected to incarnate on the planet to see if it could be the schoolhouse of the future, they came down through the different levels. Visitors from other planets came to teach them and more and more souls chose to come to your planet to learn. As they had children, so these new souls incarnated on the planet and the population expanded.

"Mankind is in for an awakening and with that awakening will come peace and a closeness of all nations, as you realise you have to pull together to cope with these immense revelations which will lift the planet into its future consciousness, beyond the power of evil and pain and into peace and harmony.

"Man has searched for his origins through many lifetimes – and now it will be there for him to see, to feel, to acknowledge. This will throw science on its head; anthropology will be viewed anew. It will take some time for man to trace his roots, to herald a new beginning and end all doubt.

"The original visitors are coming to Earth again – to guide and help. They want to help mankind to a better future. They want to help build a life of peace and tranquillity, a life of love and joy, in the clear knowledge that nothing will be polluted any more, not lands or seas, nor minds, thoughts or deeds.

"There are currently life forms on your planet who hail from elsewhere, who have traversed the cosmos to help man at this time. These beings are humanoid in appearance, only lighter in matter and much taller. They glow with a radiance of Light and love only obtained once your body has raised through sufficient vibrations to start to shed the physical and all it entails. They are manifest in human form so as not to scare the masses, but some retain their Light bodies to show their true state.

"These so-called alien races which come to help the planet now, thought the human race was intelligent enough to realise what it was doing to the planet and could sort it out alone. Once they realised mankind would need assistance they decided to come and help. Even with the enormous energy and flying power of their vessels, it will take some time to travel the distance they need to cover.

"Governments are trying to cover up information about UFOs. They cannot accept what is to happen, and do not want spacecraft to come and frighten the populace. They do not realise that humankind has made its own decision about alien races. What a shock it will be to those in power, when much of the populace accepts so readily! They do not give their people credit for intelligence and sense. This may sound like science fiction, but it is fact. America has been secretly in touch with beings from another dimension for some time now.

"There is a galactic ship in your cosmos which is approaching Earth, beaming in Light to locate Lightworkers on your planet. It is within Earth's boundaries in space. It has been there for some time now, just watching as the plan unfolds on your planet. They will show their hand, but not quite yet. The time has to be right; it has to be appropriate for them to let you know they are there. Let everyone know they come in peace; they do not want to scare anyone. They just want you all to know life cannot continue in the vein it has for centuries; it needs to improve.

"The cosmos itself is seated within an ocean of energy, and these waves of pure Light and strength can be harnessed as energy and power. The concept is very complex; and as yet is not understood by man. These visitors will use this energy as they traverse across the galaxy to greet your world.

"These spacecraft follow a beam of natural neutrons, which flows through the universal sector of which Earth is a part. This currently flows via Sirius, and brings this energy to your planet. Sirius have always had links with your planet, sending their goodwill through the ether to keep Earth on track. They struggle to understand why humankind is not now as advanced as they, and are horrified at the misdeeds man does to his fellow man. They send Light and love to beam across the planet to try to raise the consciousness of mankind – but, lamentably, this gets buffeted in transit.

"This energy will uplift the consciousness of all who are willing to listen: it will uplift all areas of Light and ease the pain in the darkness. The Light of the Universe will be brought to the Earth, whereupon man will be able to walk his truth and Light in safety and love. This Light harbours the very essence of mankind within its construct.

"Man's own space travel is in its infancy. Scientists could learn a lot if they let ships approach, but they are very wary. Once man understands what is happening to the planet and realises that the ships are there as 'saviours', he will readily accept their appearance.

"You will know the civilisations who come to help; your instincts will tell you all is okay. They are messengers of Light and love and they will bring great peace. Do not be frightened or anxious of these events; they herald a great adventure and a chance for the Earth to be free again: free of tyranny and war, free of pestilence and doubt. The end is in sight, though this is not actually an end but a beginning, the beginning of a new world, with new colours and vibrations. Look forward to this with great joy. All will be well.

"The raising of the group consciousness is underway. It is a long haul, but it should take all of mankind through the veil into the next dimension. The planet will not change, but man's attitude to man will change and it will become a time of peace and plenty. Contact with the Spirit plane or extraterrestrials will become as easy and commonplace as listening to the radio or watching television.

"You chose to be on planet Earth at this time to experience the great changes affecting your planet. This is something you will never forget, and it will raise your consciousness along with the planet's. Everyone who is on Earth today chose the time of their birth, whether they remember it or not, they chose to play their part in this wonderful adventure. Help others to recognise that you should all be working together for the betterment of the planet and everything upon it.

"A Galactic Council has been raised to work with the Earth at this crucial time, to help raise her vibration and bring her back into harmony with the rest of the Cosmos. They will show their status to those who will listen – but there will also be those who will see them as the enemy and fearing attack will take a stance as protectors of the planet, when in fact the Galactic Council are those who come to care and protect. So many souls wish to see these so called 'aliens' arrive but others will view them with terror and aggression!

"The Galactic Council are an inter-dimensional group who come from different dimensions, advanced star systems and galaxies. Be open to these visitors. They will see your colours and know you are of their Realm, open to the beginnings of a new Earth. A new place in the cosmic orbit of your Universe and others linked in symmetry. The Galactic Council is in touch with us all to ensure Earth rotates correctly within its space time context, to bring it back into a state of equilibrium, and to keep mankind on its true path, ensuring that Earth continues as a planet of Light for many millennia to come.

"It has to be established that they mean no harm, you are of their essence, so like an Ancient ancestor, they come to assist in the placing of your planet back on her pedestal and returning mankind to its original blueprint of true worth. The Light of the Universe will be brought to the Earth whereupon man will be able to walk his truth and Light in safety and love. This Light harbours the very essence of mankind within its construct.

"You need to herald their coming. In doing so, you may be seen as 'kooks' and 'lunatics', but the truth of what you say will be proven as they show their ship to the world."

With this exhortation, Shomas turns and departs, leaving Olivia with her mouth agape. This was the most intense lesson yet. The fact that she could be related ancestrally to someone from another planet blows her mind.

When she talks to Jane about it, though, Jane isn't surprised; she has heard it before. Jane is perfectly comfortable with the knowledge that there are other intelligent life forms throughout the Universe.

"Shomas told me about some years ago about an interesting planet called Maldek," she says, "which was apparently about the size of Earth and once existed between Mars and Jupiter. It exploded about 75,000 years ago, creating an asteroid belt. This great interplanetary event brought devastation and chaos to the other planets in the vicinity as fragments of Maldek littered the solar system. The debris and impact of the explosion cratered the inner planets, altering their orbits and leaving Mars' surface a scarred and barren wasteland.

"The indigenous people of Maldek were rescued and resettled on Phobos, a satellite of Mars. Pictures from a Russian space probe have indicated that Phobos may still be inhabited, as what looks like a space ship has been seen coming out of that planet. As it rose, its shadow played on the planet's surface."

"That's incredible, I wonder if they really are still there?" Olivia interjects.

"It would be fascinating to know," Jane agrees. "I have read that half the atoms in our bodies have been scientifically proven to hail from beyond the Milky Way. Scientists are starting to find that our origins are not as local as we thought they were.

"I have also read in *Nexus* magazine that The Rosetta space probe discovered organic compounds in the nucleus of a comet which are possibly the building blocks of life on Earth. According to researchers in Paris, these organic molecules were produced in interstellar space well before the formation of our solar system. If these molecules were indeed produced in interstellar space, and if they played a role in the emergence of life on our planet as scientists believe, this really would put the beginning of life into a new context.

"Science," Jane adds, "is now picking up on many of the same things, long believed by those of us working for Spirit."

Olivia crosses the room to look out of the window at a dull grey sky, heavy with cloud. Somewhere beyond those clouds are stars...and other planets, other galaxies, and a multi-dimensional universe. She is amazed at the concept that somewhere out there could be the origins of life as we know it. And here she is, a tiny speck on an ever revolving orb in that huge expanse of space.

CHAPTER TWENTY-FOUR
THE NEW MILLENNIUM

Spring has definitely sprung at long last, as the cold days of winter are discarded. Daffodils lift their bright yellow faces to the morning sky, nodding cheerfully in the soft breeze, and the scent of the hyacinths is intoxicating. The green of the leaves coming into bud brings the garden back to life with a new energy, and songbirds are filling the air with their joyous melodies. The sun glints on the water in the bird bath, and trees resound with fledglings chirping for their mothers, who flit to and fro from their cosy nests collecting food.

Olivia has arrived bright and early so as to enjoy a full day chatting with her grandmother and to Shomas. She sits with Jane in the room upstairs, holding a large crystal in her lap, as they talk about prophesy, time, and the future of the planet.

"You are too young to remember the millennium, Livvy, but there was chaos!" her grandmother recalls. "Everyone was convinced that computer clocks would stop ticking from midnight on the last day of 1999, and that all computers around the world would crash rather than turn to 01.01.2000. The airports closed at midnight on that last day of December incase the flight controls ceased. We all sat with bated breath, to see what the new day would bring.

"In tarot readings, the 20th century is often represented by a card showing a fool and a dog on a cliff edge – and people wondered, were we going over the edge to our fate, or would we be dragged back from the brink by the dog? The card representing the 21st century pictures an Angel – would this be the end or just the beginning of Paradise?

"I had been up to Derbyshire, and driving back on the first day of 2000, there were hardly any other cars on the M1. In over 150 miles, I only saw six cars! By the time I reached the M25, normally clogged up with long queues of traffic, it was empty. As I drove past Heathrow Airport, it was also eerily quiet, as not a single plane was leaving the ground. I drove along for miles without seeing a soul and began to think I really was one of the few people left on the planet!"

Olivia is fascinated, "I never really thought about the millennium, Granny, or realised it had been such an issue."

"After the first few hours were over, it was realised that everything was fine. All of the computers continued to work as usual, and everyone went back to doing what they always did, as though nothing had happened. But, in 2012 there was panic again, this time connected to the ancient Mayan calendar. The story started with the doomsday date of 21st December 2012, which was linked with the end of a long 'count period', or cycle, in the Mayan calendar. There were prophecies that this date would herald the end of the world!"

Jane picks up a book of Shomas's writing and finds a passage from 2012. She reads it to Olivia: "'Those who spread alarm about the Mayan calendar did not realise the hornet's nest they would unleash. The media, with its relish of conspiracy theories, magnifies such issues out of proportion and turns them into major stories. It creates 'thought forms' within the masses, which spiral out of control. So many people with little knowledge of our world, or our work, are led by this kind of rabble rousing and nothing can be said to alleviate their worries. This will only settle once this doomsday date is well passed. Newspaper, television and radio editors should stop and think before they speak – but too many of them thrive on the chaos that ensues.

"'Most people underestimate the power of thought, the power of mind over matter, and how constructive or destructive the strength of a single thought form can be. You may have experienced the disappointment associated with harsh criticism, for example, whether it be justified or not, and you will also have felt good when kind words are used to encourage you. Words create thoughts, and thoughts have power. Be aware of the impact of idle gossip and of repeating rumours. Communicate thoughtfully and heal dissention. Never speak unkindly or in anger. Consideration moves you closer to compassionate living. The future is created by what you think and do today.'"

Olivia thinks of all the times when someone has said something hurtful to her, or she to them. She did not realise that these thoughts were tangible and could have such an impact. She then thinks about the newsmongers who set a story free just to see how far it can run and the effect it can have. Do they realise the devastation they can create with their words?

Jane continues to read an extract of Shomas's story from that time.

"'There was a major energy shift at the beginning of October 2012; a lot of people on the planet were affected by low energy, feeling off-centre and a little strange. This was imperceptible to the mass of the human consciousness, but it did affect those who work for the Light. The planet, and all upon her, moved up through the energy fields and up through the veils, into a realm of consciousness far higher than has been attained on the Earth for a millennia and more.

"'All who work for the Light need to come together to pray for the Earth, pray for her future and for the future of all who live upon her, whether they be man, beast, flora, fauna, minerals, oceans and every living organism on her surface. Pray for her health and vitality. Pray for her to raise in consciousness as smoothly as possible, and to maintain her place in the Universe for many, many millions of years to come.

"'We need all who worked for the Light to visualise the leylines extending from the planet out into the solar system and on into the cosmos and to link to other Light beings on other planets in order to hold the strength of the grid in place. We know that this will be hard to maintain, but it is essential to ensure a smooth transit through this troubling time. We know all Lightworkers hold the planetary logos in high esteem and are willing to help keep the planet tightly bound to the Universe.'"

Pausing from the journal, Jane then tells Olivia, "In order to overcome the mass doomsday thoughts sparked by the Mayan calendar controversy, all Lightworkers concentrated on visualising the planetary grid to keep it in place and hold it secure until March 2013, by which time people's fears had been allayed and, for the most part, they had forgotten the Mayan prophecies."

She flips forward in the journal of Shomas's writings, this time choosing a passage from 2013:

"'We are delighted to welcome the planet and all upon her to a new level of consciousness: not a death but a rebirth, a refreshing of your spiritual home and a recharging of your batteries. It has been a wonderful experience for those who have recognised imperceptible amounts of energy change. This is a transient time for mankind: you are merely coming through the veils, to reach a higher level of consciousness, a level unparalleled in Earth's recent history. This has lifted the mind-set of the masses to a higher level than has been known for the past thousand years. We know this is hard to understand for the layman; but for those working in the Light, this is a time of great celebration.

"'Earth is going through a time of upheaval at the moment; there are wars and conflicts in many areas. There are tidal waves and earthquakes, pestilence and disease, all of which take their toll. Life on Earth is tough at the best of times, but currently it is tougher than usual. And here, we have had a huge influx of people from Earth coming home. It has been a challenging time for us to process them all, but they are safe and sound and housed where appropriate.

"'The darkness which has shadowed your planet for so long is beginning to move. Much of the sloth and decay on the planet will become a thing of the past. The degradation and destruction caused by wars, famine and greed is slowly on the move away from the consciousness of most on planet Earth, as she is starting to move into the Light, away from the darkness which has held her in its grasp for so long. There is still a very long way to go, this is not an instant fix but it is the start of raising the consciousness of the planet; above materialism and above the need for power and control over all other forms of life. It is a slow but gradual move to the thousand years of peace which we promise you for the future. Help mankind to recognise that you should all be working together for the betterment of the planet and everything upon it.

"'We need everyone to understand this vibrational move is done out of love and self preservation. If Mother Nature doesn't throw off this mantle of decay and pollution then she will wither and die, causing her special place in the Universal grid to be destroyed, which in turn will affect thousands of planets within your galaxy. She wants to refresh and renew, with the human race upon her, raising their consciousness.

"'Man must first experience the thrill of rising through the veils into the future: one thousand years of peace and love. One thousand years when man loves his neighbour, no matter what colour or creed. One thousand years where he loves everything that lives and breathes upon the Earth, in the oceans, in the forests and in the sky above. What a wonderful experience that will be.

"'All negativity will eventually slip away, as people come to the realisation that wars achieve nothing; no ground is gained, no prizes won, so what is the point? Angry men who wish to rule and control will lose their hold, and the world will be freed of famine and pestilence. The levels of darkness cannot reach into the fourth dimension to tighten their grip, so all will be at peace. Life will be wonderful again: an idyll, a paradise, as it once was all those years ago.

"'Good and Evil have battled for aeons, but this time we intend to take the upper hand. There are so many Lightworkers on your planet, and we want you all to know that you are helping us in the battle of wills, moving everyone forward to a new realm of love, Light and contentment.

"'Hatred and anger are negative emotions and are not in God's remit. As anger is a negative reflex, watch yourself from without; stand back and let anger be alone, and it will wither and die. When you have anger, it unbalances your body and creates a 'dis-ease' in your system. This disease makes you very vulnerable to the forces of evil, so you need to be positive and good.

"'Many on Earth at this time are surrounded by a lot of negativity; they hold this to them like a protective cloak. Tell them to let it free, push it away and bring in more Light. The weight of the world is upon their shoulders, but we can help them carry it if they let in more Light.

"'Whilst talking of anger, we need you to know that logic can override the heart; logic is not the way. The logic of a calculating mind takes you on a strange pathway, but not to your destiny, not to the future you desire. Listen to your heart: let it lead you, let it take you where it will, and you will have many wonderful surprises. Trust us, we won't let you stumble or fall if you allow us to lead you all the way. Take a huge step off the side of logic, off the treadmill of convention, out of the strait-jacket you have been locked in, and be a free spirit guided by the heart, blown by the winds of change.

"'Lift the thoughts and fears of all you contact; raise their vibrations to such a level that when the consciousness of the planet raises, all on her will rise too. Help to raise everyone's awareness. Let everyone know we are here. Tell them all will be well. A small drop of knowledge spreads as in a pool of water; the ripples run to infinity. Follow your dream, follow your heart, and take heed of your intuition.

"'Earth needs to know that there are people worldwide who care enough about her to pray for her future, and for the future of all upon her. She has been so fed up with the destruction caused by the need for man's so-called progress: removing oil, gas and coal from the caverns beneath her surface to further his need for a so-called perfect world. Pray to give her the strength to go through the raising of her consciousness, bringing in the Light and bringing everyone to the foothills of paradise. This is just the start, but a milestone nonetheless.

"'Look at future events with serenity, and maybe even a sense of adventure. You are all spiritual beings, children of God (or your spiritual equivalent), changing and evolving and moving ever upward on a spiral of understanding towards your ultimate reunion with the Creator.

"'Over the next year, you will find Earth going through a number of changes. It will speed up as it moves constantly through space and time: only by milliseconds, but enough to make a difference. The strong winds and changes in the seasons have been due to time slips over the years. The amount of change ahead will be imperceptible, but this will create a quickening of the days.'"

Jane stops reading and gives Olivia a thoughtful look. Some of the concepts she has learned from Shomas over the years are really quite complex; is it too much to understand all at once? Yet her granddaughter doesn't look puzzled or overwhelmed, so Jane decides to carry on and tell her other things she has learnt over the years.

"There are all sorts of forces that effect the planet Earth, which in turn effect all of us living on her," she explains. "Early in our 'writing career' Shomas told me about the forces of magnetism and the phenomenon of 'pole reversal'. The magnetic poles are constantly moving and have actually reversed many times in Earth's lifetime. After drilling through the Earth's crust and extracting a sample, geologists have found evidence identifying geologic and fossil records from hundreds of past magnetic polarity reversals. These show iron ore pointing in one direction in part of the sample and then pointing in the opposite direction in the same sample but further along the core, demonstrating where Magnetic North had drawn them to rotate in different directions.

"This is not a moving of the actual North and South Poles, it is a moving of Magnetic North – which had flipped to South, and South to North during the time-span of that single sample, which represented a few hundred thousand years. Scientists estimate that the Magnetic North pole migrates northward about forty miles per year. These transitions are very random, but the magnetic poles reverse polarity roughly every two to three hundred thousand years. The magnetic fields push and pull at one another, taking between eighty and a thousand years for the transition of the poles to complete. There is scientific proof that these polarity reversals do not affect the rotational axis of Earth; it is purely a geomagnetic phenomenon.

"Let me read to you what Shomas had to say about this: before I had even heard of magnetic poles," Jane suggests.

"'As the rotational pull of the planet changes subtly, the poles will sway in the breeze as they flex their muscles, and this will affect weather belts. Bands of the planet normally gripped with cold will be warm, and the tropics will cool as the icy north pole passes through their space. We know this all sounds absurd, but believe us: it has happened before and will happen again. It is difficult for us to pinpoint exact dates and times, but trust us the planet is flexing her muscles currently.'"

Jane smiles, "When I learned about science confirming this, I was stunned. My Guides always blow me away when they 'prove' what they have written. Historians have found records from Egypt and China, which mention reversals of summer and winter, and slight changes in the position of sunrise and sunset – all of which I have heard about from Shomas. Over and over, the information imparted by our Spirit Guides is confirmed as true.

"The Piri Reis map, an ancient world map used by mariners of the 16th Century, shows Antarctica as a continent without the massive ice cap we know today. Glacial evidence proves that ice from the South Atlantic moved through Brazil and west into South Africa at one time, and into Central India and north of the Equator at another period. And, in frozen arctic ice, giant mammoths have been found with fresh tropical plants in their stomachs, indicating climate and continent change."

"Geophysicists believe the reason Earth has a magnetic field is because its solid iron core is surrounded by a fluid ocean of hot, liquid metal, which creates electric currents, and these in turn create the magnetic field," Jane continues. "Changes in that field can have a powerful affect.

"That's incredible, but also scary," Olivia comments with eyes open wide. "I think of the Earth as stable beneath my feet, but it doesn't sound like it has ever really been."

"My Guides have advised that the Earth is due for another pole reversal sometime in the future, but they also told me not to panic." Jane reassures her. "Let's look at what Shomas says about this."

"'Your planet is in need of help,'" she reads, "'and as such she is being re-aligned to restore her energy channels. These are just changes which will manifest in different ways to lift the levels of the planet and its people nearer to the Source.

"'Mankind continues to use the planet's resources ceaselessly. He is taking all the Earth can offer, but never replenishes what he has taken. More and more rubbish is being dumped into landfills, which are producing more methane into the atmosphere. Methane and fluorocarbons, are known to interfere with, and create holes in, the ozone layer, which is your planet's protective 'skin'. The ozone layer absorbs most of the sun's medium-frequency ultraviolet light, so without it, there could potentially be damage to all exposed life forms on the surface. The ozone layer needs protecting. We know man understands this and it is in hand.

"'Deforestation is also a major factor, as it drives climate change and has a negative impact on the environment. The indigenous people of the rainforest say that these forests are the lungs of the planet and need protection. They are very distressed at the way man is destroying them for his own gain, causing a loss of habitat for millions of species. Eighty percent of land animals and plants live in forests, and cannot survive the deforestation that destroys their homes.

"'The weather patterns have been abnormal for the last few years, breaking all temperature records. There are glacial melts and winds are becoming stronger all over the world, causing much damage. The seas rise and pound the shores, but the increased rain will replenish the reservoirs. There are weather anomalies all over the world. Global warming is influencing storms, which are caused by changes in atmospheric conditions.

"'This upheaval is not done to hurt or cause pain. It is all done to heal the planet and to ensure her survival, so that man may also survive. Without Mother Earth, nothing would endure. She needs to be aligned to help her to heal herself. She is a living being and deserves your respect.

"'As the Earth progresses and gets back on her feet, there will be a greater awareness of the oneness of the planet and the people who live upon her. There will be a greater understanding of where mankind began and where he is heading. Time is a great Healer. As time progresses, man will help and heal the planet and all upon her by developing the skills which are tucked deep in the recesses of his mind, as yet unused in these days of high technology.

"'The basic parameters of the planet are due to change as it moves up the levels, and as man's awareness of spiritual matters rises too. Trust your intuition and you will be shown the right path. Healers will be on hand to help, and your Guides are right behind you, giving you the little push you need sometimes to help you on your way. As the vibrations rise, so will the consciousness of those who seek the Light, and the truth, and want a better world to live in. It won't happen just yet but not too far into the future, then there will be peace again; and everyone will love, respect and help everyone else, this is as it should be.'"

Jane closes the journal, and puts it down on a table. "What do you think about all this?" she asks her granddaughter.

Olivia looks troubled. "My friends and I talk about the climate crisis. We are the generation that is really going to have to face it. But when we talk I feel powerless. It's different talking about it with Shomas. When he describes the Guides, Angels and all the others working together to heal the planet, I feel hopeful again, and I want to help too. It's exciting to hear about mankind rising to a new level, and to know there is a better future ahead, but when is this change supposed to take place?"

"We know that it will happen, but no-one can say precisely when," Jane answers, "the Guides have difficulty grasping the concept of time in their realm. As I have said before, they have no clocks or watches, no calendars or date lines. When they make predictions of things to come, there is no guarantee of a time span. Our 'four score years and ten' is an infinitesimal amount of time in relation to the aeons of time and space since the beginning of creation. The Guides live in the larger time frame, so their perception of the passage of time is very different to ours. Sometimes when I get messages, I am confused by the time scale. When I am told something is imminent, for example, I expect it to happen the next day or the one after, but I am interpreting the word 'imminent' in relation to our time scale, not theirs. To them 'imminent' might mean in a few months, a few years, or a few decades. This has to be taken into consideration when Guides make statements about what is to happen to the Earth.

"The Guides say that the Healing of the planet has already started," Jane adds. "At some point there will be a major shift – and although we do not know when it will occur, everyone who works with the Light will recognise it when it happens."

She picks up a journal and reads another piece of writing from Shomas on the subject:

"'As the vibrations of the planet rise, all the malevolence in the world will gradually be left behind and the world will become a far more peaceful planet. This will take a long time, but it is long overdue. With the rise in vibrations will come a greater awareness of Earth's needs. Man will show more consideration for her resources. As the vibrations rise through the levels of consciousness, it will become obvious that people are lighter, more pleasant, more caring. Many won't know what is happening, but they will still feel the affect. People will smile more, and be more courteous to one another.

"'Your planet is on the brink of change. There is a long uphill struggle before all is well, but we know you have the strength of character to come through. It will be frightening, but also exciting. Encourage everyone to help and respect each other in a unique bond. The Earth needs to recharge herself, and with everyone's help she can do this. If you could see what is to come, you would be so happy, but we cannot tell you everything yet, as you could not comprehend the enormous changes in store.

"'Within your lifetime you may start to see this long-awaited shift in the raising of consciousness. Progression through the vibrations will be slow, and will take many years. Human life-spans aren't long enough to encompass this change in its entirety, but you will see it happen nonetheless: in this lifetime, and in future incarnations.

"'The planet will live and breathe and be beautiful again. Man will re-build for the future, taking a long look at the damage he has caused and put it right. Until then, keep moving forward and help each other. There is hope for a better world to come. Stop taking all the fossil fuels and destroying the Earth; give future generations a chance to live with pure clean air, to swim in unpolluted seas and rivers, and to experience the delight of your wondrous world.

"'Many people on Earth are becoming more spiritually aware, helping to raise the consciousness of the planet. There are Lightworkers who dedicate their lives to protecting other species on your planet; we thank them and ask them to show the way for others to follow suit. We need you all to help make Earth the vibrant, beautiful planet she was always meant to be.'"

Jane closes the book on this positive note. Olivia is right, she reflects. People are going to need hope in order to face the challenges ahead.

"Have you heard about 'The Queen's Commonwealth Canopy'?" she asks her granddaughter. I saw a wonderful documentary in which Her Majesty Queen Elizabeth II and Sir David Attenborough discussed it. The Commonwealth Canopy is an initiative to create a vast network of native forests across Britain and the Commonwealth nations, saving natural habitats and protecting them forever in the Queen's name. Twenty nations have already signed up, committing to the preservation of established indigenous forests, as well as to planting new woodland."

"That's brilliant!" Olivia exclaims, "I love knowing that the Queen cares so much about nature. I have heard that Prince Charles and his sons have a strong interest in conservation too."

"We all have our part to play when it comes to Healing the Earth, and our Guides are always there to help. I have some advice about this from Shomas, which I can read to you," Jane says, as she returns to the journal she was previously reading.

"'Make sure you put your world before materialism, before your own needs, think of the Earth first. Relinquish material wealth that will not fit into your more perfect future. Leave behind anything, physical or mental, which does not help to move you to higher vibrations and a consciousness that will benefit the planet.

"'Just give peace and love wherever you go, and help others to understand what they need to do to improve their future. You may experience a difference in lifestyle when you put the planet first, but you will be pleased with the outcome. We want you to progress, not to go backwards; and as you progress, there will be less need for many of the things you surround yourself with now. You will retain all that is essential, but not anything which would hurt the Earth's Spirit.

"'The plan is made; you just have to follow it. We have come to help you. The time has come for the planet to change and you will all change with her – not in personality, but in your thoughts and deeds. In the next phase of the planet you will be full of love, for her and for your fellow man. It will be a wonderful experience, and you are lucky to be alive at this time.

"'Help everyone, good or bad, to understand what is happening to the planet, so they will see the Light and help others. Tell everyone to learn to be positive, kind and gentle, so they will in turn teach that to others too. There will be many who will not believe what you have to say at first, but as they start to understand they will want to learn more. Some will question how you know these things. Just tell them you have a guiding Light that shows you the way of what is to come.

"'The Spring Equinox brought more Light into the Earth. It is a changing time for everyone on your planet, as well as for us. We ask you all to place Light into the centre of the Earth: concentrate on placing it into the central crystal at the heart of the planet, so that a million shards of Light will radiate up through the Earth into portals of Light in every country all over your world. Please meditate on the Light of the crystal to penetrate the realms of darkness.

"'Man is becoming much more aware of the need to help his environment. We are so looking forward to the vibration coming to a point whereby we can really push with some momentum and see things snowball. We will be clapping our hands with delight, leaping up and down and dancing for joy when this finally happens; there will be a great cheer from this side when everything starts to slot into place. There is so much to come in the future, you will be fascinated by the many new experiences which will be on offer. There is so much for you to learn, you will love it.

"'Remember to take time for yourself. We know it is a noble thing to give yourself for others, but try to think of yourself also – in a caring, unselfish way. Rest and relax. Don't take the burdens of the world on your shoulders all the time. Remember to enjoy all that is good about the world, and about each other. You cannot heal out of exhaustion or despair, only love.

"'We want you all, once you realise your potential, to speak to audiences about our work, explaining reincarnation and karma in layman's terms so that people understand them. We need you to herald our messages to the world, for this is part of a huge plan to raise the consciousness of the planet.

"'There is much negativity in the world; so many people think there is nothing they can do. But they are wrong: everyone can contribute. Our plan for the future is to bring joy where there is suffering. We beseech you all to raise your consciousness and to help us to help others.

"'I give you these messages as a record to be looked back on as the plan for your planet's unfolds. Share these messages with others. There will be quite a few who will be receptive, but some will block any attempt at understanding. Don't worry, just help those you can and the rest will come around in time.

"'Take each day as it comes, as they say. There will be times when you feel you are banging your head on a brick wall. Don't worry, just persevere and do your best. You all came to Earth at this time to help mankind and you will. You may have suffered in this life, but it has given you much strength and compassion. Don't lose those gifts. There will be pitfalls to come, but we shall guide you over them where others may fall down.

"'Life will be beautiful again, as it was in the beginning, and as it was meant to be. The future is coming, full of hope, joy and love. Open your arms, embrace it, and lead the world on its happy path. Lift your head, lift your heart, show your Light and lead on. Shine like a star so that others can follow. Don't hide your Light: show it, glow with it, build it ever stronger until all can see and follow your guidance.'"

Jane stops reading and closes the journal.

"Thank you, Granny," Olivia says. "That was exactly what I needed to hear."

Jane gets up from her chair and gives a big stretch. They have talked most of the morning away, while outside the window the garden is bright with sun and the sky is cloudless.

"Let's eat some lunch and then go for a walk," she suggests. "It is always good to talk about Spirit – but we must take care of our bodies too, and enjoy the natural world around us."

"That's a lovely idea," Olivia agrees, gently pushing Chloe from her lap and rising. "But I will make lunch this time," she adds, resolving to be better at helping others. Shomas is right, she already feels a little lighter as she follows Jane into the kitchen.

CHAPTER TWENTY-FIVE
ASCENSION

The sun is struggling to get a watery hint of light through darkening clouds, but summer is coming, and a riot of colour is rising in the garden. Olivia has been helping Jane move some of her larger plants to another flower bed, and on finishing she is suddenly mesmerised by a great spotted woodpecker on the pear tree, it is the first time she has ever seen one in Jane's garden. He is so beautiful and keeps rat-a-tat-tating on the tree, looking just like a toy bird on a pole, as he slides effortlessly up and down the branches, tapping and flicking pieces of bark across the lawn. What a bonus to an otherwise dull morning!

Once the gardening work is done, the two women head back inside: Jane settling at her desk to write some letters and Olivia running upstairs to meet with Shomas. Today he has promised to tell her about Ascension. As soon as she has entered into her meditation, he appears and launches straight into his talk.

"Many people across the world are waiting with bated breath for Ascension. Ascension is a word, just a word, conjured up by those who are 'in the know'. They think it will be a big bang and that suddenly their lives will be altered irrevocably; but this is not the way. Ascending is a process of tiny footsteps; it is a ladder you climb with love and care, and as you reach the pinnacle, you bring all others with you to see the Light.

"There are no fireworks, no carousels, no whoops of excitement; it will creep up on you all, and you will feel a gradual sense of upliftment and enlightenment as you stand tall within the Light of the Creator. Your Earth has been a long time in darkness; it has suffered wars and pillages for aeons. But all will slide into insignificance as the Light takes over, bringing peace and love to you all.

"Ascension is simply a raising of awareness, a raising of the Light within the hearts and minds of everyone. Those who are closest to us will lead the process for the good of all mankind. The people waiting impatiently for Ascension will discover it is not an instant fix. It will take time but will eventually be a huge step forward for all.

"There is no exact date for Ascension; it depends on all of you: on how you relate to others, how you heal your world, and how you protect all species. Ascension, as we say, is like climbing the rungs of a ladder. Each step is equally important to the last, but each traveller will reach different rungs in their own time frame. There will be many rungs to climb, and many levels to reach, as the consciousness of the planet rises and everyone on Earth rises with her.

"Let us speak for a moment about levels. Across the Universe there are many different levels of awareness and knowledge, and on each level there are 'layers' of consciousness each appertaining to different aspects of time and space. On Earth, few of you see the layers, or understand the opportunities they offer for expanding consciousness. These levels are time frames in space, and as Lightworkers, once you learn to perceive the different levels you will be able to see Spirit. And Healers will see the workings of a body as though they have x-ray vision and be able to help and heal the problems they see. This is a skill available to all of you, once you realise your potential.

"Each life has so many layers or multiple dimensions of reality, all aspects of which change according to the layer in effect at that time. You feel the essence of all that is within your bodily matrix, but do not realise the power that this wields. Much of the Light across the cosmos is now fine-tuning for the date of elevation to another level of awareness, affecting the entire universal grid. The process is already beginning and Earth is due for another upgrade. It will resonate to the sound of Angel song which will lift it through the veils. This will bring many constructs into harmony. It is a major event in the cosmic paradigm, and as such will escalate the rising of awareness across your planet. Even those with little knowledge or understanding of our world will hear the call to drop arms and bring in peace.

"You will feel it like a fever. It will rise up in you, elevating your soul consciousness to a level never reached before, and where we will welcome you all to a new level of understanding. At long last man will appreciate his worth on your planet, and will wish to benefit the land and all species upon it.

"As the Ascension begins, Lightworkers will be champions of the Earth, ambassadors of the rise in consciousness across the whole planet. They will see the Light and follow it first, taking the first steps in the Ascension process. Just watch; time will tell you when.

"Take your Light and be a herald to all who understand and even to those with little understanding. Show everyone that this is the way. There will eventually be a time when all mankind will know what it is we have to offer and will step onto the path of Light. As we have said, Ascension will not be an instant fix; it will take many years. The planet will lift slowly and surely through the veils, rising away from the darkness and dross of hate, war and discrimination to a higher level of peace and harmony. All mankind is at a cusp in time. Ascension has been coming in small footsteps for quite a while now. The process will help all those on the planet to become affixed to the Light matrix, allowing the darkness in their hearts to slip away.

"Back in December 2018, many of the planets in the cosmos aligned, which forced a 'cosmic interference' across your planet. It was quite a major event from our point of view, creating a Portal of Light which could be seen across universes. Many beings across these aligned planets had their consciousness raised, and this increased the awareness of that entire Light band. It was a huge stepping stone forward on the Ascension path for everyone and brought much joy.

"Each new year sweeps away the dross and debris of the past and brings in the Light of the Future. You will move from an industrialised way of life to one that is lighter, brighter and more productive. The energy of the planet, and all upon her, will elevate to a new plane of existence. Look to the future, it will be bright!

"Eclipses affects humanity on the spiritual plane. The planetary alignment having a drawing effect on Lightworkers: pulling at their energy and affecting them for days. But an eclipse also brings a whole new energy to the planet, a changing in the atmosphere. This is a positive thing, it is all a part of the dawning of a new age, a change in the whole remit of mankind."

Olivia is spellbound as Shomas paints a vivid picture of the future. It is so different to the constant gloom and doom she reads in the daily papers.

"A Portal of Light is opening," Shomas tells her, "and all who want to follow the path of Light will traverse through it. Then we shall come along behind and pick up any strays who wish to follow. Those of lesser determination may long for home.

"There is a lot of work to be done over the next few years to herald this new era. Mankind is waiting for a big leap in evolution, but in truth this is a slow process, a gentle flow. No-one gets the big switch; it would be too traumatic for the main populace. Life is hard and would be harder if these moves were too rapid, as the affect on your bodily structure would be extreme. We prefer to take you tenderly from one step to the next in a gracious flow of love and Light. You will need time to absorb new energy flows. It will not come easily for those consistently elsewhere in minds and bodies.

"The veils between the different levels of existence are preparing for the Third Wave. Each wave pushes Lightworkers further up the ladder. The general populace will follow the leaders. As each wave moves up through the veils, those already on that rung of the ladder move up another step. Imagine it like an escalator: each time new people join on the bottom, those before them move higher. With every good deed you perform, all move forward another step.

"Magical things are in the air, bringing peace and harmony to your planet in a way unprecedented to this date. Just be patient, it will happen as and when it should. There is nothing to be done to increase the speed that this experience will take, it is in the stars.

"Ascension is a buzz word, a light to dangle to attract attention, but it will take years to bring the whole planet to a level where it may ascend. Little steps, tiny movements day-by-day, will bring results – but the overall Ascension process takes time, so please do not be disappointed, it will happen, maybe in your lifetime, maybe not, but it is on the cards.

"Man has fallen so far from grace that it will take a long time to resolve, but resolve it must, before each rung of the ladder is offered as a step to the beauty beyond. You must all take your Light and shine it brightly. Be prepared to take the first steps, lift your face to the future, and gradually all of humanity will follow.

"We rely on you to be the Light which glows at the forefront of this Ascension. Many people will not understand what is happening; they may get bodily imbalances and feel very unsettled. Let everyone know we are in their corner, we want you all to succeed. We shall build a bridge from your world to ours to help progress lost souls, as there are always so many at such a time.

"You should also know that there is currently a meeting of worlds in the Ether, and this is affecting the mind-set of Earth's whole populace. It is nothing to do with Ascension, although many believe it is. There is a Light waiting to descend to Earth soon, and this will bring a new energy and fulfilment to the work of everyone connected to the Light. I will tell you more at the proper time.

"The new age has been a long time coming. Now that you are about to enter the Age of Aquarius, the tides will change. Man's thought patterns will become more spiritual and he will feel a greater desire to protect all species and the land on which you live. With this dawning of the Age of Aquarius, it is the time for him to stand up and be counted as a representative of the Earth, and as an ambassador of all that is good in his world.

"This new age is a change in the whole remit of mankind. It is a doorway, an opening to a new dimension with access to information pertinent to your future. At this time, we need you to understand that life is changing dramatically for all of you. It will bring a new purpose to life which has not been seen on Earth for many millennia. All we need you to do right now is re-tune to our new frequency. This is simple, just ask! It will lift you to a new level of consciousness, allowing you to maintain contact with our realm.

"The old age has gone, and with it the trappings of financial dogma and the need for industry. The new age casts a new reflection on the planet and all upon her. This age moves with nature, and heralds the start of a more 'caring and sharing' planet – where every soul that incarnates on Earth helps to feed the crops, calm the seas and look out for all the beautiful creatures of your world to ensure they stay alive for generations to come.

"Pray for peace. Pray for calm in the world. Pray for a song of joy to herald across the wastelands of the Universe. Over the days, the weeks, the months ahead, bring your voice to the fore to tell others of life as it should be, as it was meant to be – a life where heralds of Angels sing to the glory of God, waking mankind as a whole to the unity and love only found in worlds which slumber in the Heavens. Take solace in the knowledge that man will again revere the Earth, and be blessed by the sharing of his life with others and with all the beasts of land, sea and air.

"Feel the love of the Angels in your heart and in your head. Allow the Light of the Master's plan to lead you effortlessly to the place of peace with others of like minds. We offer you our blessings to bring you to that place, where nothing will spoil the idyll of life as it should be. We bless you and caress you with the warmth and love of a thousand ancestors whose lives were blessed on Earth, and who bring that love and harmony back to you, to the forefront of your life today and forever.

"Always try to give of your best to all who enter your life. They come for a reason, they come to test your resolve, bringing you challenges to keep you on your path to the Light. But, do not let them detract you from your purpose. You are ambassadors and heralds for the Light. Let go the need to be right, and choose peace as the path to follow. To lead others on paths of purity, you need to be on that path yourself.

"We are moving the entire planet up through the veils in a plan to improve the psyche of mankind. You will find that everyone will improve in their graciousness and acceptance of the Light. This is an important landmark in the lifetime of humankind. It is the start, the very beginning, of an improvement in the Light emanating from your world. It will shine like a star in the night sky for all the Angels to see. All here will rejoice to see there is a spark of Light and Love on Earth again."

With that, Shomas bows and takes his leave. Olivia is no longer disconcerted by his abrupt departures; she simply sits in silence, gathering her thoughts, and then goes downstairs to tell Jane about all she has learnt today.

Jane reaffirms that even when all seems to be going wrong, Spirit always has man's best interests at heart, wanting only for everyone to pull together to create a better future for all.

The day has brightened and the dark clouds have passed so Jane and Olivia settle on a seat in the garden, and watch the wonder of nature. There is so much happening in the world and so many big changes ahead, yet the birds still sing, bees buzz amongst the herbs, and the flowers dazzle with their colours and scents. The two women sit awed and grateful for this little haven which brings them peace.

CHAPTER TWENTY-SIX
THE LIGHT

The sun is high in the noonday sky when Olivia comes to visit her Grandmother again. Jane, as always, is in the garden tending her plants and filling the bird feeders. After several busy weeks at the Theatre during the high point of their summer season, Olivia is excited to return to her regular visits – not only to see her Granny, but also to share wisdom and insights with Shomas again. She has missed them both.

After the normal banter about the family, and hugging a lovely, cooling iced tea, Olivia climbs the stairs to the room Where the Magic Happens. She pauses as she enters Jane's special room, full of light and energy and crystals of every hue, and thinks about all that has happened here and how much she has changed in the process.

Olivia sits herself comfortably in the big armchair near the window, feeling a thrill of anticipation. The sun casts shadows across the walls as she goes into a deep meditation, where she will meet Shomas, who she knows will take her on another magical journey of discovery. He soon arrives and bows his head in greeting and to her surprise he begins by talking about Jane.

"I sit at your grandmother's feet," he tells her. "Not in a subservient way, but just to be there for her at all times, as I often did when we were children in Tibet. We have been together in quite a few other lifetimes, sometimes as men, sometimes as women. Each time I would keep an eye on her, or she would keep an eye on me. It is a real joy that in this lifetime she knows I am here, linked to her in the Spirit realm. It gives me great pleasure that she feels the love that I send."

Olivia smiles, as she knows how close their bond is after all this time, and the love they share.

"I am so glad that you too, are a seeker of the Light," he tells her with a tender look, "not only for your grandmother's sake. Everyone here appreciates those who work for Spirit on Earth.

"We want to thank all those who work in the Light, and we send love and blessings to all of you. Whenever you work for the good of all, we energise you, protect you, and bring you closer to the Light. Keep sending your energy to the centre of the planet, so that a myriad of blessings will scatter across the Earth to ease the pain and heartache of the many nations. We are so pleased to have this opportunity to work with you to heal the planet and to guide you in your lives. We send our love to you all and want you to trust that we shall always be by your sides.

"We watch you all in your busy lives, rushing here, there and everywhere. Take time to stop, take time to think before your actions, take time to see the rest of the world before your eyes. Remember to reach out to help others in some small way, no matter how small, to give them the confidence that someone cares. Help those who struggle with affliction to pull themselves out of the mire and find the road to recovery. Take a hand, a mind, a heart, and show it love and tenderness to bring it back onto the path of true Light. If you do this, it will snowball: the person you help will want to help others, and so it goes on from person to person across the globe.

"Allow other drivers to merge into traffic instead of blocking their path by going first; this will ease their whole day and make them more likely to help another. Let someone go in front of you in a queue in the supermarket or coffee shop, and see how their spirits elevate as they continue their day. These are simple steps, easy to do, but how many will take the time in the busy world of yours.

"It is better to smile than raise a fist in fury; better to hold out a hand than to stamp your feet in frustration: better to live a life of peace and harmony than anger and hatred. You are all our children and we want you all to smile, to hold your heads up high, confident that you know you are doing the right thing in casting off material wealth for a store of human kindness and happiness. It doesn't take much to change a day for someone: one good deed will traverse like ripples on a lake, and their whole day will be brighter, lighter and Healed in some small way.

"How many elderly people do you see with heads bowed, as they trudge through a lonely day? Open a door for them, offer to give them your seat on the bus, catch them if they appear unsteady, offer to grasp for something too high on a shelf for them to reach. Some will moan, but for others this may be the only sign of kindness and help they have received in a while, and it will restore their faith in humanity and lighten their daily load.

"Take care, and be confident in the knowledge that we hold the safety net for your life, once you acknowledge your true purpose. The more you help others, the more help will come your way."

"But how can I help?" Olivia asks. "There seems to be so much sadness and anger in the world right now. What can we do to help alleviate that?"

"Bring your thoughts to a central universe, a universe where your planet is the focal point for good, not evil," he advises. "You will be amazed how many planets in your cosmos watch Earth with anticipation as it evolves to a new level of lightness. State your intention to serve the Light and there will be many here who will help and guide you.

"In the near future, peace will reign at last across many continents currently charged with animosity. It has to happen; it can't go on as it does now. There are many Lightworkers across your planet, all adding their help in differing ways – and whether your role is big or small, each part adds to the whole. One act of kindness does not cure all, but a million acts will be enough to bring your world back from the edge. Hold out your hand, clasp another, each a link in a chain around the world, holding the planet close and dear to your hearts.

"Too many people today value individuality over community. 'Freedom' should be a beautiful word, but it has become tainted, used to justify selfish ends. Over the past century your world has seen hundreds of wars fought by thousands of innocent men and women in the name of freedom. Freedom for whom? No matter where you are in the world, you are never totally free from the petty trials and tribulations of governments and rulers. We want to offer you all *true* freedom: freedom of expression; freedom to pave your own path for the future; freedom to sing your own song, whose chorus will open the hearts and minds of many others on your planet. We want you to have the freedom to open your hearts to others less fortunate than yourselves, and to bring them forward into the light of goodness and well being. We want you to have the freedom to traverse your beautiful world in peace and harmony with all lands, with all nations.

"When man first came to Earth, he had the freedom to walk the lands and live peacefully. To be at one with the animals, the birds, the fishes; and to be at one with the trees and the plants, respecting their growth and development into their richness of colour and flavour. But with each progressive century, man has chosen to rule, conquer and destroy the idyll put into his care. Why, we ask, why does man destroy the perfection he constantly seeks? Man is a complex creature. Given a whole world to treasure, it is only now that he is realising how much he has lost.

"Lightworkers must help to bring faith back to the lands: not a faith of idolatry, but a faith that all will be well if you treasure every infinitessimal part of the whole planet. The Light we offer fills the Halls of Knowledge throughout your world with love and peace. We offer you the chance to start again. There are veils of darkness currently drawn across your planet which are due to rise. The play has been acted out and has been deemed a failure. It is time to start again and the role of the Lightworkers is to show the way. Bring Light back to your planet. Bring Light into every corner of the whole. Do not leave a stone unturned in the quest to put right all that has been done wrong, in so many previous lifetimes. Now is the time of Light and love. Now is the time to bring all that you hold dear to fruition, in the name of the Father, in the name of Light.

"More and more souls are being drawn to the Light as your world starts moving upward through the veils. These veils, these levels, are there for a purpose: to protect mankind from seeing the future. Seeing through the veils would give you access to alpha states[16], which can be highly dangerous for the uninitiated. No-one is allowed through the veils until they are ready, as this would be too much for most to handle. We want you to walk not run, this has to be done a step at a time. You are all capable of so much more than you realise and so many of you are now starting to see the Light.

"We hold out our hands to you all," Shomas says with great kindness in his eyes, "to help you to progress towards the Light in all that you do. We do not expect you to give up your day jobs in pursuit of the Light, just bring Spirit into that work too. Help others and be a Healing presence. Speak and act with kindness. Lighten the load of all around you, bring them into harmony with a calm demeanour. Bring everyone forward to be part of the revolution to heal and repair your world."

Olivia thanks him for these words. Shomas bows and takes his leave – but then, instead of vanishing, he suddenly turns back again. There is something else he want to tell her.

"Those on Earth who follow the Light have been working hard for so long. As you begin to do this work, we acknowledge that it can be hard. This is a difficult period for the world at large, but we anticipate it will resolve in our favour, and we hope to see it happen in your lifetime. This is your path, chosen before your birth, to help us to bring about the dissolution of darkness, and we thank you for the part you play. Have faith that all will yet be well.

"It is all part of the Master's great plan that life unfolds as it does. Where every soul can choose their own life path to the future. But man is a wilful being and often strays off his chosen path, following the rocky road of discontentment. Until one day he realises that the true path to his destiny has been planned from the outset, and lies smooth and straight, so he can reroute and follow his dreams.

"Mankind is evolving at a faster rate than ever before. The Angels, Archangels and Spiritual hierarchy are moving forward at the same pace, so everyone is progressing into a new evolutionary space in time. We want everyone to know that as life is changing; they need to run if they are to keep up. So many will refuse to acknowledge the pace at which they need to change for the better. They want everything, and they want it now, but won't put in the effort to achieve it. Effort is going to be needed now. We cannot spoon feed everyone. We will help as much as we can but all of you need to help yourselves too.

"We love and cherish you all, and want you all to be free to challenge the confines of space and time and traverse the Universe as your ancestors did, at the very start of civilisation. We will work with you, but you must work too – for yourselves and for each other. Open your hearts and minds and bring in all that is good and wholesome, for you and your family. Expand this to cover your city and your Earth, then take it to the frontiers of space and beyond. Show that Earth still has Light, and always will have, as long as workers of Light hold their planet dear. Walk tall, for you have been recognised, and will see the Light descend upon Earth to raise the vibration of the planet above its current state.

"Strengthen the resolve of the populace to make the Earth a place of peace. Be a herald, a Pied Piper of souls who are lost to the mundane but want to wield their swords for the purpose of the Light in beauty and sanctuary. The Light of Love heals all.

"In the peace and calm you are holding today, we send healing to all those whose hearts and minds are broken, to all those in pain who wish to be mended. We lead them on a path to harmony of the spirit so they will know where to find their God in their lives, where to find an oasis of tranquillity wherever they may be, despite all the chaos in the world. Over time they will find an inner peace which will harmonise their souls. They will find a place of refuge, bringing harmony to their very essence. We bless them at this time, and we bless you, and all of the Lightworkers. We want you to know how much we care for you, and for mankind as a whole.

"Pray for peace and pray for calm. Pray for love and Light to enter every portal in every soul, so the whole world will know what it is like to feel perfect even if only for a minute. Each time this happens, this doorway to the Heavens will open further and further to allow each heartbeat to fall into rhythm with its neighbour, until all the world will beat in time with each other and bring harmony and joy to planet Earth.

"The children of your world find it easier to be in harmony with each other: boy, girl, white, black, they play and run and laugh together as a whole. This joy at working and playing together, lives in their ease of manner. They see no differences between them, and they feel at ease in all situations. Adults need to feel the same, bringing themselves in line with others – not as conformity, but in a way where they can no longer see a difference in colour, in faith and in culture. All look at the same sky, all breathe the same air all raise the same Light to the glory of their God.

"Bless you all, our children who live in harmony with others. Bless you all who lay down your sword to offer peace and solace to your fellow man. Bless you all who work for the betterment of mankind as a whole. We love you, we cherish you, and we thank you for your singularity of thought that all men are equal and that all life should be protected and healed. Blessings, dear ones. We love you and care for you and your kith and kin always.

"And blessings to you, Olivia, as your work with the Light unfolds. Blessings to your grandmother, who helped to set you on this road. Jane is a Goddess of Light. She brings Light to the shares of Earth, and she opens her heart to bring love to all who meet her. She has worked as a Seer in the Temples of Light in Atlantis and Lemuria, she will show you how to open to the Light and teach you many Healing skills. We are always in her space as she holds a special Light for us."

With that, Shomas softly fades away and Olivia returns to the room. She is thinking about that last statement and about her grandmother's love of 'random acts of kindness' as she goes downstairs and enters the room where Jane is waiting for her.

Unusually for her, Jane is watching a film. When Olivia asks her what it is, Jane replies *'Pay it Forward'*. It's all about random acts of kindness."

Olivia sits down beside her, smiling. Of course that's what it is.

.

CHAPTER TWENTY-SEVEN
HOW IT IS MEANT TO BE

Olivia and Jane wake early and decide to sit in the garden for a while revelling in the quiet and peace before starting their day. Summer is turning to autumn but the air is warm despite the time of year and the two women are enjoying the chance to be outside. Olivia suddenly feels Shomas's presence.

"Shomas is here," she tells her grandmother.

"I know," says Jane, "I can feel him waiting to speak with you. You can visit with him right here, Livvy, you don't need to be in my special room. The crystals there were helpful when you were learning how to link with Shomas, but now you are more experienced you can make the connection from anywhere. Go ahead and try."

Olivia sits up in the garden chair: feet on the ground, spine straight, shoulders relaxed. She begins her meditation. Used to the quiet of the upstairs room, at first her attention is distracted by the sound of bird song, a gust of wind, a car passing on the road, but she focuses on her breathing, following her breath into a meditative state. This time instead of travelling to the Crystal Cave or any of the other places she has previously been, she is still in her grandmother's garden and Shomas sits on the grass beside her.

"We are blessed with the stillness of life in this garden," Shomas begins. "We are blessed to witness the calm and meditative quality of your life outside of the stresses of your world at large. We are blessed to hold solace in the quiet of your surroundings."

Olivia agrees. The stillness of the garden is intoxicating, so calming and peaceful. If only the whole world could be the same! She feels Jane rise from her seat and leave them as Shomas starts his lesson for the day.

"Man has opened his heart to us: not completely, but much more than it has been for a thousand years. We can tell you of lives and loves that have been lost and found over aeons, reawakening in this lifetime to bring harmony to all around them. Let there be peace in all lands, peace for all nations, around the world.

"So many in your world still want to rule in totality over their own lands and the nations beyond, there is no need for dictatorship. Man on the whole has a kindly heart and responds better to a carrot than a stick.

"Earth is in a strange place currently, betwixt and between energy systems; the Light on Earth keeps being extinguished by the power and energy of the darkness. So many on your planet are angry at this time, leading to so many insurrections. The ruling factions, ignoring the needs of their populace, are sowing the seeds of chaos. This has to stop.

"We need you to help people realise just how important it is right now to keep to the Light, and to hold it strong. This is the time for decisiveness in this make-or-break war against darkness, inadequacy and doubt. Hold the Light strong in your part of the world. Keep the lamp high so others of like minds can see it. Call on them to bring their light to shine brightly with yours and others across the land.

"All of this turmoil will resolve. It is the storm before the calm of life itself. This is the time to stand and be counted, raising your Light as a beacon of hope for others to see that the future will be bright. Step forward with your head held high in the knowledge that all will be well for the future. There will be hope where all hope has gone, and truth amongst all the lies. Remember that we are here to hold, cherish and support you through these dark times and into the Light ahead.

"Offer everyone a way to a more peaceful existence. Show them that working in the Light, and for the Light, is the best way forward. The world needs leaders, true leaders to lead by example. You will know what you do is right if it is for the benefit of planet Earth and all that lives upon her.

"Take the light and love of our realm to the four corners of the Earth. This is important, it will bring you all into harmony with us. There is a wave of positive energy on its way to your world. It has been travelling through the cosmos for centuries, and is slow moving, but when it arrives it will take the planet by storm. It has traversed from beyond the Pleiades, and is on its way to you. This wave will bring a new paradigm. It will destroy negative karma and bring those of little understanding into the regime of the Light. It will lift your energies higher than they have been for a long while.

"Everyone on Earth will receive this gift of positivity. It will traverse the planet slowly and methodically before returning back into the Universe, leaving joy in its wake. This has been prophesied for some time, and many have seen it coming.

"You will benefit immensely from this, both individually and communally. Governments worldwide will sit up and take notice as souls are blended in harmony. Just watch and see the repercussions. This is a big event in time, and will be discussed for millennia to come."

Shomas gazes across the lovely garden, its colours glowing with Jane's love and care. Then he rises from the grass, indicating that today's lesson is done. He smiles warmly at Olivia, and leaves her with these words:

"Thank you for working for the Light. It is important work to do. With every heart you touch, every mind you alter, every soul you help to find their true path, you help to Heal your beautiful planet. We are pleased to see so many Children of the Light expanding and growing in consciousness, bringing love, light and generosity of Spirit to the Earth plane and everyone else upon it. Love, Light, Peace and Joy to you all."

Olivia feels touched and honoured, to be even a small part of this, as she watches him depart, his essence fading, then gone altogether. The garden now seems more solid and ordinary, although still beautiful. There is still magic here, a lingering presence.

She stands there with her heart wide open, taking in the sound of the birds, the scents of autumn, the clear white Light. The sense of change coming. Then she suddenly turns and runs inside. She has so much to tell Jane.

CHAPTER TWENTY-EIGHT

CONCLUSION

As was said in the Introduction, this book has been written over many years, using Automatic Writing, mainly by Shomas and the Elohim, but also from others in the Spirit World and this is what they told me:

"We the Elohim, as Brothers of Light, are many; and we bring the love and the wisdom of the Ancients to your presence. We bring our love and Light to heal the planet for the future, offering information pertinent to man's role on Earth.

"This is the time to look to your fellow man for words of wisdom which will help Earth through this time. You can all heal the world with our words; we need everyone to receive our messages so they will work as a group consciousness to stop war, want and waste. The future is rosy for those who wish to see.

"We wish for you to reach the hearts and souls of all who teach on the Earth plane, to open their eyes to see that not all children are the same. We ask them to see the Light reflected in the souls of those children who have especially come to Earth to help and heal hearts and souls at this time, and encourage them to grow accordingly.

"You are each a child of the stars, a being of the Universe; you have been given these gifts of Light to help others. To show man the way into the Light, and the part he should play to help Planet Earth forge its place back into alignment with its lineage and place in space...to return it to its original blueprint, not to lose all that is good, but to rectify all that is bad in your world. Thank you dear ones."

"With love and affection, you will all be moved onward and upward through the echelons of our world to pull yourselves up and beyond the abilities you have now, to achieve a level where you can link directly to us at all time. Your lives are about to change and change in a big way. You are about to step into the freedom that self-confidence brings: no more worry, no more doubt; and once you move forward, you will find all contact with us is simple, all links to us are pure.

"Blessed be all souls, as they move above and beyond the remit of the purpose of the planet and into the realms of Spirit to be our foot soldiers on Earth to lead the nations through the mire.

"This is an enlightening time, a time of great worth for those of you who live your lives working for us and beyond the veils of Light. Your work for the planet keeps it free from its drudgery; it releases it from the nucleus of hate, which holds it in stasis. You will find new souls who are eager to experience all you have to offer, as it is enlightening and enlivening for all those seeking the truth.

"All the messages you receive are written as a record to share with those who will listen. Tell everyone about the messages, people can accept or reject the information we give, as they please. Go now, our children of Light; we love you and protect you always."

I hope this book will be read with an open heart, that it answers a lot of questions and explains things clearly. Each chapter has the teachings of Spirit which will have provoked thought and may have made you smile. Everyone in Spirit thanks you for caring for your world and working for the good of others, as well as yourselves. Live, love and Heal the world and work towards a better future for everyone.

I know for some, the concepts in this book may have proved difficult to comprehend. I can only say: this is information I have received and I trust it, but it is up to you to choose for yourself what you wish to believe and what you don't. We all have free will; we all have the freedom to choose the way we think or act and the path we wish to take for our future. It is up to you to use that free will and to accept what has been written, or not. All I hope is that you have enjoyed the book, and will think a little more about our planet and taking care of her and everything upon her.

The world, belongs to us, and we can make it whole again with a little effort. If we pull together, we can be assured that the next generations will live long and healthy lives. Live your own life to the full; make the most of every minute, but do it with care: care for yourself, care for others and care for the ecosystem, so that everyone who follows will also be able to live lives at least as full as yours.

Our Spirit Guides have our welfare at heart, and, with profound and gentle persuasion, they hope to change the ways of man towards a brighter and happier future where there are no wars, and where peace and happiness prevail.

Your Guides wish to give you all the confidence to stand up and be counted, and to move forward in the faith that everything you do in their name is pure. Everyone in the Spirit Realm would like to thank you for caring for your world.

I completed this book on Earth Day. How very apt! Take care of your world, take care of the land you call home, and may peace prevail within this lifetime and for many, many more years to come.

QUOTATIONS

The following words show that many 'Masters' of our world have wanted peace for the Earth for a very long time.

"There are only two ways to live your life,
one is as though nothing is a miracle,
the other is as if everything is."
Albert Einstein

"When one door closes another door opens
but we so often look so long and so regretfully upon the closed door,
that we do not see the ones which open for us."
Alexander Graham Bell

"All things are possible, to him who believes."
Mark 9:17 - 24

"Live in harmony with one another, be sympathetic,
love as brothers, be compassionate and humble.
Do not repay evil with evil or insult with insult
but with a blessing because to this you were called
so that you may inherit a blessing."
From a Letter from St. Peter

"I always knew that deep down in every human heart, there is mercy and generosity.
No one is born hating another person because of the colour of his skin, or his
background, or his religion. People must learn to hate, and if they can learn to hate,
they can be taught to love, for love comes more naturally to the human heart than its
opposite. Even in the grimmest times in prison, when my comrades and I were pushed
to our limits, I would see a glimmer of humanity in one of the guards, perhaps just for a
second, but it was enough to reassure me and keep me going.
Man's goodness is a flame that can be hidden but never extinguished."
Nelson Mandela

"To be free is not merely to cast off one's chains,
but to live in a way that respects and enhances the freedom of others."
Nelson Mandela

"As we let our own light shine,
we unconsciously give other people permission to do the same."
Nelson Mandela

"May the eternal flame of love, forever be in our hearts,
forever shine in our eyes and forever teach our feet to dance."
from a poem by Rumi

"The sun, with all those planets revolving around it and dependent upon it,
can still ripen a bunch of grapes, as if it had nothing else in the Universe to do."
Galileo

"We are at a unique stage in our history.
Never before has mankind had an awareness of what we are doing to the planet
and never before have we had the power to do something about it.
Simply put, we have a responsibility to care for our planet.
The future of humanity, and indeed all life, now depends on us."
Sir David Attenborough

"We will witness more extinction of animal, plant, and human races,
because of man's lack of understanding of the 'balance of life.'
Our vision is for people of all continents, regardless of their beliefs in the Creator,
to come together to pray and meditate. To unite spiritually as a global nation.
To commune with one another, thus promoting an energy shift to heal our Mother
Earth and achieve a universal consciousness toward attaining Peace.
Give thanks for the pure food, gifted to us by our Earth, so the
nutritional energy of medicine can be guided to heal our minds and spirits.
The fate of the entire World depends on your decision. Each of us has been
put here at this time to personally decide the future of humankind.
You are desperately needed to save the soul of this world.
Did you think you were put here for something less?
In a Sacred Hoop of Life, there is no beginning and no ending."
Chief Arvol Looking Horse

The Final Analysis
Mother Teresa of Calcutta

"People are often unreasonable, illogical and self-centred; Forgive them anyway.
If you are kind, people may accuse you of selfish, ulterior motives; Be kind anyway
If you are successful, you will win some false friends and some true enemies;
Succeed anyway
If you are honest and frank, people may cheat you; Be honest and frank anyway
What you spend years building, someone may destroy overnight; Build anyway
If you find serenity and happiness, they may be jealous; Be happy anyway
The good you do today, people will often forget tomorrow; Do good anyway
Give the world the best you have, it may never be enough;
Give the world the best you've got anyway
You see, in the final analysis, it is all between you and God;
It was never between you and them anyway."

BIBLIOGRAPHY & APPENDIX

An Introduction to Crop Circles by Andy Thomas: Wessex Books 2011 ISBN 978-1903035375

Quest for Contact by Andy Thomas and Paul Bura: SB Publications ISBN 978-1857701289

Painting of Shomas courtesy of Spirit Artist Freda Robinson

Nexus Magazine NexusNewsfeed.com & ScienceDaily.com

Chief Arvol Looking Horse: White Buffalo Teachings, the Lakota/Dakota/Nakota Nations

DNA http://preventdisease.com/news/13/012313
Scientists-Present-Evidence-on-Expanding-DNA-Strands.html

Blue Planet II - bbc.co.uk/blueplanet2

The Queen's Commonwealth Canopy (QCC) - http://queenscommonwealthcanopy.org

The Old Testament of The Bible

Notes:

1. **Spirit Realm & Spirit Guides:** The Spiritual Realm is unseen by human eyes, but we are connected to it, and what goes on in the Spiritual Realm directly affects our physical world. Spirit Guides are non-physical beings, who are assigned to us, often before we are born, to help nudge and guide us through our life. We are more than physical entities; we possess a soul or Spirit destined to exist for eternity.

2. **Light:** In this book frequent mention is made of Light. This term is often used in Spirituality. Divine Light represents truth which is given by God himself and this Light allows God, Angels, or humans to communicate through spiritual means, rather than through physical capacities.

   Light is a nemesis of evil forces. As such, it is an absence of darkness and a quality that helps us see, and understand, more clearly. People who are of the Light smile more readily and take life as it comes, they do not dwell on life's problems, they bounce back with resilience. Cosmic energy, creative force and optimism are all aspects of Light.

   In the Bible, God takes man 'from darkness, and leads us into Light'. In Hinduism, Diwali, the Festival of Light, is a celebration of the victory of Light over darkness. And Buddhist scriptures speak of numerous Buddhas of Light, including a Buddha of Pure Light, of Incomparable Light, and of Unceasing Light.

3. **Lightworkers:** Lightworkers are those who work in the Light and for the Light. They try to help others to see the true path they should be following, to ease the conflict in their lives, and to bring all mankind and Planet Earth to a place of peace.

4. **The Elohim, The White Brotherhood, The Twelve Elders of the Universe who work with Melchizedek:**

   Ascended Masters: These are highly evolved beings, some of whom have lived on Earth. They are part of the Spiritual Hierarchy overseeing the Earth and other planes at this time. Many Ascended Masters belong to the White Brotherhood and the Order of Melchizedek. They bring Light into the hearts and minds of humanity to further their development. They guide, protect, inspire, heal and assist in the progress of mankind.

   The Elohim: Are mighty Beings of Love and Light who use the creative powers of thought, feeling and word to help mankind and planet Earth. They carry the highest vibration of Light that we can comprehend in our state of evolution. They are the most powerful aspect of the Consciousness of God. Serving directly under the Elohim are the Nature beings.

   The White Brotherhood: These are advanced Spiritual beings of Light who also assist humanity in their evolution. They are supernatural beings of great power who spread spiritual teachings and are often known as the Masters of the Ancient Wisdom or Ascended Masters. They are in charge of renewing or reawakening creation.

   The Twelve Elders of the Universe who work with Melchizedek: The twelve Melchizedek planetary receivers. The Melchizedek energy strives to bring higher wisdom to humankind.

5. **Planes:** A Plane is a state of consciousness that transcends the physical Universe. They are not "places" that exist somewhere else; they are all around us, all the time.

   The Physical Plane: Where we currently reside as human beings. All objects are solid, space maintains a constant structure. Particles can only travel up to the speed of light.

   The Etheric Plane: Space and time are inconsistent and fluid.

   The Astral Plane: A non-physical dimension, where consciousness goes after physical death. Objects are no longer solid, so you can pass through them easily. Time merges and reality doesn't exist. Physical beings travel to the Astral plane during their sleep state, partly active or dormant, dependent upon their evolutionary growth. When they wake their physical and higher bodies interlock again.

   The Causal Plane: Is where energy fields of our past, present and future events reside.

   The Mental Plane: Energy can jump from one place to another instantaneously, so can appear to be in two places at once. This is the plane of ideas and concepts.

   The Spiritual Plane: Where Spiritual beings reside. It is completely non-physical, objects do not exist in form. Time and space are irrelevant, and everything is in a constantly changing state of being. This is the dimension of the soul, the plane of consciousness. Here you intermingle with others as pure thoughts, emotions and energy, there is no need for language.

   Akashic Plane: All knowledge of the Universe is recorded on this plane, everything that happens in the Universe as and when it occurs. The records show events exactly as they were experienced from the beginning of time.

Inner Plane: Pure potentiality, thought, love and spirit. Concepts from this plane move outwards, as form, to the outer plane

Outer Plane: Where thought becomes matter. We think and it manifests.

6. **Veils/Our side:** A veil is something hidden from mankind, a separation between man and God. It is a metaphor representing that we are separate from Spirit. We are led to believe that this physical reality, on Earth now, is all that exists because the veil blocks our view of the Spirit Realm beyond and our memories of previous incarnations. When Spirit beings speak of 'our side', they mean their side of the veil, therefore out of our view. We can, however, maintain relationships with Guides and loved ones who dwell in Spirit, as we are spiritual beings, encased in physical bodies.

7. **Dimensions:** A dimension is a state of consciousness which vibrates at a certain rate. There are numerous dimensions, each higher than the one before. Each higher dimension gives a wider perspective of reality, a more expansive level of knowing. For humans to have access to a higher dimension, we need to vibrate with its resonance and establish ourselves therein.

We on Earth are three dimensional beings on the Third Dimension. This dimension is a state of consciousness which is quite limited. On this dimension, we cannot merge with one another or walk through walls. Physical objects are solid and we can't read another person's mind. Everything on the planet is subject to gravity.

The space between the Third and Fourth Dimensions is where discarnate spirits get 'stuck' until freed to go to higher dimensions.

The Fourth Dimension is time, when occupied by a three-dimensional object. When we move to this dimension we shall experience spiritual awakening and upliftment. Everything around us will feel lighter, less rigid. Time will no longer be linear, with no real awareness of past and future. Time, in this dimension, can be stretched and condensed. Manifestation is much quicker in the Fourth Dimension. When we experience joy, love and gratitude, this is Fourth Dimensional consciousness.

The Fifth Dimension is where no fear, anger, hostility or guilt exists. We will have mastery over our thoughts. Manifestation is instantaneous. People will communicate through telepathy and have the ability to read each other's thoughts and feelings with ease. There is no distinction between past, present or future.

The dimensions are a means of organising different planes of existence according to their vibratory rate. There are varying other dimensions in the world of Spirit where everything is possible. Our evolution will continue with ascension to higher dimensions.

Each dimension has its own electromagnetic boundary and its own karmic laws and principles. With an overseer for each dimension and a connection to Source which is fundamental to its nature. Dependent on your level of consciousness, you may travel to other vibrations or dimensions. Each individual may go up or down in vibration or harmonic frequency according to their thoughts, words, feelings or actions in each moment.

Earth is not a dimension in its own right, it is part of the Milky Way. Pleiades is our sister galaxy on the same dimension.

8. **Levels/Estates**: Different levels can be accessed dependent upon your achievements.

9. **Vibrations:** A vibration is a movement of our energy through space, and may be experienced as mental or physical feelings. If we have a high vibration, we feel ready to tackle the day and create more of what we want in life. When things go 'right', we can experience a special feeling inside confirming that this is the correct decision or action. If our vibration is low, it provides warnings which, if we are aware of them, allow us to take action to improve our mood and hence improve our vibration.

10. **Frequency:** The higher the frequency, the greater the energy of the vibration.

11. **Life Force Energy:** Spiritual Energy is the manifestation of divine, pure love which comes from the Source/God or your equivalent. It is an energy which defies description and is considered the eternal life force which binds the soul to the body. It is the universal life force which exists in all living matter. It is a life sustaining force which survives death and can return through reincarnation. Healing is a conduit for the transference of this energy to an ailing person.

    Chi/Qi is both the male and female life force energy, which is in perfect balance and flows through the body to activate the energy vortices or chakras.

12. **Deva**: A deva is a powerful supernatural being of nature (or nature spirit). They are invisible to the human eye, except to those humans who have an extra-sensory power to see beings from other planes through their third eye. They shine with their own intrinsic luminosity and are capable of moving long distances at great speed. It is believed that there are many different types of devas all performing different functions on Earth to help the ecology of the planet.

13. **Karma:** Refers to the spiritual principle of cause and effect. Where the intent and actions of an individual influence their future. Good intent and good deeds create good karma and future happiness, whilst bad intent and bad deeds create bad karma and future suffering. Karma is the sum of a persons actions in this and previous incarnations, which can affect your current or future lifetime.

14. **Original Landmasses:** The tropical rainforests used to cover two thirds of what used to be called Gondwanaland, which literally means 'Land (wana) of the Gonds'. This land mass which included Africa, Madagascar, India, Australia, Tasmania, Antarctica, South America and the Falklands, was originally part of Pangaea (whole/entire Mother Earth) but drifted apart during the Jurassic/Mesozoic periods.

15. **DNA:** Holds all the genetic information in a person. It is believed that activation of higher strands of DNA will allow a human body to process more data and expand our consciousness. A healthy human brain can process more than 400 billion bits of information per second but we are only consciously aware of 2,000 of those at

any given time. Our conscious mind allows us to be aware of roughly one percent of reality. The rest of the information is processed by our subconscious.

Some geneticists believe that by activating our DNA beyond the two strand helix will allow us to anchor high frequency energies that can heal and change our body. Our life-span could increase and we could activate dormant abilities, such as clairvoyance and telepathy. It is essential that we acknowledge changes to our genes and the evolution of our species, in order to understand why these changes are happening. If scientists and spiritual teachers are correct, we may be evolving to have more strands of DNA. Therefore activating these higher strands could be the key to enlightenment. It is said that some children already are being born with more DNA.

16. **States of Mind:** When you are actively awake you are in a Beta state of mind. When you allow your imagination, creativity and intuition free rein you are in an Alpha state, which makes you more receptive and less critical, allowing for better memory recall and (because you are calmer) better decision-making. This is a natural state for meditation and self-hypnosis and helps relieve stress and reduce anxiety.

Monkey Mind: Humans have around fifty thousand separate thoughts each day. A 'monkey mind' is when our mind never settles on one topic at a time. Irrational fears and anxious imaginings made real by our constant attention, swing from thought-branch to thought-branch all day long. Our ego is the chattering monkey of our internal monologue. With this going on, it becomes nearly impossible to be present and focused on the moment we are in. It becomes infuriating and exhausting, so should be avoided if at all possible. Mindfulness and meditation can help calm the Monkey Mind.

17. **Enlightenment:** A state of understanding. In Hinduism and Buddhism, it is the highest spiritual state that can be achieved.

18. **Gaia:** A goddess in Greek mythology who personified Earth.

19. **Weeble:** A 1970s roly poly toy, egg shaped and weighted at the bottom so it could never be knocked over. The advertising slogan was 'Weebles wobble but they don't fall down'.

20. **Divine Consciousness:** A metaphor for truth and goodness.

21. **Portal:** A portal links a specific location on one plane to a specific location on another. Some portals are like doorways. Others are locations like a circles of standing stones, that exist in multiple planes at once. Some are vortices, typically joining an Elemental Plane with a very similar location on the Material Plane.

22. **Hall of Records:** Housing the knowledge of history from the beginning of time.

23. **Kirlian Photography:** Discovered in 1939 by Semyon Kirlian, it depicts an energy field, or aura, surrounding living things, reflecting the physical and emotional states of the subjects at the time of the photograph. It is believed that Kirlian photography can be used to diagnose illnesses.

24. **Lost Souls, Negative Entities/Negative Attachments, Error:** Lost souls are beings trapped between Heaven and Earth. They might have unfinished business or are unable to find the Light because they are consumed with lingering darkness. Discarnate humans, aliens, negative thought forms or error can attach themselves to a living person, draining their energy and influencing their thoughts, feelings and personality. They have not fully left the physical, etheric, and astral planes so attach themselves to someone open to them. Entity attachments can be removed by identifying what thoughts, emotions, and behaviours they aim to induce and cutting these off, transmuting or replacing them with their positive opposite.

25. **Solstice**: Latin for Sun Stands Still

26. **Twelve climatic regions of the Earth**: Tropical wet. Tropical wet and dry. Semi-arid. Desert. Subtropical dry (Mediterranean). Humid subtropical. Humid oceanic climates. Humid continental. Subarctic climates. Icecap climates. Tundra climates. Highland climates.

27. **Planetary Logos:** Governs Earth's Planetary body. Divine law in action. Controls man's destiny on the Planet. Assists those who wish to connect to their higher self.

28. **Maldek:** once existed between Mars and Jupiter. It exploded 75000 years ago and became an asteroid belt. This interplanetary event brought devastation and chaos, as fragments littered the solar system, cratering the inner planets, altering their orbits and leaving Mars' surface a scarred and barren wasteland.

29. **Vega:** is the fifth-brightest star in the night sky, and the second-brightest star in the northern celestial hemisphere, after Arcturus. It is only 25 light-years from the Sun, and, together with Arcturus and Sirius, one of the most luminous stars in the Sun's neighbourhood. Vega is arguably the next most important star in the sky after the Sun. Vega was the northern pole star around 12000 BC and will be again around the year 13727AD

30. **The National Federation of Spiritual Healers:** In 2009 it was decided to use The Healing Trust as the working name of NFSH. For further information about this organisation and to join please contact 'office@thehealingtrust.org.uk'

Lightning Source UK Ltd.
Milton Keynes UK
UKHW020006090620
364668UK00009B/847